Praise for *Same Kind of Different as Me*

This book is more than a memoir—it captures the presence of the only spirit that can transform the problems facing our society. When one person sets aside their own needs and misconceptions then steps purposefully and prayerfully into the life of another, miracles happen. Both lives are improved and the world gets a glimpse of real live grace. I am grateful to Ron and Denver for sharing their story and pray it will continue inspiring people to invest themselves in the simple, personal solutions that can change our world.

—The Honorable Rick Perry
Governor of Texas

Prepare to be inspired and changed as you read this tapestry of two men's lives stitched together by the power of God's love. Ron Hall and Denver Moore invite you to walk with them on their journey of growth, pain and joy. One man's story of worldly success, the other of complete poverty, brought together through the vision and perseverance of a Godly woman. Their story is a message for us all to reach out beyond ourselves and make a positive difference in the lives of others.

—Karol Ladd
Author of *The Power of a Positive Woman*

In his letter to the Corinthians, the apostle Paul wrote, "And now these three remain: faith, hope, and love. But the greatest of these is love."

Same Kind of Different as Me is the story of the faith, hope and love of one woman, Deborah Hall. Her faith in God, her hope for a better world, and her undying love forever changed the lives of two men: her husband Ron, a wealthy international art dealer, and Denver Moore, a homeless man for whom living on the streets was "a step up in life."

Telling the story in their own words, Ron Hall and Denver Moore regularly alternate between warming and wrenching your heartstrings. The unique two-author style and the open and candid way in which these men write add up to an engaging, emotional and life-changing experience.

Same Kind of Different as Me opened my eyes in a new way to a problem that remains largely out-of-sight, out-of-mind all across our nation. As Mayor of Fort Worth, Texas, where much of this story takes place, my resolve to address homelessness strengthened dramatically as a result of this book. Ron Hall and Denver Moore deserve tremendous credit for raising awareness in such a compelling way.

An important read for anyone with a heart for his or her fellow man, *Same Kind of Different as Me* is truly a work for the ages.

—Mike Moncrief
Mayor, City of Fort Worth

Same Kind Of Different As Me is a compelling story of tragedy, triumph, perseverance, dedication, faith, and the resilience of the human spirit. Deborah Hall's story is one of fierce dedication to helping others through the teachings of the Lord. Her passing left an enormous void in the lives of all who knew and loved her. Through her ministry to the homeless, her spirit touched the hearts of thousands of people. During this time period in her life, Deborah brought together the souls of two men from opposite ends of society. Their spirits have now touched a multitude of people all over the world. As these two men prayed, both together and separately during Deborah's last few months on earth, they formed an unimaginable bond. They tell their stories of dealing with the devastation of Deborah's illness and ultimate passing. These two remarkable men have dedicated the proceeds of this book to carry on Deborah's vision of helping the Lord's most unfortunate children. This is a must read. You can't put it down. Ron and Denver, you truly are my heroes.

—Red Steagall
Texas Poet Laureate

The most inspirational and emotionally gripping story of faith, fortitude, and friendship I have ever read. A powerful example of the healing, restorative power of forgiveness and the transformational, life changing power of unconditional love. Many talk about it, a few live it. The people in this story unquestionably do. Ron, Denver, and Debbie sincerely, humbly and unabashedly share their story, warts and all, leaving any reader permanently changed. From modern day slavery, still in existence today, to infidelity, to the miraculous, supernatural interventions of GOD and his Angels, this amazingly TRUE story reminds us of the limitless power of love.

—Mark Clayman
Executive Producer for the Academy award–nominated *The Pursuit of Happyness*

Denver Moore and Ron Hall's story is one that moved me to tears. The friendship that forms between these two men at a time when both were in great need is an inspiration to all of us to be more compassionate to everyone we come in contact with. This is truly a wonderful book!

—Mrs. Barbara Bush

Same Kind of Different As Me was a blessing to read. Ron and Debbie Hall took me on their journey of becoming the earthly hands and feet of Jesus. On their way, they found a true friendship in Denver Moore that only God could have brought together. Moreover, the servant-hearted, humble volunteers at the Union Gospel Mission were an exhortation for me to truly live what I believe. I laughed and I cried, and I praised God for real life, walking-around examples of what it means to "love them like Jesus."

—Melodee DeVevo
Casting Crowns

same kind
of different
as me

same kind
of different
as me

RON HALL &
DENVER MOORE
WITH LYNN VINCENT

THOMAS NELSON
Since 1798

NASHVILLE DALLAS MEXICO CITY RIO DE JANEIRO BEIJING

Author is represented by the literary agency of Alive Communications, Inc., 7680 Goddard Street, Suite 200, Colorado Springs, CO 80920

Published in Nashville, Tennessee, by Thomas Nelson. Thomas Nelson is a registered trademark of Thomas Nelson, Inc.

Thomas Nelson, Inc. titles may be purchased in bulk for educational, business, fund-raising, or sales promotional use. For information, please e-mail SpecialMarkets@ThomasNelson.com.
Although this is a work of nonfiction, some of the names have been changed.

Library of Congress Cataloging-in-Publication Data is available.

ISBN:978-0-8499-1910-7

Printed in the United States of America

09 10 11 12 13 RRD 16 15 14 13

1

Well—a poor Lazarus poor as I
When he died he had a home on high . . .
The rich man died and lived so well
When he died he had a home in hell . . .
You better get a home in that Rock, don't you see?

—NEGRO SPIRITUAL

Denver

Until Miss Debbie, I'd never spoke to no white woman before. Just answered a few questions, maybe—it wadn't really *speakin*. And to me, even that was mighty risky since the last time I was fool enough to open my mouth to a white woman, I wound up half-dead and nearly blind.

I was maybe fifteen, sixteen years old, walkin down the red dirt road that passed by the front of the cotton plantation where I lived in Red River Parish, Louisiana. The plantation was big and flat, like a whole lotta farms put together with a bayou snakin all through it. Cypress trees squatted like spiders in the water, which was the color of pale green apples. There was a lotta different fields on that spread, maybe a hundred, two hundred acres each, lined off with hardwood trees, mostly pecans.

Wadn't too many trees right by the road, though, so when I was walkin that day on my way back from my auntie's house—she was my grandma's sister on my daddy's side—I was right out in the open. Purty soon, I seen this white lady standin by her car, a blue Ford, 'bout a 1950, '51 model, somethin like that. She was standin there in her hat and her skirt, like maybe she'd been to town. Looked to me like she was tryin to figure out how to fix a flat tire. So I stopped.

"You need some help, ma'am?"

"Yes, thank you," she said, lookin purty grateful to tell you the truth. "I really do."

I asked her did she have a jack, she said she did, and that was all we said.

Well, 'bout the time I got the tire fixed, here come three white boys ridin outta the woods on bay horses. They'd been huntin, I think, and they come trottin up and didn't see me 'cause they was in the road and I was ducked down fixin the tire on the other side of the car. Red dust from the horses' tracks floated up over me. First, I got still, thinkin I'd wait for em to go on by. Then I decided I didn't want em to think I was hidin, so I started to stand up. Right then, one of em asked the white lady did she need any help.

"I reckon not!" a redheaded fella with big teeth said when he spotted me. "She's got a *nigger* helpin her!"

Another one, dark-haired and kinda weasel-lookin, put one hand on his saddle horn and pushed back his hat with the other. "Boy, what you doin' botherin this nice lady?"

He wadn't nothin but a boy hisself, maybe eighteen, nineteen years old. I didn't say nothin, just looked at him.

"What you lookin' at, boy?" he said and spat in the dirt.

The other two just laughed. The white lady didn't say nothin, just looked down at her shoes. 'Cept for the horses chufflin, things got quiet. Like the yella spell before a cyclone. Then the boy closest to me slung a grass rope around my neck, like he was ropin a calf. He jerked it tight, cuttin my breath. The noose poked into my neck like burrs, and fear crawled up through my legs into my belly.

I caught a look at all three of them boys, and I remember thinkin none of em was much older'n me. But their eyes was flat and mean.

"We gon' teach you a lesson about botherin white ladies," said the one holdin the rope. That was the last thing them boys said to me.

I don't like to talk much 'bout what happened next, 'cause I ain't lookin for no pity party. That's just how things was in Louisiana in those days. Mississippi, too, I reckon, since a coupla years later, folks started tellin the story about a young colored fella named Emmett Till who got beat till you couldn't tell who he was no more. He'd whistled at a white woman, and some other good ole boys—seemed like them woods was full of em—didn't like that one iota. They beat that boy till one a' his eyeballs fell out, then tied a cotton-gin fan around his neck and throwed him off a bridge into the Tallahatchie River. Folks says if you was to walk across that bridge today, you could still hear that drowned young man cryin out from the water.

There was lots of Emmett Tills, only most of em didn't make the news. Folks says the bayou in Red River Parish is full to its pea-green brim with the splintery bones of colored folks that white men done fed to the gators for covetin their women, or maybe just lookin cross-eyed. Wadn't like it happened ever day. But the chance of it, the threat of it, hung over the cotton fields like a ghost.

I worked them fields for nearly thirty years, like a slave, even though slavery had supposably ended when my grandma was just a girl. I had a shack I didn't own, two pairs a' overalls I got on credit, a hog, and a outhouse. I worked them fields, plantin and plowin and pickin and givin all the cotton to the Man that owned the land, all without no paycheck. I didn't even know what a paycheck was.

It might be hard for you to imagine, but I worked like that while the seasons rolled by from the time I was a little bitty boy, all the way past the time that president named Kennedy got shot dead in Dallas.

All them years, there was a freight train that used to roll through Red River Parish on some tracks right out there by Highway 1. Ever day, I'd hear it whistle and moan, and I used to imagine it callin out about the places it could take me . . . like New York City or Detroit, where I heard a colored man could get paid, or California, where I heard nearly everbody that breathed was stackin up paper money like flapjacks. One day, I just got tired a' bein poor. So I walked out to Highway 1, waited for that train to slow down some, and jumped on it. I didn't get off till the doors opened up again, which happened to be in Fort Worth, Texas. Now when a black man who can't read, can't write, can't figger, and don't know how to work nothin but cotton comes to the big city, he don't have too many of what white folks call "career opportunities." That's how come I wound up sleepin on the streets.

I ain't gon' sugarcoat it: The streets'll turn a man nasty. And I had been nasty, homeless, in scrapes with the law, in Angola prison, and homeless again for a lotta years by the time I met Miss Debbie. I want to tell you this about her: She was the skinniest, nosiest, pushiest woman I had ever met, black or white.

She was so pushy, I couldn't keep her from finding out my name was Denver. She investigated till she found it out on her own. For a long time, I tried to stay completely outta her way. But after a while, Miss Debbie got me to talkin 'bout things I don't like to talk about and tellin things I ain't never told nobody—even about them three boys with the rope. Some of them's the things I'm fixin to tell you.

2

Ron

Life produces some inglorious moments that live forever in your mind. One from 1952 remains seared on my brain like the brand on a longhorn steer. In those days, all schoolchildren had to bring urine samples to school, which public health workers would then screen for dread diseases. As a second grader at Riverside Elementary in Fort Worth, Texas, I carefully carried my pee to school in a Dixie cup like all the other good boys and girls. But instead of taking it to the school nurse, I mistakenly took it directly to Miss Poe, the meanest and ugliest teacher I ever had.

My error sent her into a hissy fit so well-developed you'd have thought I'd poured my sample directly into the coffee cup on her desk. To punish me, she frog-marched me and the whole second-grade class out to the playground like a drill sergeant, and clapped us to attention.

"Class, I have an announcement," she rasped, her smoke-infected voice screeching like bad brakes on an 18-wheeler. "Ronnie Hall will not be participating in recess today. Because he was stupid enough to bring his Dixie cup to the classroom instead of the nurse's office, he will spend the next thirty minutes with his nose in a circle."

Miss Poe then produced a fresh stick of chalk and scrawled on the red-brick schoolhouse wall a circle approximately three inches above the spot where my nose would touch if I stood on flat feet. Humiliated, I slunk forward, hiked up on tiptoes, and stuck my nose on the wall. After five minutes, my eyes crossed and I had to close them, remembering that my mama had warned me never to look cross-eyed or they could get locked up that way. After fifteen minutes, my toes and calves cramped fiercely, and after twenty minutes, my tears washed the bottom half of Miss Poe's circle right off the wall.

With the strain of loathing peculiar to a child shamed, I hated Miss Poe for that. And as I grew older, I wished I could send her a message that I wasn't stupid. I hadn't thought of her in years, though, until a gorgeous day in June 1978 when I cruised down North Main Street in Fort Worth in my Mercedes convertible, and security waved me through the gate onto the private tarmac at Meacham Airfield like a rock star.

It would have been perfect if I could have had Miss Poe, a couple of old girlfriends—Lana and Rita Gail, maybe—and, what the heck, my whole 1963 Haltom High graduating class, lined up parade-style so they could all see how I'd risen above my lower-middle-class upbringing. Looking back, I'm surprised I made it to the airfield that day, since I'd spent the whole ten-mile trip from home admiring myself in the rearview mirror.

I guided the car to the spot where a pilot stood waiting before a private Falcon jet. Dressed in black slacks, a starched white shirt, and spit-shined cowboy boots, he raised his hand in greeting, squinting against the Texas heat already boiling up from the tarmac.

"Good morning, Mr. Hall," he called over the turbines' hum. "Need some help with those paintings?"

Carefully, and one at time, we moved three Georgia O'Keeffe paintings from the Mercedes to the Falcon. Together, the paintings were valued at just shy of $1 million. Two years earlier, I had sold the same collection—two of O'Keeffe's iconic flower paintings and one of a skull—to a wildly wealthy south Texas woman for half a million dollars. When she tore a personal check for the full amount from her Hermès leather checkbook, I asked her jokingly if she was sure her check was good.

"I hope so, hon," she said, smiling through her syrupy-sweet Texas drawl. "I own the bank."

Now, that client was divesting herself of both a gold-digging husband

and the O'Keeffes. The new buyer, an elegant, fiftyish woman who owned one of the finest apartments on Madison Avenue and probably wore pearls while bathing, was also divorcing. She was hosting a luncheon for me and a couple of her artsy, socialite friends that afternoon to celebrate her new acquisitions. No doubt an adherent to the philosophy that living well is the best revenge, she had used part of her king's-ransom divorce settlement to purchase the O'Keeffes at nearly double their former value. She was far too rich to negotiate the $1 million price tag. That suited me just fine, since it made my commission on the deal an even $100,000.

My client had sent the Falcon down from New York to retrieve me. Inside, I stretched out in a buttercream leather seat and perused the day's headlines. The pilot arrowed down the runway, took off to the south, then banked gently north. On the climb-out, I gazed down at Fort Worth, a city about to be transformed by local billionaires. It was much more than a face-lift: Giant holes in the ground announced the imminent construction of great gleaming towers of glass and steel. Galleries, cafés, museums, and upscale hotels would soon rise to join banks and legal offices, turning downtown Fort Worth from a sleepy cow-town into an urban epicenter with a pulse.

So ambitious was the project that it was systematically displacing the city's homeless population, which was actually a stated goal, a way to make our city a nicer place to live. Looking down from three thousand feet, I was secretly glad they were pushing the bums to the other side of the tracks, as I despised being panhandled every day on my way to work out at the Fort Worth Club.

My wife, Debbie, didn't know I felt quite that strongly about it. I played my nouveau elitism pretty close to the vest. After all, it had been only nine years since I'd been making $450 a month selling Campbell's soup for a living, and only seven since I'd bought and sold my first painting, secretly using—stealing?—Debbie's fifty shares of Ford Motor Company stock, a gift from her parents when she graduated from Texas Christian University.

Ancient history as far as I was concerned. I had shot like a rocket from canned soup to investment banking to the apex of the art world. The plain truth was, God had blessed me with two good eyes: one for art and the other

for a bargain. But you couldn't have told me that at the time. To my way of
thinking, I'd bootstrapped my way from lower-middle-class country boy into
the rarified atmosphere that oxygenates the lifestyles of the Forbes 400.

Debbie had threatened to divorce me for using the Ford stock—"The
only thing I owned outright, myself!" she fumed—but I nudged her toward
a cautious forgiveness with shameless bribes: a gold Piaget watch and a
mink jacket from Koslow's.

At first, I dabbled in art sales while keeping my investment-banking day
job. But in 1975, I cleared $10,000 on a Charles Russell painting I sold to a
man in Beverly Hills who wore gold-tipped white-python cowboy boots and
a diamond-studded belt buckle the size of a dinner plate. After that, I quit
banking and ventured out to walk the art-world tightwire without a net.

It paid off. In 1977, I sold my first Renoir, then spent a month in Europe,
spreading my name and news of my keen eye among the Old World art elite.
It didn't take long for the zeros to begin piling up in the bank accounts of Ron
and Debbie Hall. We didn't enjoy the same income level as my clients, whose
average net worth notched in somewhere between $50 and $200 million. But
they invited us into their stratosphere: yachting in the Caribbean, wing shooting in the Yucatán, hobnobbing at island resorts and old-money mansions.

I lapped it up, adopting as standard uniforms a closetful of Armani suits.
Debbie was less enamored with the baubles of wealth. In 1981 I called her
from the showroom floor of a Scottsdale, Arizona, Rolls-Royce dealer who
had taken a shine to an important western painting I owned.

"You're not going to believe what I just traded for!" I said the instant she
picked up the phone at our home in Fort Worth. I was sitting in the "what,"
a $160,000 fire-engine-red Corniche convertible with white leather interior
piped in red to match. I jabbered a description into my satellite phone.

Debbie listened carefully, then delivered her verdict: "Don't you dare
bring that thing home. Don't even drive it out of the showroom. I'd be
embarrassed to be seen in a car like that, or even have it in our driveway."

Had she really just called a top-of-the-line Rolls *that thing*? "I think it
would be fun," I volunteered.

"Ron, honey?"

"Yes?" I said, suddenly hopeful at her sweet tone.

"Does that Rolls have a rearview mirror?"

"Yes."

"Look in it," she said. "Do you see a rock star?"

"Uh, no . . ."

"Just remember, you sell pictures for a living. Now get out of the Rolls, get your Haltom City butt on a plane, and come home."

I did.

The same year Debbie snubbed the Rolls, I opened a new gallery on Main Street in Fort Worth's blossoming cultural district, an area called Sundance Square, and hired a woman named Patty to manage it. Though we displayed impressionist and modern master paintings—Monet, Picasso, and their peers—worth several hundred thousand dollars, we were careful about posting prices or keeping too much inventory on-site, as a good number of derelicts had not yet been convinced to move to their new accommodations under the freeways to the southeast. Greasy and smelly, several came in each day to cool down, warm up, or case the place. Most of them were black, and I felt sure they all were also alcoholics and addicts, though I had never taken the time to hear their stories—I didn't really care.

One day, a drug-dazed black man, filthy in thread-worn army fatigues, shambled into the gallery. "How much you want for that picture?" he slurred, jabbing his finger at a $250,000 Mary Cassatt.

Fearing he might rob me, I tried to humor him while evading the truth. "How much you got in your pocket?"

"Fifty dollahs," he said.

"Then give it to me, and you can walk out the door with that picture."

"No, suh! I ain't givin you fifty dollahs for that picture!"

"Well, this isn't a museum and I didn't charge admission, so if you're not buying, how am I supposed to pay the rent?" I then invited him to leave.

A few days later, he returned with an equally nasty-looking partner and perpetrated a little smash-and-grab, bursting out onto the sidewalk with a sackful of cash and artisan jewelry. Patty hit the real-live panic button we'd had installed, and I ran down from the upstairs suite, commencing a classic movie-style chase, with the robbers ducking down alleys and leaping trash cans, and me in hot pursuit, yelling, "Stop those men! I've been robbed!"

I sprinted at first, but slowed down a little after it occurred to me to wonder what I would do with the bums if I caught them. (I yelled louder to make up for running slower.) By the time the police collared them a few blocks away, the crooks were empty-handed, having left a ten-block trail of jewelry and $20 bills.

The incident firmly fixed my image of homeless people as a ragtag army of ants bent on ruining decent people's picnics. I had no idea at that time that God, in His elaborate sense of humor, was laying the groundwork for one of them to change my life.

3

Nobody ever told me how I got my name Denver. For the longest time, nobody ever called me nothin but Li'l Buddy. Supposably, when I was just a little bitty fella, PawPaw, my granddaddy, used to carry me around in the front pocket of his overalls. So that's why they called me Li'l Buddy, I guess.

I never really knowed much about my mama. She was just a young girl, too young to take good care of me. So she did what she had to do and gave me over to PawPaw and Big Mama. That's just the way things was on the plantations and the farms in Red River Parish. Colored families came in all different shapes and sizes. You might have a growed woman livin in a shotgun shack, pickin cotton and raisin' her own brothers and sisters, and that would be a family. Or you might have a uncle and aunt raisin' her sister's kids, and that would be a family. A lotta children just had a mama and no daddy.

Part of that come from bein poor. I know that ain't no popular thing to say in this day and age. But that was the truth. Lotta times the men would be sharecroppin on them plantations and look around and wonder why they was workin the land so hard and ever year the Man that owned the land be takin all the profits.

Since there ain't no sharecroppin now, I'm gon' tell you how it worked: The Man owned the land. Then he give you the cotton seeds, and the fertilizer, and the mule, and some clothes, and everthing else you need to get through the year. 'Cept he don't really *give* it to you: He let you buy it at the store on credit. But it was his store on his plantation that he owned.

You plowed and planted and tended till pickin time. Then at the end of the year, when you bring in the cotton, you go to the Man and settle up.

11

Supposably, you gon' split that cotton right down the middle, or maybe sixty-forty. But by the time the crop comes in, you owe the Man so much on credit, your share of the crop gets eat up. And even if you don't think you owe that much, or even if the crop was 'specially good that year, the Man weighs the cotton and writes down the figgers, and he the only one that can read the scale or the books.

So you done worked all year and the Man ain't done nothin, but you still owe the Man. And wadn't nothin you could do but work his land for another year to pay off that debt. What it come down to was: The Man didn't just own the land. He owned *you*. Got so there was a sayin that went like this: "An ought's an ought, a figger's a figger, all for the white man, none for the nigger."

When I was just a little fella, folks said there was a man named Roosevelt who lived in a white house and that he was tryin to make things better for colored folks. But there was a whole lotta white folks, 'specially sheriffs, that liked things just the way they was. Lotta times this was mighty discouragin to the colored men, and they would just up and leave, abandonin their women and children. Some was bad men. But some was just ashamed they couldn't do no better. That ain't no excuse, but it's the God's honest truth.

I didn't know hardly nobody that had a mama and daddy both. So me and my big brother, Thurman, lived with Big Mama and PawPaw, and we didn't think nothin of it. We had a sister, too, Hershalee, but she was already grown and lived down the road a ways.

Big Mama was my daddy's mama, 'cept I didn't call him Daddy. I called him BB. He'd come around the house ever now and then. We lived with Big Mama and PawPaw in a three-room shack with cracks in the floor big enough to see the ground through. Wadn't no windows, just wooden shutters. We didn't mind the holes in the floor when it was hot out, but in the wintertime, the cold would stick its ugly head up between the cracks and bite us. We tried to knock it back with some loose boards or the tops of tin cans.

Now, Big Mama and PawPaw made quite a pair. Big Mama was a *big* woman . . . and I don't mean just big-boned. She was big sideways, north to south, all the way around. She used to make up her own dresses outta flour sacks. In those days, flour sacks was kinda purty. They might come printed up with flowers on em, or birds. It took seven or eight right big ones to make Big Mama a dress.

On the other hand, PawPaw was kinda smallish. Standin next to Big Mama, he looked downright puny. She coulda beat him down, I guess. But she was a quiet woman, and kind. I never heard a' her whuppin nobody, or even raisin' her voice. Wadn't no mistakin, though, she did run the place. PawPaw didn't run nothin but his mouth. But he took care of Big Mama. She didn't have to go out in the fields and work. She was busy raisin' her grandbabies.

She wadn't just my grandma, though. Big Mama was my best friend. I loved her and used to take care of her, too. She was kinda sick when I was a little boy, and she had a lotta pain. I used to give her her medicine. I don't know 'xactly what kinda pills they was, but she used to call em Red Devils.

"Li'l Buddy, go on and get Big Mama two a' them Red Devils," she'd say. "I needs to get easy."

I did a lotta special things for Big Mama, like takin out the slop jar or catchin a chicken in the yard and wringin its neck off so she could fry it up for supper. Now, ever year PawPaw raised us a turkey for Thanksgivin. Fed him special to get him nice and fat. The first year she thought I was big enough, Big Mama said, "Li'l Buddy, get on outside and wring that turkey's neck off. I'm fixin to cook him up."

I'm tellin you what, that turned out to be a tough row to hoe. When I took out after that Tom, he lit out like he was runnin from the devil hisself. He zigged and zagged, kickin up dirt and squawkin like I was killin him already. I chased that bird till I thought my legs would give out, and till that day, I didn't know a turkey could fly! He took off just like a aeroplane and set hisself down way up high in a cypress tree.

That bird wadn't no fool, neither. He didn't come back till three or four days after Thanksgivin. Made us have to eat chicken that year.

When that turkey flew the coop, I thought I was gon' get my first whuppin for sure. But Big Mama just laughed till I thought she would bust. I guess that's 'cause she knowed I did the best I could. She trusted me like that.

Matter a' fact, she trusted me more than she trusted my daddy and my uncles—her own sons. Like that money belt she kept tied around her waist— I was the onlyest one she let go up under her dress to get the money out.

"Li'l Buddy, get up under there and get me out two dimes and a quarter," she'd say. And I'd get that money and give it to whoever she wanted to have it.

Big Mama always had somethin for me. Some peppermint candy or maybe some bottle caps so I could make me a truck. If I wanted a truck, I'd get a block a' wood and nail on four bottle caps, two on the front and two on the back, and I had me a truck I could roll around in the dirt. But them times was few and far between. I never was a playin child. Never asked for no toys at Christmas. Didn't have that in my personality.

I guess that's why I acted like I did when the first tragedy come into my life.

— — —

One night when I was about five or six, Big Mama's legs was givin her fits and she had asked me for two a' them Red Devils and went on to bed. Wadn't long after that, me and Thurman went on to bed, too, even though our cousin, Chook, said he was gon' sit up for a while beside the fire. He'd been stayin with us.

Me and Thurman had a room in the back of the house. I didn't have no proper bed, just a mattress set up on wood boards and cement blocks. I kinda liked it, though, 'cause I had a window right over my head. In the summertime, I could leave the shutters open and smell the warm earth and look up at the stars winkin at me.

Seemed like there was more stars in those days than there is now. Wadn't no 'lectric lights blottin out the sky. 'Cept for the moon cuttin a hole in the dark, the nights was just as black as molasses, and the stars glittered like broken glass in the sun.

Now, I had me a little cat that I had found when he was just a little furball of a kitten. I don't even remember what I called him now, but he used to sleep on my chest ever night. His fur tickled my chin, and his purrin was just like a tonic to me; had a rhythm soothed me right to sleep. That night, though, seemed like I'd been sleepin quite a while when that cat jumped off my chest and scratched me. I woke up with a holler, and the cat hopped up in the window and started meowing real hard and wouldn't quit. So I got up to see what was wrong with the cat, and in the moonlight, I could see smoke in the house.

First I thought I was 'lucinatin and rubbed my eyes. But when I opened em up again, that smoke was still there, turnin round and round. First thing I did was shoo my cat out the window. Then I ran into Big Mama's room, but I didn't see no fire. I knew the house was burnin, though, 'cause that smoke started pilin up real thick. Even though I couldn't see no flames, it felt like there was fire burnin my throat and my eyes. I started coughin real bad and ran to the front door, but PawPaw had already gone to work and locked it. I knowed the back door had a wooden latch on it that I could barely reach.

I ran back to my room and tried to wake up my brother. "Thurman! Thurman! The house on fire! Thurman, wake up!"

I kept shakin and shakin him, but he was hard sleepin. Finally, I jerked the covers off him and rared back a fist and hit him upside the head just as hard as I could. He jumped up then, mad as a wet cat, and tackled me. We rolled on the floor just a-scrappin, and I kept tryin to yell at him that the house was on fire. He caught on after a minute, and me and him jumped out the window into the johnsongrass outside. Even though he was bigger than me, Thurman plopped down on the ground and started cryin.

I tried to think real fast what could I do. Big Mama was still in the house, and so was Chook. I decided to go back in and try to get em out. I jumped up, grabbed the edge of the window, and shimmied up the side a' the house, climbin the boards with my bare toes. When I got inside, I ran out into the front room, stayin down low under the smoke, and there was Chook, sittin by the fireplace with a poker in his hand, just starin with his eyes all glazed up.

"Chook! The house on fire! Help me get Big Mama; we got to get out!" But Chook just kept pokin in the fireplace like he was in a trance.

I looked up and seen sparks shootin down outta the chimney and spinnin off into the smoke like whirligigs. That's when I knowed the chimney was on fire and probl'y the roof. I was coughin and coughin by then, but I had

to try to save my grandma. I scrunched down low and found my way back
to her room. I could see her face, sleepin hard like Thurman had been, and
I shook her and shook her, but she wouldn't wake up.

"Big Mama! Big Mama!" I screamed right in her ear, but she acted more
like she was dead than sleepin. I could hear the fire in the chimney now,
roarin low like a train. I pulled and pulled on Big Mama, tryin to drag her
out the bed, but she was too heavy.

"Big Mama! Please! Big Mama! Wake up! The house on fire!"

I thought maybe the smoke had done got her, and my heart broke in half
right there where I was standin. I could feel tears runnin down my face, part
from grief and part from the smoke. It was gettin real hot, and I knowed I
had to come on up outta there or I'd be done in, too.

I ran out to the front room, hollerin and screamin and coughin at Chook,
"You got to get out, Chook! The smoke done got Big Mama! Come on up
outta here!"

Chook just turned and looked at me with eyes that looked like he was
already dead. "No, I'm gon' stay here with Big Mama." I can't explain why,
but he wadn't even coughin or nothin. Then he went back to pokin in the
fireplace.

That's when I heard a crackin noise that made me freeze and look up:
The roof was fixin to cave in. The smoke started to get so thick I couldn't
see Chook no more. I got down on my hands and knees and felt my way till
I felt the feet of the potbelly stove, then I knowed I was close to the back
door. I crawled a little farther till I could see a little crack of daylight slidin
up under the door. I stood up and stretched just as high as I could to where
I could just barely reach that wooden latch with the tips of my fingers. Then
the door burst open and I rolled out, with the black smoke boilin out after
me like a pack a' demons.

I ran around to find Thurman on the side of the house by Big Mama's
room, just a-squallin. I was cryin, too. We could see tongues of fire lickin
down from under the eaves till they grabbed hold of some boards and
began to burn down the sides of the house. The heat pushed us back, but I
couldn't stop hollerin, "Big Mama! Big Mama!"

The fire swirled up into the dawn like a cyclone, roarin and poppin, sendin out the black smell of things that ain't s'posed to be burnin. The horriblest thing was when the roof fell in, 'cause that's when Big Mama finally woke up. Between the flames and the smoke, I could see her rollin round and callin out to the Lord.

"Help me, Jesus! Save me!" she hollered, thrashin and coughin in the smoke. Then there was a loud crack and Big Mama screamed. I saw a big piece of wood crash down and pin her on her bed. She couldn't move no more, but she kept hollerin, "Lord Jesus, save me!"

I only heard Chook holler one time then he was quiet. I stood there and screamed and watched my grandmother burn up.

4

As I mentioned, I did not start out rich. I was raised in a lower-middle-class section of Fort Worth called Haltom City, a town so ugly that it was the only one in Texas with no picture postcard of itself for sale in the local pharmacy. No mystery there: Who would want to commemorate a visit to a place where a shabby-looking house trailer or cars stripped for parts squatted in every other yard, guarded by mongrel dogs on long chains? We used to joke that the only heavy industry in Haltom City was the three-hundred-pound Avon lady.

My daddy, Earl, was raised by a single mother and two old-maid aunts who dipped Garrett snuff till it ran down their chins and dried in the wrinkles. I hated to kiss them. Daddy started out a comical, fun-loving man who retired from Coca-Cola after forty-odd years of service. But somewhere during my childhood, he crawled into a whiskey bottle and didn't come out till I was grown.

My mama, Tommye, was a farm girl from Barry, Texas, who sewed every stitch of clothing we wore, baked cookies, and cheered me on at Little League. As a girl, she and her sister and brother all rode a horse to school—the same horse, all at once. Her brother's name was Buddy, and her sister's name was Elvice, which was pronounced "Elvis," a fact that would later become something of a problem.

Tommye, Buddy, Elvice, and later, Vida May, the youngest, all picked cotton on the blackland farm owned by their daddy and my granddaddy, Mr. Jack Brooks.

Now, most people are not in the market for Texas blackland farms, as they are not at all romantic. The topography is mainly flat, so there is a scarcity of sunset-washed knolls from which to gaze upon your plantation house and declare that some Irish love of the land will soon seize your soul. In fact, the land itself is miserable, cursed with soil that may well be the original inspiration for cement. The flimsiest morning mist will cause a man in work boots to pull up a mud stump every time he takes a step. A half-inch rain will motivate even the most determined farmer to throw his tractor in low and head for the blacktop if he doesn't want to spend the next day cussing while he digs out his John Deere.

That is not to say my granddaddy's place outside Corsicana, about seventy-five miles southeast of Fort Worth, wasn't pleasant in a rural way. My brother, John, and I spent our summers there by choice, an option we considered far superior to three months of hunting down our daddy at the Tailless Monkey Lounge. Nine months of that a year was enough for us.

So every June, when Mama drove us out to the home place, we leaped out of her Pontiac and ran toward Granddaddy and MawMaw's green-asphalt-shingled farmhouse with the joy of soldiers on furlough. Raised in the 1920s, the house was built like a box. I don't remember when they got indoor plumbing, but while I was a boy, a cistern squatted by the back door to catch rainwater running off the roof. MawMaw had a white porcelain pan sitting on the back porch. When we came in for supper, we'd draw some water out of the cistern and wash our hands with a bar of Lava soap, which is about like washing with sandpaper. But Lava is the only kind of soap that'd get the dirt off a man who'd been working the fields on a blackland farm.

Granddaddy worked like a mule and was a true redneck. That's because he wore khaki pants and a long-sleeved khaki work shirt and work boots six days a week. His entire body was snow-white, except for his bronzed, leathery hands and, of course, his neck, which was covered east to west with thick wrinkles colored Indian red like plowed furrows on more gracious land. He was a decent, honest man who would help anyone who needed helping. He was also the hardest-working man I ever knew.

My uncle Buddy tells the story about my granddaddy as a poor young man heading back to Texas after World War I. After kicking the crap out of the Germans in France, Granddaddy, in his twenties, had to try to figure out how to keep a wife, raise four kids, and pay for a little farm. Along the way, he asked a neighbor, an old farmer named Barnes, how he did it.

"Jack, you watch me," Mr. Barnes said. "You work when I work and go to town when I go to town."

As you might expect, Mr. Barnes never went to town. And seldom did my granddaddy. During the dust bowl and Great Depression, he hung on tight, so skinny he had to carry rocks in his pockets to keep from blowing away. At a time when even banks had no money and a man couldn't get a nickel's worth of credit even if his name was Rockefeller, he made it by picking cotton all day and hauling it on a mule wagon to the gin at night. He slept on the cotton till it was his turn to get ginned, drove back to the field at sunrise, and repeated this cotton waltz until the harvest was done.

Most summer days, John and I were with Granddaddy in the fields, picking cotton or riding shotgun on the tractor. When we weren't with Granddaddy, we leaned toward trouble. MawMaw kept a big peach orchard near the road that passed by the farm. I loved the smell of the orchard when the fruit hung ripe and sweet. Ripe peaches also make mean grenades. One day John and I had a contest to see who could lob one far enough and hard enough to nail a passing car.

"Betcha I can hit one first!" John called from his battle station, high in a tree loaded with ripe fruit.

In another tree, I lined up squishy ammo in the crotch between two branches. "Betcha can't!"

It took us several tries, but one of us, we still don't know which, finally managed to bust out the windshield of a 1954 Ford Fairlane. The driver, a woman, pulled over and marched up to the farmhouse to lodge her complaint with MawMaw. To hear her tell it, you'd have thought we'd shelled her with field artillery. When Granddaddy got home, he cut a switch out of one of those peach trees and wore us out. He also tanned our hides the time we, without permission, repainted the entire chicken house, including the tin roof, a frightening shade of baby blue.

Still, Granddaddy himself loved to pull pranks. When I think back on it,

I guess some of his pranks weren't pranks so much as him teaching boys to be men. Once, he threw John and me in the stock tank to teach us how to swim before he remembered he didn't know how to swim either, and couldn't rescue us. Both of us learned to swim real quick.

One Christmas we spent at the home place, John and I opened up two shiny packages and each found a pair of boxing gloves. Right there on the spot, Granddaddy loaded us both in his 1947 Chevy pickup and took us into Barry to the filling station, which in those days doubled as a place for old men to play checkers, drink coffee, and talk about the weather and cattle prices. Secretly, Granddaddy had already called the daddies of every kid in town within three years of our ages, and that morning they came barreling up to the filling station on clouds of yuletide dust, and formed a pickup-truck boxing ring. John and I had to fight every kid in town, and both of us had bloody noses before breakfast, which we thought was great. Granddaddy wore himself out laughing. That, and riding new calves every Christmas morning, their warm breath carving curlicues in the daybreak chill, are my favorite Christmas memories.

On the farm, MawMaw did her part milking cows, raising kids and a garden, putting up peaches, green beans, and squash for winter, and cooking Granddaddy two chocolate pies a day. He ate one at dinner and the other at supper and remained a six-foot-one, 140-pound string bean his whole life.

Folks used to say Granddaddy looked like Kildee, the black shoeshine man who worked in the Blooming Grove barbershop. Old Kildee was a beanpole, too, and didn't have a tooth in his head. He used to entertain folks by squinching up his chin to touch his nose. Granddaddy once gave John fifty cents to give Kildee a kiss, which John happily did, not only because he earned four bits to spend on candy, but also because everyone loved Kildee.

To this day, Kildee is the only black man buried in Rose Hill Cemetery in Blooming Grove, Texas, laid to rest right there amid the expired ancestors of the finest white families in Navarro County.

In other parts of the country, maybe dead folks didn't worry so much about the color of neighboring corpses. But the civil rights movement that began to gather steam in the 1950s hopped right over Corsicana, Texas, the way a soaking spring rain can skip over parched land despite a farmer's most fervent prayers.

— — —

In the 1950s, the Southern social order was as plain to the eye as charcoal in a snowbank. But from the perspective of a small fair-skinned boy, it was about as much a topic for considered thought as breathing in and out. White families in Corsicana lived mostly on farms or in neat rows of freshly painted homes in town. Colored folks had their own section across the railroad tracks near the cotton gin and the commission company's cattle pens. I don't know if the area had a proper name, but I never heard it called anything but "Nigger Town."

At the time, that didn't seem to be a bad thing because these were nice folks who lived there, and many of them worked for my granddaddy. As far as I knew, all their first names were "Nigger" and their last names were like our first names: Bill, Charlie, Jim, and so forth. Some of them even had Bible names like Abraham, Moses, and Isaac. So there was "Nigger Bill" and "Nigger Moses," but none of them were ever called by a proper first and last name like mine, Ronnie Ray Hall, or my granddaddy's, Jack Brooks. And really, there seemed no reason in those days to know their last names as no checks were ever written to them, and for sure there were no insurance forms to fill out or anything like that. Not that I thought about it in such detail back then: That was just the way things were.

Nigger Town was made up, row upon row, of one- and two-room shacks built of gray plank lumber that looked like it had been salvaged from a shipwreck. Some people used to call them "shotgun shacks" because, I found out later, they were so small that if you stood in the front door and fired a shotgun into the house, the blast would blow straight out the back door. The houses were all lined up like cars on a used lot and stuck so close together that a really fat person coming out the front door would have had to walk all the way around the block to get in the back.

Maybe they had been built somewhere else because there wasn't room enough between them to swing a hammer. It seemed as if someone had just craned them in and plopped them down on sawed-off bois d'arc stumps, so you could see all the way underneath them. But that was a good thing as those open cellars made a perfect place for mongrel dogs and chickens to take cover from the scorching Texas sun.

Granddaddy hired lots of colored folks, and a few white men, to help farm his cotton. Every morning before light, we'd drive a truck into Nigger Town and start honking the horn. Anybody—man, woman, or child—capable of chopping weeds and wanting to work that day would stagger from their shacks, dressing as they came, and climb aboard. There weren't any safety rails or rules about hauling folks: Granddaddy just tried to drive slow enough to keep from throwing anybody off.

After a morning chopping cotton, we'd load up all the workers and haul them to the filling station, which doubled as a grocery store. The colored workers would line up before the glass front of the white-porcelain meat counter and choose a thick slice of baloney or pickle-loaf and a chunk of cheddar cheese. Granddaddy, standing by the cash register, would pay the bill, throwing in a box of saltines and a couple of raw onions for everyone to share. They'd all take their lunches, wrapped in white butcher paper, and go sit on the ground behind the store. There was a cistern out there for drinking, with a can strapped with black tape so they wouldn't make a mistake about which one to drink from.

With the coloreds taken care of, we'd hop back in the truck and carry any whites who were working that day back to the farmhouse for dinner. MawMaw always put on a spread, stuff like fried chicken, fresh black-eyed peas, homemade rolls all hot and buttery, and always a pie or a cobbler. Even as a little boy, it bothered me that the colored workers ate lunchmeat on the ground behind the filling station while the white workers gathered like family for hot, home-cooked food. Sometimes I had the urge to do something about it, but I never did.

At the end of every workday, Granddaddy paid all the workers the same, three or four dollars apiece, and carried them back to town. He always gave them a square deal, even making no-interest loans to colored families to carry them through the winter when work was scarce. Jack Brooks made these loans on a handshake and didn't keep books, which made it hard for MawMaw to know who owed him money. But the Negroes in Corsicana respected him so much that after he died in 1962, several came unbidden to pay both their respects and their debts.

From the time I was six or seven, I worked out in the fields, chopping cotton beside them.

One day when I was about fourteen, some of those fellows and I were chopping a long row, pouring sweat and fighting off grasshoppers the size of small foreign cars. Grasshoppers on a blackland farm are evil creatures that cling to your clothes like burrs and spit a foul brown juice at you when you try to peel them off. That day, the air buzzed and sweltered around us till it seemed like Granddaddy had planted his cotton on the surface of some bug-ridden alien sun.

To pass the time, two men chopping on either side of me began to discuss their social calendar for the evening. A man everyone called Nigger John—he had worked for Granddaddy since I could remember—hacked his hoe into a fresh patch of johnsongrass and bull nettles. "When the sun gets low," he told his friend Amos, "I'm gon' get on up outta here and go down to Fanny's Place and get me a beer and a woman. Wish I could go right now 'fore I burn up."

"I'm goin with you," Amos announced. "'Cept I can't decide whether to get me one woman and two beers, or one beer and *two* women."

John shot Amos a sly grin. "Why don't you get two women and give one of em to Ronnie Ray here?"

Now I knew Fanny's was what the coloreds called a "juke joint," which by legend meant a dark, smoky den frequented by persons of questionable character. But at age fourteen, it had never occurred to me that a man could simply "get him" a woman, much less two. I put my head down and listened close, pretending to bear down on a particularly stubborn clump of weeds.

John wasn't buying. "What you so quiet for, Ronnie Ray?" he teased. "You mean to tell me you ain't never had a warm beer and a cold woman?"

At that juncture of my young life, I was obviously no man of the world. But I wasn't stupid either. I straightened up, tipped back my straw hat, and fixed John with a grin of my own. "Ain't you got that backward, John? Don't you mean a *cold* beer and a *warm* woman?"

For the next minute and a half, it seemed John and Amos might require medical attention. They fell on each other howling and gasping, hoots of laughter floating like music out over the fields until John finally recovered enough to lift the corner on the curtain of my innocence.

"Nah, Ronnie Ray, I ain't got nothin' backward!" he said. "The women at Fanny's so hot, they got to sit on ice blocks to cool em down enough so they can get down to business. Miss Fanny don't be wastin no ice on no beer."

Well, that busted open the dam. John knew Granddaddy and MawMaw were teetotalers and came to regard it as his solemn duty to make sure I didn't see another birthday without having experienced the pleasure of a warm beer. After several days of ribbing, he and Amos finally threw down the gauntlet.

"You come on down to Fanny's tonight, and we'll fix you up," John promised.

So on a steaming night in August, I eased Granddaddy's '53 Chevy down the hill from the farmhouse, engine quiet, then popped the clutch and drove the ten miles to Corsicana. My chopping buddies were waiting for me just across the tracks.

I had never been to Nigger Town without Granddaddy, so I was plenty nervous as the three of us walked down dirt roads lined with shotgun shacks and not a single lightbulb. Mostly, folks just sat out on their porches, eyes watching in a black night broken only by a coal-oil lantern, a struck match, or the orange glow of a cigarette. It seemed we'd walked halfway across Texas before the sound of guitar music floated toward us and, like a dream, a low building took shape in the dark.

Inside, Fanny's was smoky, red, and dim. At the head of a dirt dance floor, a buxom woman crooned the blues, steaming up the place like a tropical rain on hot sand. John and Amos introduced me to their friends, who greeted me like a local celebrity and handed me a Pabst Blue Ribbon, warm as advertised, then slipped away.

For most of the next hour, I sat alone at a corner table, fixated on silhou-ettes of shirtless men drenched in sweat and women in dresses that clung to their bodies, locked together in a slow, sexual kind of dancing I'd never seen before. I'd heard the music before, though, real, live blues sung by people with names like Lightning Hopkins and Big Fat Sarah over scratchy air-waves beamed live from Laredo at midnight by Wolfman Jack.

I pretended to swig on the PBR. But when I was sure nobody was looking, I let it slosh on the dirt floor as I discovered that the smell of beer nauseated me, kicking up memories of me looking for my daddy at the Tailless Monkey Lounge.

5

It didn't take long for Big Mama's house to burn down to a heapin pile of smokin red coals. When the flames had died down, I sat there next to it just a-cryin, not understandin why God would take away the person I loved the most.

After a little while, somebody come and took me and Thurman to live in Grand Bayou with BB, my daddy. I didn't know him very well, and I still don't know what he did for a livin, just that he worked in the city—Shreveport, I think, down past where my aunt Pearlie May lived. Maybe he was workin on the railroad stackin hisself some paper money 'cause he was rich enough to buy him a car, a big ole two-door like a Pontiac.

BB was a big man, heavyset. He wadn't six feet tall, but he looked it, and even though I was just a little fella, I could tell he was popular with the ladies. BB liked the ladies, too, and used to keep three or four of em on a string at the same time. That's why on Sunday mornings, he wouldn't set foot in the New Mary Magdalene Baptist Church. One or two of his women was already married, and they and their husbands was part of the congregation.

That didn't mean BB didn't love Jesus—he just had to find a different way to visit Him on Sundays. So me and him and Thurman would go to church kinda like we was goin to a drive-in picture show. Now, the church house wadn't too far off the road. It was painted white and had a real nice pecan tree spreadin some shade over some raggedy grass out front. Instead of parkin and goin in through the big double doors like the rest a' the folks, BB'd pull his Pontiac right up beside the church house. They musta knowed we was comin 'cause when BB drove up, the preacher'd come over and slide

27

up a window right next to the car so we could sit in that Pontiac and listen to the Word of God.

I couldn't see nothin inside the church, but I'd hear the choir and the congregation singin some spirituals. I had some favorites, and I would sing along.

> *He's got the rivers and the mountains in His hands,*
> *He's got the oceans and the seas in His hands,*
> *He's got you and He's got me in His hands,*
> *He's got the whole world in His hands.*

I hoped He had Big Mama and Chook in His hands. I was purty sure He did.

After the singin was done, the preacher'd commence to preachin. He had a style about him, liked to start out soft and low like he was singin a lullaby. But 'fore long he'd work hisself up into a righteous sweat. I remember the way he said "God"—kinda long and drawed out, sounded like "Gaw-ud."

And he just *loved* to talk about sin.

"Now *sin* is when you misses the mark that Gaw-ud is aimin for you to *hit*," he'd say. "Bein' lazy is a *sin* 'cause Gaw-ud is aimin for you to be *diligent*. Bein foolish is a *sin* 'cause Gaw-ud is aimin for you to be *wise*. And bein lustful is a *sin*, 'cause Gaw-ud is aimin for you to be *chaste*. Can I get a witness?"

"Amen!" the church would holler. "Praise Jesus!"

I couldn't see nobody sayin' it 'cause I was way down below the windowsill. But I remember that the folks inside seemed mighty enthusiastic. After the sermon, the choir would sing some more. Then someone would pass the offerin plate out the window, and BB would drop in some coins and pass it back in.

Me and Thurman wadn't with BB but for a few weeks when he left the house one night and didn't come back. One story goes that his car broke down on Highway 1. Another says it was sabotage. Either way, he pulled off the road out there by the Grand Bayou Social Club, and a man charged outta the woods and stabbed BB to death. Folks said the man that killed him was the husband of one of the women BB was messin with. I never found out if that man was one of the ones that worshipped with us on Sundays.

— — —

The next day, my uncle James Stickman come by and picked me and Thurman up in his wagon, pulled by mules. We went to live on a farm where my uncle James and aunt Etha was doin a little sharecroppin.

A lotta folks called croppin a new kinda slavery. Lotta croppers (even white ones, what few there was in Louisiana) didn't have just one massa— they had two. The first massa was the Man that owned the land you was workin. The second massa was whoever owned the store where you got your goods on credit. Sometimes both a' them men was the same Man; sometimes it was a different Man.

The Man that owned the land was always wantin you to plant less and less food, and more and more crops he could sell for cash money. In Red River Parish that meant plantin cotton from the doorstep to the edge of the road. That Man wound up bein your massa 'cause seemed like no matter how many bales a' cotton you turn, you always end up in the hole. The first year me and Thurman was with Uncle James and Aunt Etha, I think we turned two or three bales a' cotton. The next year, we turned five bales, but we was still in the hole. Didn't get no money, didn't get nothin but the privilege of stayin on for the next season to pay off what we owed. I was just a little fella, but I still couldn't understand how we could work so hard ever year, and ever year end up in the hole.

I always knowed white folks didn't think much of black folks back then— thought we was mainly lazy and not too bright. But I found out years later they thought black *croppers* had the extra burden of bein a little bit like boll weevils—ruinous. Someone told me they read where a planter said a cropper has nothin, wants nothin, expects nothin, don't try to have nothin, but wastes and destroys everthing.

That planter hadn't met my uncle James. He worked hard bringin in all that cotton for the Man, and he expected to be paid so he could provide for us. He was also the kind a' man who would speak his mind. Nobody messed with him—not even the Man. After 'bout three years, Uncle James got tired a' bein in the hole, and he told the Man he was tired of it and was fixin to move us all to a big plantation where he heard he could get a better deal. I reckon the Man didn't argue much or worry 'bout what Uncle James owed, 'cause he never did come after us.

The plantation where we moved stretched wide and deep, field after field stitched off with rows a' pecan trees. And ever one a' them fields was dedicated to King Cotton. First year we got there, the cotton flowers was just a-bloomin, and I remember seein rows and rows, acres and acres, of red and white flowers marchin off to meet the blue sky in ever direction.

The Man at that plantation hired on Uncle James and Aunt Etha to pick cotton and also do a little more croppin. Big Mama's sister, my great-aunt, lived there, too. I don't remember what I used to call her, 'cept Auntie. Maybe that's 'cause I was scared a' her and some a' that mumbo jumbo she did with powders she grinded up from leaves and roots. 'Specially after that time she made it rain.

Uncle James did his plowin with a mule named Ginny. Now, in those days used to be a big argument over which was the better animal, a horse or a mule. I grew up to be a mule man myself. Mules live longer than horses, don't get sick as much, and don't complain about a swelterin summer. And you can train up a mule to mind. He turn right when you say "Gee" and left when you say "Haw," and come when you whistle. That ain't the case with horses, which act kinda persnickety 'bout doin what they're told. A mule don't stomp on your cotton bushes, neither, like a horse do with his big ole clumsy feet. And you don't need to waste time feedin a mule, neither. Ginny knowed how to get up in the woods and hustle for herself.

When Uncle James got out in the fields with Ginny, Thurman and me would follow along behind the plow. Sometimes we'd get to horsin around and bouncin dirt clods off each other's heads. But only when Uncle James wadn't lookin. When he *was* lookin, we acted like we was all business, droppin cottonseed in the spring and huntin for armyworms in the summertime. When we was busy and quiet, I thought a lot about Big Mama, and my belly hurt.

Aunt Etha worked right out in the fields with us, too. She was a right purty red-bone woman, tall and gracious. She worked right alongside Uncle James, choppin cotton, scrapin the rows, and pickin, too. But when the sun got high, she gen'lly picked up her skirt and headed back to the house, 'cause she was in charge of the cookin.

You might think in those days that the women did all the cookin, but that wadn't true. It was just that the women did their cookin in the house, and the men did their cookin in the woods.

Prohibition was gone, but you still couldn't get no store-bought whiskey in Red River Parish. I'm tellin you, the woods was sproutin corn-liquor stills like toadstools.

A lotta folks think moonshiners was all hillbillies and rednecks sittin on the porch drinkin white lightnin outta Mason jars in the broad daylight. And sometimes that was the truth. Uncle James told me one time about some no-account white cropper he knew that spent mosta his days lyin out in the yard with a jug a' liquor, wallerin with the pigs and just as happy. Uncle James didn't think much a' him.

But right respectable folks was shinin, too. I knowed some colored folks worked on other farms and plantations owned by white men—bankers and such. Wadn't a one of em wadn't cookin up some liquor somewhere on his place. The Man had him a still tucked up in the woods so he could make a little sippin whiskey. When I got older, he took me up there a time or two.

"Climb up yonder and let me know if you see anybody comin," the Man'd say to me, and I'd climb up in a tree and watch for the sheriff.

Anyhow, Aunt Etha did all the cookin at Uncle James's. Anything we'd kill, she could make a meal out of it—possums, coons, rabbits, it didn't matter. Possums was a little extra trouble, though, 'cause you got to know how to deal with a possum. First you got to throw him in a fire outside and burn the hair off him. Then you got to scrape him down and put him in a pot and boil him, or maybe put him in a pan by the fire and let him roast with his head still on him. You can't get the grease out a possum 'less you do that.

Aunt Etha raised us a garden, too, 'cause there wadn't no such thing as goin down to the Piggly Wiggly. Only store you go to was the Man's store and that was just for a little salt, pepper, and flour 'cause we never did figure out how to make that. So mostly, whatever we was eatin was comin out of the woods or the ground. Aunt Etha's garden was fulla good things like field peas, butter beans, onions, sweet taters, and ash taters. I remember the sweet smell when she'd cut up a mess of wild peaches or pears and cook em down with sugar. It was a fine mornin when she rolled out the biscuits and put out the preserves, tastin sticky and sweet, like heaven in the summertime.

We growed our own greens—collards, turnip, and mustard—all simmered down with fatback and a little bit a' salt, with a great big ole slab of corn bread on the side. We got the cornmeal by takin the corn that we growed down to the little grindin mill over by the Man's store. The white folks at the store would grind the corn for us and give us the meal, and the Man would put the grindin on our bill. I never did know how much it was exactly.

He gave us our milk for free, though, for takin care of his cows. 'Cept we'd get blamed if one em went dry.

Now Christmas was killin time. Every year, the Man gave us two hogs to raise. We killed em at Christmas and hung em in the smokehouse. I was in charge a' the smokehouse, and I had to build the fire and keep it goin, which was the best job 'cause I got to sneak me a little piece of meat ever so often.

Aunt Etha used to love to make cracklins, which is somethin you don't see much of no more. She'd light the fire under a great big cast-iron wash pot and fill it up with slabs of pork fat. Then she'd cook that down till the pot was fulla hot bubblin lard with crispy little curlicues of hard fat floatin on the top. Them was the cracklins, and the smell of em fryin up would cause folks to drop their hoes in the field and follow their noses to the smokin pot like ants to a church picnic. We'd eat em like they was candy and make cracklin corn bread with the scraps.

Them hogs gen'lly lasted us for mosta the year, 'cause we didn't let nothin go to waste. Now the white folks was kinda picky about which parts a' the hog they'd eat. Not us. We ate the pig snout and the pig tail and everthing in between—from the rooter to the tooter!

You can't be wastin' nothin when that's all the meat you got to last you for a whole year. Even then, we had to stretch it out some, fillin in with other kinds a' meat. I guess we'd eat about anything 'cept for a skunk. I drug a skunk in the house one time, and when Aunt Etha saw it she started hollerin, "You get that skunk outta my house, boy!"

Uncle James whupped my tail, but not right then 'cause I stunk too bad. I had to go back down to the creek and wash off that stink with some lye soap, then go *back* and get my whuppin.

I got my share of whuppins, usually with a switch off a pecan tree. Sometimes, I'd go way down the road past where I was s'posed to go, and talk to a little girl I liked, 'cause I thought that was worth the whuppin when I got back. I got more whuppins for that than anything else.

"The heart of a child is fulla foolishness," Uncle James'd say with a stern face, quotin the Scriptures. "But the rod of correction will sure 'nough drive it out."

Sometimes when I'd get in trouble, though, he'd get a little smile in his eye. "I ain't gon' whup you this time," he'd say. "But do that again and I'm gon' whup you good." One time I had whuppins stacked up about four high. Uncle James was a good Christian man.

While he took care of our foolishness, Aunt Etha took care of our bodies and souls. Mostly, we never got very sick, but when we did, my auntie sure 'nough had the cure: Somethin she called "cow-lip tea."

Now cow-lip tea was brown and thin, kinda like the Lipton tea the Man sold at his store, but a durn sight more powerful. Cow-lip tea come from them white toadstools that sprout up outta cow patties. But there's a secret to makin it: You got to use the toadstools *and* part of the cow patty, too. That's where cow-lip tea got its name. "Cow" from the cow patties and "lip" from "Lipton." Least that's what Aunt Etha always told me.

The way you make cow-lip tea is you get the toadstools and a little dried cow patty and grind em up in the sifter. You can't use no fresh green cow patty to make no good tea, 'cause you can't grind it. So you take that dried patty, and after you get it ground up like fine powder, you put it in a rag and tie a knot on top. Then you add a little honey to a boilin pot and drop that rag in the water till it bubbles up and turns good and brown. Now you got cow-lip tea.

If I was sick, Aunt Etha'd always make me drink a canful.

"All good medicine tastes bad!" she'd say, then put me in the bed underneath a whole pile a' covers, no matter whether it was summertime or wintertime. In the mornin, the bed'd be soppin wet and the sheets'd be all yella, but I'd always be healed. I was nearly grown before I figured out what I was drinkin.

6

I spent every summer at Granddaddy and MawMaw's until 1963, when I enrolled at East Texas State, which at the time was the cheapest college in Texas. By that time, girls, their pursuit, and eventual capture were pretty much the center of my universe. But the little college my family could afford was stocked mainly with farm girls. By contrast, my buddy Scoot Cheney and I had heard that Texas Christian University, ninety miles west in Fort Worth, was slopping over with Rich Girls. And while I'd grown up nearby, I'd never been on the campus.

In our fantasies, Rich Girls would jet around town in dent-free, late-model sports cars, belong to country clubs, and live in houses that didn't have wheels on them. We were certain they would also be miles better looking than farm girls.

Though I never met one, I had etched in my mind an image of what Rich Girls looked like. When we were about ten and twelve, my brother, John, and I had a favorite game we played that went something like the card game slapjack. We'd sit on MawMaw's porch, slowly turn the pages in the Sears catalog, and try to be first to smack a hand down on the prettiest girl on each page, who would then become the imaginary girlfriend of whoever slapped her first. Later, I was sure the girls at TCU would look like the girls in the Sears catalog.

As it turned out, that was pretty close to the truth. But my first encounter with such a delicious creature fell victim to a wardrobe disaster.

My dear mama, Tommye, had always made all our clothes, so when I packed my bags for college, they were full of shirts she had carefully and lovingly sewn from feed sacks. But when I got to East Texas State, I noticed that most of the boys wore khaki pants and madras shirts, the kind made with that natural dye from India. Feed sacks, apparently, were out.

Worried, I called my mama. "Everybody here is dressed different than me. They're all wearing madras shirts."

"What's madras?" she asked.

I fumbled around for an explanation. "Well, it's kind of like plaid."

Now, Mama meant well, but to her plaid was plaid. She drove down to Hancock's Fabric Store and bought several yards of it, and whipped me up a matching shirt-and-shorts set.

In the meantime, Scoot and I landed our first blind dates with TCU girls, a pair of Tri Delta pledges. We were taking them to Amon Carter Stadium to root on the TCU football team, the mighty Horned Frogs, before a sell-out home crowd. The friend who fixed us up told me that my date, Karen McDaniel, looked like Natalie Wood.

Well, a date like that called for a new outfit, so on the way in from East Texas State, Scoot and I detoured by my house so I could pick up the one my mama had just finished. She beamed with pride when she handed it over, a pair of longish shorts and a short-sleeved, button-up shirt, both blue with black and green stripes as wide as highway centerlines. I knew it wasn't madras, but I figured it was better than a feed sack. When I modeled it for Mama, she bragged about how handsome I looked.

Then Scoot and I headed over to the TCU freshman girls' dorm.

"A movie star," is what I thought when Karen McDaniel stepped out onto the dorm's front porch: She had teased-up dark hair and big blue eyes that batted like strobe lights. I had never seen anybody who looked like that in Haltom City. As it turned out, Karen had never seen anybody who looked like me. Ever.

I had finished off the shorts set Mama made me with knee-high black socks and a pair of brogan-style, lace-up shoes. As I headed up the crowded dorm steps to introduce myself, another adorable brunette walked out of the dorm onto the porch. But when she saw my clothes, she screeched to a halt so fast it looked like she'd dropped a two-ton anchor. "Well, lookee here!" she blared, causing every head within fifty yards to turn my way. "It's Bobby Brooks, dyed to match!"

She turned out to be Jill, Scoot's date, a pixyish Tri Delt with eyes like Bambi. Having pronounced judgment on my mama's handiwork, she then looked down at my shoes and wrinkled her perfectly upturned nose as though examining roadkill. "What kind of shoes are *those*?"

I shrugged, sweat beading up on my reddening face. "I don't know . . . just shoes, I guess."

"Well, the boys at TCU wear *Weejuns*," Jill said.

Scoot thought that sounded mighty exotic. "What are 'Weejuns'?" he asked me, leaning in close.

"I don't know," I said skeptically. "I think they're those pointy-toed things the queers wear."

"They are not!" the girls protested in unison, scandalized. "They're penny loafers!"

We walked the two blocks to the stadium, and while most couples were holding hands, Karen maintained a mortified distance. Inside the stadium, the whole student body seemed to ogle me as if I were the victim of a fraternity prank. I don't remember who won or lost that football game, or even the name of the opposing team. I only remember feeling as if Bozo the Clown had died and I'd inherited his clothes.

7

I got my first cotton sack when I was about seven or eight. It was a big white flour sack. You prob'ly don't know much about pickin cotton so I'm gon' tell you how it was: hot. Lord-a-mighty, it was hot. Hot enough for the devil and his angels. Then there was the bugs and skeeters. Zoomin in off the bayou, seemed like they was big as gooses and twice as mean.

Ever day, we'd light out just about the time the sky at the edges of the fields turned a little pink with mornin, but you could still see some stars. I'd pick all the day long, pluckin me four or five pieces of cotton outta every boll I could find. When the bolls busted open, they was hard and kinda crackly. After a while, they turned my hands raw. The cotton was soft like a feather, but it got heavy mighty fast. Ever day, the Man say I had about twenty pounds in my sack. Seemed like no matter how long I picked or if my sack felt extra heavy that day, the Man say it was twenty pounds.

Sometimes he'd give us a token to spend at his store. I'd go in there and buy me a piece a' candy or a hunk a' cheese.

That's how I met Bobby. The Man's store was kinda on the front half of the plantation, and I had to walk by his house on my way back to Uncle James's. It was a big white one with a black roof and a great big ole shade porch all the way around it. One day, I was walkin down the red dirt road that ran by it, when this white boy about my age wearin overalls like me come out and started walkin with me.

"Hey," he says to me, traipsin along.

"Hey," I said.

"Where you goin?"

"Home."

"Where's home?"

"Over yonder," I said, jerkin my chin in the gen'l direction.

"Wanna go ride bikes?"

Well, that stopped me in my tracks. I turned and eyeballed this fella. He was kinda regular lookin, about my same size with some freckles on his nose and a curly mess of brown hair with some red in it like somebody'd dusted his head with cinnamon. While I was lookin at him, I was sizin him up, tryin to figure out what did he want, and why was he tryin to take up with somebody like me.

Finally, I gave him an answer: "I ain't got no bike," I said and started walkin again.

"You wanna go shoot BB guns then? You can use mine."

Now, that was an invite. I didn't have no BB gun, but I wanted one real bad so I could get out in the woods and bring me down some blackbirds or maybe a possum.

"Yeah, I'll go shoot BB guns with you. You sure your mama won't mind?"

"Nah, she don't care long as I'm home 'fore dark. You stay here; I'll run get my gun."

From that day on, me and Bobby was partners in crime. Turned out he was the Man's nephew come to visit. He didn't know he wadn't s'posed to be my friend.

When I wadn't workin, I'd slide over to the back porch of the Man's house and whistle. Bobby'd ease out the back door and we'd meet up. We was purty tight. If he had somethin to eat, I did, too. Sometimes at dinner, he'd eat some a' his food and slip the rest in his pocket and sneak out the house. Then we'd walk down the road where the Man couldn't see, and I'd eat me a chicken leg or a sandwich or somethin that he brung me.

Purty soon his people figured out we was friends, but they didn't really try to keep us from associatin, 'specially since I was the only boy on the place right around his age and he needed somebody to play with and keep outta trouble. They detected he was givin me food, so they put a little wood table outside the back door for me to eat on. After a while, once Bobby'd get his food, he'd come right on out and me and him'd sit at that little table and eat together.

When I wadn't workin, me and Bobby was in business, workin on bikes, swimmin, or makin slingshots outta tree twigs and inner tubes. Sometimes Thurman'd go with us, but mostly it was just me and Bobby.

We'd go huntin and kill us some birds with his Daisy Rider BB gun. I was a purty good shot and could drop em right out of the sky. I had a rope belt that I wore round my overalls, and ever time I killed me a blackbird, I'd tuck his feet up under the rope and let him hang there upside down. Once we'd shot a bunch, I'd take em home to Aunt Etha and she'd make a pie.

Now the next year that Bobby come to the plantation, I got up the courage to ask the Man if I could pick scrap cotton and earn me a bicycle. Up to then, I'd just been ridin old heaps me and Bobby built outta junk parts. Didn't even have no tires on em, just rode em on the rims. I needed a *real* bicycle so me and Bobby could do some serious ridin.

Now scrap cotton is the little pieces danglin off the cotton bushes and also inside the dirty bolls that's layin on the ground after the fields done been picked. Since Uncle James and Aunt Etha wadn't makin no money, I had to scrap cotton if I was gon' get me a bike.

I was ready to pick that scrap just as long it took, but Bobby had a plan. He'd come out and pick with me, scrapin the last wisps off the picked-over flowers, actin like he was gon' keep some a' that scrap for hisself. But all the cotton he picked, he put it in my sack. And when the Man wadn't lookin, he'd go in the cotton shed and fill up his sack with the *picked* cotton, the good cotton, then come out and empty it into mine. We'd hide it under the scrap.

Ever summer, me and Bobby had a new project, but that scrappin went on for a *long* time. Ever year, we scrapped them fields and the Man weighed what we picked—and what Bobby stole!—and ever year, the Man put me off, tellin me I ain't scrapped enough to get no bike. Went on like that for three years, till finally, right around Christmas, the Man come down to Uncle James's and said for me to come up to his house, only he never did say why.

"Just come on up and you'll see," he said.

We hoofed it on back up there, and when we got close I could see it sittin up on the big wraparound porch, shinin just like a dream: a brand-new Schwinn, red and white with a rubber squeeze-horn on it.

I turned and looked at the Man. He was smilin just a little.

"Is that *mine*?" I asked him. I couldn't believe it.

"It's all yours, L'il Buddy," he said. "You get up there and take it on home."

"Thank you, sir! Thank you, sir!" I ran off whoopin like a wild boy, jumped on that fine machine, and burned off down the road to show my uncle and auntie. That Schwinn was the first new thing I ever had. I was eleven years old.

8

On November 22, 1963, I pulled on a store-bought madras shirt, khaki pants—and yes, *Weejuns*. Scoot and I, along with two other fellows, piled into my baby-blue, four-door 1961 Chevy Biscayne and headed out for our second adventure with sorority girls. The occasion was TCU's homecoming, and Elvis blared on the radio the whole way into town.

Those were the days before interstates, and our route heading in from Commerce, Texas, took us through downtown Dallas. As I guided the Biscayne onto Elm Street, the traffic suddenly slowed to a crawl. We pulled up next to the School Book Depository at the intersection of Elm and Houston, right behind a white sedan—the last car in our way before I could have gunned my car into the clear, with a straight shot to Stemmons Freeway.

The white sedan moved ahead, but just as we were ready to pull through the intersection, a police officer stepped into our path, whistle shrieking, one arm out like a fullback.

"Dang it!" Scoot said, checking his watch. "Now we're gonna be late!"

It seemed like it was going to be a long wait, so I cut off the engine and we all got out and sat on the hood. First we heard sirens and motorcycles coming from our left, and we all turned to see what was coming. A cheer swelled toward us, rolling through the crowd like an ocean wave. Then we saw it: a convertible Lincoln limousine with eagle-eyed G-men riding the running boards and bumper.

Although it was over in less than ten seconds, it seems like slow motion now: Texas Governor John Connelly in the front seat. President John F.

Kennedy in the back, waving, on the side nearest us. And Jackie, dazzling, sitting next to him in her powder-pink pillbox hat.

Then, fast-forward: The crowd suddenly, inexplicably, exploded like a school of spooked fish. We didn't know why. All we saw was our chance to shoot through the intersection and get back on the road to TCU. The four of us jumped off the hood and clambered into the Biscayne.

We roared through the intersection toward the on-ramp right behind the presidential limo. For moments, we had no idea we were living history. Then the radio announcer broke in: "The police are reporting gunshots near the presidential motorcade in Dallas."

Then, moments later, another announcement: "The president's been shot."

"My God!" I yelled. "He's right in front of us!" I floored it, and we chased the limo down the freeway past Market Hall where a crowd of thousands was waiting to hear JFK speak, all the way to Parkland Hospital, where I whipped the Biscayne into the parking lot right up beside the empty limousine.

I cut the ignition. We sat there, stunned. The radio announcer called the play-by-play: The shots seemed to come from the School Book Depository . . . a massive manhunt in downtown Dallas . . . waiting to hear the president's condition. We'd been there maybe twenty minutes when a Secret Service agent, trim and intimidating, strode toward us from the emergency room exit.

He poked his crew cut into my window, and I could see my reflection in his mirrored sunglasses. "What're you boys doing out here?" he said, dead serious.

He listened to our explanation then said, "Well, unless you want me to take your mug shots and fingerprints, you'd better move along."

"Yes, sir," I said.

Reluctantly, I started the car and we pulled slowly out of the Parkland lot. We hadn't been on the freeway for more than ten minutes when the radio announcer made his grim report: "The president is dead."

It didn't take us long to realize we were some of the last civilians to see him alive. ·

9

Ever Sunday, a field hand drivin a mule wagon wound down the dirt plantation roads gatherin up folks to haul em off to praise the Lord. There was about twenty families that worked on the Man's place. They'd climb into the mule wagon, the men handin up the ladies, then handin up the babies, then climbin on last, and the field hand would drive em all to the New Glory of Zion Baptist Church. To tell you the truth, I don't really remember 'xactly what the name of it was, but all them churches was "New" this and "Glory" that, and for sure just about all of em was Baptist.

Ever plantation had a colored church, and that was where most a' the socializin went on. Our little clapboard church sat in a wide field and had a cross over the door that never saw no coat of paint. Seemed like God used the tin roof for a pincushion, 'cause it was fulla holes that the sunlight fell through, and made the wooden benches look kinda pokey-dotted. Sometimes it'd come a rain and the preacher'd have to sweep the mess out the front door.

The preacher, Brother Eustis Brown, was just another field hand. But he was the onlyest man I knowed besides Uncle James that could read the Bible. I learned a lot of Scripture from listenin to Brother Brown. That's 'cause he'd preach the same sermon ever week for *months*.

Let's say he was preachin on the evils of lust. Brother Brown'd say, "Now listen, church: The book of First John say we know the lust a' the flesh, the lust a' the eyes, and the boastful pride of life—all that is not from *God*, it's from this *world*! But this world is passin *away*! And its lusts are passin *away*! But if you do the will a' God, you gon' live *forever*!"

44

Ever week, he'd say them same verses, hammerin em home over and over, like he was nailin a shoe on a stubborn horse. But ever once in a while, people started complainin.

"Brother Brown, we done heard that message about a hun'erd times," one of the older women would say, somebody with gumption like my auntie, Big Mama's sister. "When you gon' change the sermon?"

Brother Brown would just gaze up at the holey roof and shake his head, kinda sad. "I work out there in the cotton with y'all, and ever week, the Lord shows me what's goin on in the congregation so I'll know what to preach on Sunday. When I start seein some changes out there," he'd say, pointin toward the plantation, "I'll be changin what I preach in here."

That's how I learned the Bible without knowin how to read.

When I was about twelve, my aunt Etha dressed me all in white and took me down to the river to get dunked. There was four or five folks gettin baptized that day, and all the plantation families brought pails and baskets of food to spread out on blankets and have us what we called "dinner on the ground." White folks call it a picnic.

My auntie wrung the neck off a chicken and fried it up special, and brought her famous blackberry cobbler, and a jug a' cool tea she made with mint leaves she got from my great-aunt. (Least I think they was mint leaves. With my auntie, you never knowed what kinda powders and potions you was gon' get.)

We didn't eat, though, till after Brother Brown preached a sermon 'bout John the Baptist dunkin Jesus hisself, and God callin down from heaven that He was mighty pleased with what kinda fella His Son had turned out to be. When Brother Brown was done preachin, he waded out into the cool green river till he got waist-deep in his white robe that he kept special for baptizin. I followed him down in my bare feet, over pebbles, smooth and shinin wet, down through the warm soft mud, into the water.

Now me and Bobby did lots of swimmin in the waterin hole, but we was mostly buck naked. So it felt kinda strange goin in the water in a full suit of clothes, and them swirlin around me all white and soft like a cloud. But I waded on out to where Brother Brown was waitin for me.

The river mud squished up between my toes while I kept one eye out for gators.

I stood sideways in front of Brother Brown, and he put his left hand behind my back. I could hear some birds a-peepin, and the water sloshin, and away off down the river, I seen some white folks on a boat, fishin. "Li'l Buddy," the preacher said, "do you believe Jesus died on the cross for your sins, was buried, and rose again on the third day?"

"Yessir, I do," I said and felt somethin graze my leg. I was hopin it was a catfish.

"I now baptize thee in the name of the Father, the Son, and the Holy Ghost!" Brother Brown said, and quick as lightnin, like maybe I was gon' change my mind, he pinched my nose shut with his right hand, and slammed me down backward in the water.

Problem was, Brother Brown kinda lost his grip and I sunk right to the bottom. I didn't know I was supposed to come right back up, so I just floated on down the river a ways, blowin bubbles and lookin up through the milky water at the clouds goin by. Aunt Etha told me afterward that the congregation panicked and charged into the river. They was still splashin around and callin my name when I popped up downriver like a bobber on a fishin line, a few shades paler and fulla the Holy Ghost!

My auntie was so glad to see me, I got two servins of blackberry cobbler that day.

10

Things was a-changin. Uncle James took sick and died, and Aunt Etha moved away. Last time I seen her, she was cryin. I couldn't figure out why God kept takin all the folks I loved the most. Me and Thurman got split up, and I went to live on a different plantation with my sister, Hershalee. Seemed like Thurman went to stay with some a' BB's people, but I ain't sure. I guess I was about thirteen, fourteen years old. Them years kinda run together in my memory. We never kept no calendar. We didn't even keep a clock. Didn't need one: When all you doin is bringin in the Man's cotton, ain't nowhere you got to be at 'cept where you're at.

I missed Bobby and wished I had another friend like him. The new Man had a couple of little daughters round about my age, but for sure I wadn't friends with no white *girls*. Besides, the white children, when they was big enough, went off to school during the day. Some colored kids did, too, but not me. And a lotta times, the Man would pull the colored kids out to go work in the fields.

It wadn't just the grown folks that put up a wall between white folks and colored folks, neither. Years later, I heard about one time in South Carolina 'bout five or six white boys used to walk to school together. Ever day, they had to get acrossed a creek tucked down there in a little shady patch of woods. Now that creek was on the way to the colored school, too, and one day the white boys decided they didn't think it was right for the Negroes to cross the creek on the same foot logs they did. So they laid theirselves an ambush. They picked up sticks and old pieces of wood and lined up on them foot logs to wait for the colored children to come walkin along.

"These here logs belong to the whites!" hollered one bully-boy when the colored children come up on the creek. "If you niggers want to get acrossed, you gon' have to wade the water!"

Well, the colored children wadn't havin that, and a shootin war commenced with sticks and rocks just a-flyin. The sorry thing was, them white boys was victorious: They pitched enough rocks to win the foot logs, and them colored kids had to wade the water to get to school.

I didn't hear 'bout that story till I was growed, but I still felt sorry for them kids. Not so much about walkin to school in wet britches as 'cause I know what it's like to get beat down for bein born with different-colored skin. And I know what it's like to walk around with my eyes down low to keep it from happenin again.

That's what I did after the draggin.

I was maybe fifteen, sixteen years old, walkin down the road that passed by the front of the plantation, on my way back from my auntie's house. That's when I seen that white lady beside her blue Ford sedan. She was bendin down a little, peekin up under the back side a' the car, but kinda ladylike, tryin to keep her white skirt outta the dirt. Her hat was white, too, a little one, just big enough to cover the top of her head, with a brown ribbon around it, like a stripe of chocolate. Like I told you before, she was dressed up like maybe she'd been to town.

I asked her if she needed any help, and she said yes. I took the jack outta the trunk and set it down under the car, pickin out as firm a spot as I could find. I cranked the jack handle around and the car swayed, inchin up enough to where I could get the tire off.

I was just puttin the lug nuts back on when them three boys rode outta the woods and asked the lady did she need any help. 'Course, the redheaded fella with the big teeth was the one that first spotted me and called me a nigger. And the next thing I knew, I had a rope squeezed tight around my neck and black terror slitherin through my belly like a water moccasin.

"We gon' teach you a lesson about botherin white ladies," said the one holdin the rope.

'Cept I hadn't been botherin her, just fixin her tire. But she didn't volunteer no other story, and I didn't say nothin 'cause for sure they wadn't gon' be believin me. I figured if I spoke, it would just add to my troubles.

I kept an eye on the boy with the rope, and when he lashed it to his saddle, I knowed what was comin and got real scared. With both hands, I reached up to try to get the rope loose. That's when they snapped their reins and took off just a-laughin.

The horses trotted at first, goin slow enough for me to run. I was stumblin along behind, my hands still graspin at the noose and me tryin to keep my feet under me. The horses was only maybe ten feet in front of me, and I could hear their feet beatin the dirt. The dust stung my eyes. I could taste it.

Then I heard a whoop and a holler. My feet flew out from under me and I crashed down in the dirt, my knees and elbows skiddin down the road. The horses pounded and pounded and I held on to the noose like a steerin wheel, tryin to pry my fingers inside of it to keep the noose from closin in tighter. The dirt was blindin me and chokin me. My shirtsleeves and the knees of my britches tore away, then my skin peeled back like a rabbit ready for the skillet. I couldn't hear no more laughin, just the terrible thunder of them horses draggin me down to die.

I expect I would a' died if Bobby and his aunt, the Man's wife from the other plantation, hadn't been drivin down the road right then. I'd about blacked out by that time, and I don't really remember too much of what happened next. I just know the draggin all of a sudden stopped. I peeked through my eyes, which had swoll up to slits and seen Bobby's aunt standin in the road pointin a shotgun at them boys on horses.

"Cut him loose!" she hollered. I felt the noose go slack and seen the raggedy end of the rope fall to the ground like a snake with the evil gone out of it. Then I heard them boys ride off laughin.

Bobby and his aunt hustled me into their car and drove me to my auntie's house. She tended to me with her roots and potions, slatherin a paste on my eyes to ease the swellin. I stayed in her bed a week till the swellin went down and I could see good again. Took about that long for my skin to scab over so I could put on pants and a shirt.

I knowed who done it. And I figured their daddies was in the Klan. But in Red River Parish, colored men had learned it was better to keep their mouths shut than tell what they know, 'less they wanted worse things to happen to their family, like maybe wakin up in the middle of the night with the house on fire.

Lookin back, I figure what them boys done caused me to get a little throwed off in life. And for sure I wadn't gon' be offerin to help no white ladies no more.

11

The first time I saw Deborah, I began plotting to steal her. Not for myself at first, but for Sigma Chi, the fraternity I pledged after transferring from East Texas State to TCU as a sophomore. It was the spring of 1965, and I was on academic probation. Deborah, meanwhile, was a sophomore on an academic scholarship, and by the time I met her was also a Tri Delt sorority girl and a "sweetheart" of Delta Tau Delta, our rival fraternity. I planned to make her a Sigma Chi sweetheart, a little inter-frat coup that carried with it the novel perk of adding an intellectual girl to our table at the Student Union.

Deborah grew up in Snyder, a tumbleweed-tossed West Texas town so flat you could stand on a cow chip and see New Mexico. It's an everybody-knows-your-business place where schoolchildren dream of traveling to exotic places like Lubbock or Abilene. Nothing green grows there outside the produce section at the Piggly Wiggly. Snyder is also the last recorded place a human ever laid eyes on a white buffalo, and today a giant plaster one keeps watch over the courthouse in the town square.

Deborah has two sisters: Gretchen, a former runner-up in the Miss Snyder beauty pageant; and Daphene, who is Deborah's twin only by virtue of the fact that the two were born on the same day. Tall and voluptuous, young Daphene grew up a party girl who never met a boy she didn't like or a book that she did. Deborah, meanwhile, was her opposite: a bookworm and as neat as a preacher's wife on Sunday. As a teenager, Deborah had the figure of a drinking straw and, being on the shy side, stuffed her mouth full of popcorn to keep the boys from kissing her at the picture show. But with

51

dark hair and eyes upturned at the corners, she was very pretty and spoke with a soft Texas lilt, perfectly pitched, like a Southern aristocrat.

It was with this weapon that she first snared me. One warm fall night in 1966, Sigma Chi was gearing up for a "woodsy," an informal event in which the fraternity trooped into the woods, hauled in coolers full of iced-down beer, and made out with their dates.

Only I didn't have a date, a fact I had been sharing with my friend Glenn Whittington when Deborah walked into the Student Union.

Glenn was the guy everybody loves—funny, affable, the perpetual match-maker. Spotting Deborah, he waved her over to our table. After some pre-liminary chitchat, he dived right in: "Deborah, do you know my friend Ron? He needs a date tonight for a woodsy."

Deborah drilled Glenn with a stare. "If your friend wants to date me," she announced in that uncompromising way of proud Southern women, "he can call me." Then she spun on her penny loafer and marched away. Never even glanced my way.

Now, up to that point, I had been into rich blonde party girls endowed with the assets necessary for the moment. I had never been with someone on an academic scholarship, someone who had actually studied for a test. This intrigued me. Plus, she was very, very pretty. I called her the next day.

She agreed to go to the woodsy with me, though we didn't make out. I learned that she had just broken up with her boyfriend, a Delta Tau Delta hunk named Frank. But by the following Monday, she'd gotten back together with him. I didn't take it personally, and we made a deal: Next time she broke up with him, she'd call me. A couple of weeks later she did.

We went out again on a Friday night. By the next Monday, she was back with Frank. This went on for weeks—she'd break up with him and call me for a weekend date. Then, by Monday, they'd reunite. You might think these capitulations would bruise my ego, but Deborah and I were really more friends than anything else. We thought the whole arrangement was hysterically funny.

Our punctuated dating ended, though, in the spring of my senior year when I tore open an official-looking envelope to find an invitation to the

Vietnam War. That led me to boot camp in Fort Polk, Louisiana; then to Albuquerque, where I smoked marijuana once and woke up next to a fat girl; and then, ultimately, to permanent duty at Fort Carson, Colorado.

Just after I left Fort Polk, I narrowly missed assignment as a rifleman in a ground unit bound for the demilitarized zone. I had just completed basic and advanced infantry training and found myself bivouacked with twenty-five thousand other freshly minted soldiers on an airfield in Colorado Springs.

"Hall! Ronald R.!" a razor-sharp second lieutenant barked. "Grab your gear and get aboard." He pointed at one in a long string of military transport jets that I knew were headed straight to the shooting war.

But for some reason he asked me a few questions, and when he found out I had three and a half years of college, he reassigned me.

"I've got good news and bad news," he said. "The good news is, there's an opening in nuclear weapons support in Albuquerque. The bad news is, you have to qualify for a top secret security clearance. If you don't, I'll put your butt on a plane just like that one."

I swore to the lieutenant that my record was clean. He shipped me off to Albuquerque, where I got the top secret clearance. Of course, I probably wouldn't have if the army had known I'd wind up smoking marijuana with a fat girl.

— — —

During my two-year army hitch, Deborah and I exchanged a few letters. Nothing purple and steamy, just keeping in touch the way people did before e-mail and free long distance. In December 1968, my tour complete, I headed back to Texas to finish my degree in night school. To earn money, I landed a job peddling Campbell's Soup to grocery store managers. I hated walking into the Piggly Wiggly wearing a three-piece suit and carrying a feather duster. In addition to lobbying managers to increase shelf space for oddball products like giblet gravy, it was my job to whisk the dirt off slow movers like green-pea soup.

I called Deborah just to say hi. She reeled off two years' worth of TCU's social history—who'd dropped out, who'd graduated, and of course, who got married. In those days, girls lined up husbands by their senior year and, if all went well, married them by spring semester. I had always thought Tri Delt sisters were the prettiest girls on campus. Jokingly I asked Deborah, "Are there any Tri Delts who aren't married yet?"

"Just me," she said. "And I have gotten *so cute*. You're just going to love me."

She was right. Gone was the pretty, slightly pugnacious scholarship student I'd taken to the woodsy. In her place was a gorgeous, educated woman, confident and full of fun. We started dating, and within a month had stopped dating anyone but each other.

In the spring of 1969, Deborah returned from the wedding of a college friend in San Antonio and told me, "Everybody down there thinks you and I should get married."

I smiled. "What do you think?"

"I think we should, too."

"Well, why don't we?"

"You have to ask me first."

I gave her a kiss and told her I'd work on it.

In July, my father loaned me money to buy a ring. But I didn't know how to propose and groused out loud to my roommate, Kelly Adams, about my dilemma.

"You want me to propose for you?" he asked.

If it worked for Cyrano de Bergerac, I reasoned, I might as well give it a whirl. I gave Kelly the ring and we went to visit Deborah at her apartment, the three of us clustered in her living room in an awkward circle.

"Ronnie's got something he wants to ask you," Kelly said to Deborah, handing over the ring. "He wants to know if you'll marry him."

Deborah rolled her eyes. "Maybe *he* should ask me?"

I grinned. "Well, will you?"

She should have told me to go back out and come in again. Instead, she said yes. "By the way," she added. "That was about the worst proposal I have *ever* heard."

We married in October 1969, and Deborah went to work teaching elementary school, while I entered the world of investment banking. I finished my degree in night school, then stayed on another year and earned an MBA. By 1971, I'd begun buying and selling paintings as a sideline. Two years later, our daughter, Regan, was born.

By 1975, the year before our son, Carson, was born, I was earning twice as much selling art as I was making as a banker. So I began to look for reasons to strike out on my own. It wasn't long before a reason arrived in the form of *The Signal*, a work by Charles Russell, the noted painter of Western art. In 1910, as a wedding gift, Russell had given the painting to the Crowfoots, a prominent Montana family whose descendants later settled in Puerto Rico. Through a contact in Santa Fe, New Mexico, I learned that a Crowfoot heir was interested in selling.

From my office at the bank, I telephoned Mr. Crowfoot in San Juan and told him I would like to buy his painting. But I was far too busy to fly to Puerto Rico, I explained, and helped him see the wisdom of traveling to Texas and bringing his heirloom with him. The truth was that while I was doing better than some men my age, I could neither afford to buy a plane ticket to San Juan nor take time off from my day job.

So Mr. Crowfoot flew to Fort Worth where I showered him with Texas hospitality, which meant big steaks and lots of liquor. By dessert, he'd agreed to sell me the Russell for $28,000. Not only that, he said he'd leave the painting in my care and allow me to delay payment for ninety days. It was an incredible opportunity, my first chance to turn a five-figure profit. I marked up the price on *The Signal* to $40,000 and started searching for a buyer.

But three months passes quickly when you're holding a ninety-day note. After forty-five days streaked by, I started to sweat. Then I had an idea: On day forty-six, with no actual prospects in mind, I drove to the airport and bought a ticket to Los Angeles. From the departure gate, I called in sick to the bank, connecting with my boss just as my boarding call blared over the PA.

After touching down at LAX, I paid five bucks for a rental car and asked the counter girl to point me toward Beverly Hills. A short trip on I-5 led me to Sunset Boulevard, where I glided off the freeway and into the rarified land of palm trees, high walls, and mansions. Winding through the famous avenue's shady curves, I popped out near Rodeo Drive, an art gallery mecca. Carrying the Russell under my arm, I walked into the first gallery I found and offered *The Signal* for sale.

Not interested, they told me. But they had a client who might be, and they called a Mr. Barney Goldberg to say I was on my way over with something he was going to like. Mr. Goldberg didn't live far away and, unexpectedly, he didn't live in a mansion. But his large hacienda-style home still looked like money. The moment I stepped onto the porch, the door swung open.

"Poopsie!" gushed a six-foot bald man who looked exactly like a cross between Gene Autry, Liberace, and Moshe Dayan. The man thrust out diamond-laden hands and wrapped me in a bear hug as though I were long-lost kin.

"No, sir," I said, shaking my head, "I'm not Poopsie. I'm Ron Hall."

"No, you are *not!*" he scolded like a doting aunt insisting that a full child take a second helping of pie. "You're *Poopsie!* And you can call *me* Snookems!"

While he was saying this, I took in his glittering ensemble: Strapped around his head behind gold aviator sunglasses, Mr. Goldberg wore a black patch over his left eye, and below that, a pearl-snap cowboy shirt and jeans, white-python-skin cockroach-killer boots with gold tips and heel orna-ments, and a solid gold, buffalo-shaped belt buckle with rubies for eyes and diamonds everywhere else. A diamond of at least three carats rode every one of his fingers except for his ring fingers—he wore ten carats on each of those.

Mr. Goldberg—Snookems—ushered me into his manly, lodgelike home, where collections of antique firearms, cowboy memorabilia, and Navajo blankets dressed every space. But it was his walls that most interested me: Every one was covered floor-to-ceiling with high-end Western art: Remingtons, Boreins, and . . . Russells.

I'm saved, I thought, mentally writing Mr. Crowfoot a check. I was certain Snookems was a prime buyer for *The Signal*. After my impromptu tour of his home, he invited me to enjoy a glass of wine before lunch—*way* before lunch. I practically sat on the edge of my seat waiting for him to make an offer on the Russell.

He took a sip of wine and began: "As you can see," he said, gesturing toward his art-laden walls, "I don't need this little thing you've brought."

My heart plunged into my stomach.

"But you are *such* a sweetie pie . . . ," he went on, "that I'm going to sell your Russell to one of my buddies and send you the money!"

Snookems beamed excitedly, as if he'd just offered to sell me Tahiti for a dollar. But since I had no other prospects, I accepted his offer. We never did have lunch, just more wine, as we hashed out the vague outlines of a deal. I stressed to him that I *had* to have the money in forty-four days, or else Mr. Crowfoot would come hunting for my scalp.

"Yes, yes, I understand," he slurred, smiling and wobbling a little as he ushered me out his front door. "*Trust* me."

Back at LAX, I called Deborah. "Great news!" I said. "I met a collector out here who's going to sell the Russell and send us the money."

Deborah sounded guarded. "What's he like?"

I hesitated, not sure an accurate description would be helpful. "Well . . . his name is Barney Goldberg—"

"Did you get a receipt or a contract?"

"No . . ."

"You do have insurance on the painting, don't you?"

"No . . ."

"Are you crazy!" she unloaded into the phone. "This sounds like a scam! You go back to that house and get that painting!"

"It's too late," I said, suddenly exhausted. "I'm out of money, and my plane is leaving in a few minutes."

I hung up and flew back to Fort Worth, guts churning. The next day I began trying to call Goldberg, to get a receipt at the very least. But each time I dialed, long unanswered rings sang through the line, mocking me across the miles. I called every day for forty-three days and never reached him. As the ninety-day clock wound down, Mr. Crowfoot began phoning me almost daily to remind me of where to send his check. Nerves ate twenty pounds off my bones.

On the forty-fourth and final day, I called Snookems again, this time from the bank, and he finally answered.

"Where have you been, and why haven't you answered your phone!" I yelled.

"*Poopsie* . . . ," he said in a mild reproach. "I've been in *Hawaii*." He pronounced it "Hi-wah-ya."

"Don't give me that Poopsie crap! Where's my money?"

"Check your account," he said calmly. "I wired it to you a couple of days ago."

I put him on hold and called down to Jean in bookkeeping, who informed me that $40,000 was sitting in my account, having been wired there by a Mr. Barney Goldberg.

Relieved beyond belief, I punched up Snookems again, thanked him, hung up, and broke into the creeping sweat that usually follows a narrowly avoided car crash. And yet . . . on a single painting, I had just cleared a profit nearly equal to my annual salary at the bank. Within a few days, I was planning a new deal with Snookems. A few weeks later, I quit the bank. And a few months later, the money started rolling in.

12

As newlyweds, Deborah and I were just your basic Sunday-go-to-meeting Methodists. We parked ourselves in the pews most Sundays, and definitely every Easter and Christmas, since in those days it was still the widely held opinion that only hell-bound heathens—and possibly lawyers—skipped church on Easter and Christmas. We kept up that pattern until 1973 when some friends from a Bible church invited us to their home for a six-week "discussion group" about life.

As it turned out, we had actually been labeled "lost," "nonbelieving," and "unsaved," possibly because we had no fish stickers on our cars. (Which reminds me of one friend who, though newly "born again," retained the bad habit of flipping off other drivers while barreling down the road in her Suburban. Even with her newfound religion, she couldn't control her middle finger, but according to her husband, the Holy Ghost prompted her to scrape the fish off her bumper until her finger got saved.)

Unsuspecting, my wife and I joined the discussion group at the Williamsburg-style home of Dan and Patt McCoy. Dan was an ex–TCU football player who was six-foot-five and 275 pounds, so when he invited us to his house, I was afraid not to say yes. That first Sunday night, we were surprised to find exactly forty people—twenty couples, we found out later, divided equally into "saved" and "saved nots." Patt had set out an attractive buffet—brownies, lemon bars, coffee, iced tea—but strangely, no one so much as grazed. I've since deduced that it's always a trap when you don't get to eat until after you hear the talk.

We introduced ourselves around and listened for an hour while a fresh-scrubbed, close-cropped man named Kirby Coleman addressed the whole group on the burning questions of existence: Why are we here? What is our purpose? What happens when we die? Quite frankly, I thought Kirby looked too young to know any of the answers.

After the group talk, he tracked us down at the buffet table. "Are you a Christian?" he asked Deborah.

He may as well have asked her if she was a human being. "I was *born* a Christian," she replied, insulted beyond belief.

"But are you *saved*?" he pressed. "Are you certain you're going to heaven?"

Deborah put one hand on her hip and pointed the other one in Kirby's face. "Well!" she said. "My *daddy* paved the parking lot at the Snyder Methodist Church, and that's good enough for me!"

Deborah Hall had had just about enough of Mr. Kirby Coleman—so much so that we went back to tussle with him again the next week. And the next. And the next. Each Sunday evening, the discussion funnel narrowed further, from general philosophizing about life to pointed evangelization. After five weeks, I had it figured out: If you hadn't accepted Jesus by the sixth Sunday, you were probably going to hell on Monday. So, on the last night after we went home, I told Deborah I was going to pray the sinner's prayer Kirby had told us about.

"I don't see the point," she said. "How could I have lived this long, been in church all my life, and still have to do that? It doesn't make any sense. Besides, it just seems too easy."

So I prayed without her, asking God to forgive my sins in the name of His Son, Jesus. Deborah, however, cross-examined the gospel like a prosecutor on a federal case. And it was eventually the lawyerly arguments in books by C. S. Lewis and Josh McDowell that convinced her Christianity could stand up to her intellectual rigor. Finally, she prayed the prayer, too.

That's how the Jesus wave that swept across college campuses in the 1960s caught us in the suburbs before it slipped out to sea. I guess we were pretty good at the whole Christian thing—or maybe we were bad at it— because we managed to alienate many of our old college friends. With our new spiritual eyes, we could see they didn't have fish stickers either, and we set about saving them from eternal damnation with all the subtlety of rookie linebackers. Looking back now, I mourn the mutual wounds inflicted in verbal battles with the "unsaved." In fact, I have chosen to delete that particular term from my vocabulary as I have learned that even with my $500 European-designer bifocals, I cannot see into a person's heart to know his spiritual condition. All I can do is tell the jagged tale of my own spiritual journey and declare that my life has been the better for having followed Christ.

13

On the land where Hershlee lived, there was three or four plantations all run up next to each other like patches on a quilt. That meant there was three or four men that worked the black folks, different ones on different parts a' the cotton. But to us, they was all the Man. When I was eighteen or nineteen, one of em gave me my own place a ways down the road from Hershalee. I was feelin pretty good about it, a man and all that, even though my house was really just a two-room shack. I didn't know no better. I thought I was movin up. My place was built right up near a sycamore tree, so it had some shade in the summertime. I had a bed, a table, two chairs, and a potbellied stove all to myself. Had my own outhouse, too. I thought I was livin high on the hog.

Used to be the thinkin in Red River Parish that there wadn't nothin lower than a sharecropper. There was, though, and I was it. There was a crack I fell through and others with me, 'cept I didn't know it at the time. See, there was croppers, and there was the children of croppers. Most a' them was croppers, too. But some of em, 'specially them that never learned how to read or figger, stayed on the land, workin for nothin but a place to live and food to eat, just like slaves. Oh, there was an understandin—that we still owed the Man. I knew he still kept books at his store and penciled down everthing I took out the door on credit. There just wadn't no way to pay it off, 'cause the Man didn't weigh the cotton no more. I knew I owed him and he knew I owed him, and that's the way it stayed.

Here was the damnable thing about it: Before Abe Lincoln freed the slaves, white folks wanted their plantations to run self-sufficient so they made sure their slaves was trained up to do plenty a' jobs. That's how come there was blacksmiths and carpenters, shoemakers and barbers, and slaves that could weave and sew and build wagons and paint signs and such. By the time I come along, though, that wadn't true no more. All them kinda jobs was white jobs in the South, and the only kinda jobs for colored folks was workin the land.

But after a while, even that started to dry up. Around the time I was three or four, white planters started buyin up tractors, which meant they didn't need so many colored hands to make their crops no more. That's when they started forcin em off their land. Whole families with little children. Daddies and mamas that didn't know no other life, didn't know nothin but how to make a crop for somebody else, forced off, sometimes at the point of a shotgun. No money. No place to live. No job. No way to get one.

Like I said before, there was about twenty colored families, 'bout a hundred souls, on the Man's plantation, each of em workin a plot of land for him. But slowly, over the years, the Man made em leave, till there was maybe only about three or four families left.

All I knowed was my life: For nearly thirty years, I sweated in the Louisiana sun, fightin off snakes, workin the earth till harvest, and pickin that cotton one boll at a time till my hands was raw, growin my own food, choppin wood all winter long to keep from freezin to death, startin all over in the spring. That ain't no bad life if your labor is for your own land. But it wadn't. And I don't guess that kinda life would be bad if it was somebody else's land, and you was gettin paid. But I wadn't. Most folks these days ain't got no idea what it's like to be that poor. Me and the other folks on the plantation was down so low we didn't own nothin 'cept the tin can that hung on our britches so we could get us a drink. We didn't even own the clothes on our backs, since we got em at the Man's store and hadn't really paid for em, according to him.

After Uncle James died and Aunt Etha moved away, I didn't have no close family but my sister, Hershalee. And after her husband died, she didn't have no croppin deal with her Man and I didn't have one with my Man. He put me up in that little shack, gave me one hog a year—not two no more—and

I worked three hundred acres for him. Never weighed in no cotton. Never got no paycheck. Ever once in a while, the Man'd slip me a few dollars, maybe five or six times in all them years.

It got to be the 1960s. All them years I worked for them plantations, the Man didn't tell me there was colored schools I coulda gone to, or that I coulda learned a trade. He didn't tell me I coulda joined the army and worked my way up, earned some money of my own and some respect. I didn't know about World War II, the war in Korea, or the one in Vietnam. And I didn't know colored folks had been risin up all around Louisiana for years, demandin better treatment.

I didn't know I was different.

That might be hard for you to believe. But you go on down to Louisiana right now, and take a drive on down the back roads in Red River Parish, and you might be able to see how a colored man that couldn't read and didn't have no radio, no car, no telephone, and not even 'lectricity might fall through a crack in time and get stuck, like a clock that done wound down and quit.

I'd been seein 'lectric lights burnin in the Man's house since I was a boy, but I was still livin by coal-oil lamp in a shotgun shack with no runnin water. What happened to me was, I got real discouraged. Felt like I wadn't good for nobody and wadn't ever gon' be able to do no better.

I knowed there was other places. I had heard my brother, Thurman, was out in California stackin hisself some paper money. So one day, I just decided to head out that way. Didn't think about it much, just walked out to the railroad tracks and waited for the train to come a-rollin. There was another fella hangin around by the tracks, a hobo who'd been ridin the rails for a lotta years. He said he'd show me which train was goin to California. When that one slowed down to roll through town, we both hopped on.

I guess I was about twenty-seven, twenty-eight years old by then. I never told nobody I was goin, so I guess I still owe the Man for all them overalls I bought on credit.

14

I was thirty-two years old when I paid $275,000 for a Williamsburg-style house in an upscale section of Fort Worth. That was a pile of money and a lot of house in 1977—especially in Texas. Dark red brick with white columns supporting a gracious balcony and a Mercedes parked out front. My art-dealing career had taken off, and we began living the society-page life. I was building my business, and Deborah was the supportive wife.

Large charities came knocking, and I often donated $5,000 paintings or hefty gift certificates to raise money at silent auctions, hoping to lure wealthy bidders to my gallery. We attended $1,000-a-plate black-tie charity balls, and Deborah and I got our picture in the paper, raising champagne glasses under starry lights.

But she couldn't quite get her mind around the logic of that kind of philanthropy.

"We pay $2,000 to get in, and half of that goes to pay for the decorator," she said. "And the *dress* I wore cost $2,000. Why don't we just send in a check for $4,000 and stay home? The charity would make more money that way."

"It's good for business," I said.

"Really? How much have you made?"

"Well . . . none, yet."

During those years, I spent a week of every month in New York, where I eventually developed a strong partnership with a dealer named Michael Altman, who is still my partner today. About four times each year, I traveled to Paris, squeezing first-class, five-star jaunts to Tokyo, Hong Kong, and Florence in between. I bought and sold expensive art, met private clients, schmoozed gallery owners and museum buyers, and managed to sneak in skiing, wine-tasting, and chateau weekends.

We stayed in Fort Worth until 1986, when I thought I'd outgrown it, then moved to Dallas where I thought I could make even more money in art. We moved into a perfectly good million-dollar home in the Park Cities that we tore down to make it nicer, painting it a color that complemented the red Jaguar convertible I parked in the driveway. The Park Cities was a wealthy enclave where the local newspaper, *Park Cities People*, periodically published a list of best-dressed ladies, most of whom spent at least $200,000 a year on clothes. I didn't mind that and would probably have been proud to appear on such a list. Deborah was, of course, appalled.

We put our children in public school. Regan spent her early years religious, pledging never to listen to rock music. Back then, she was a sharp dresser like her mom, but as a teenager, she shunned anything that smacked of wealth. At sixteen, she preferred clothes from the Salvation Army resale to anything from a mall and yearned to be a freedom fighter in South Africa.

Carson grew up a kid with a big heart, one always tuned toward God. We loved his little-boy sayings, like the one he used to describe feeling extra tired. "Mommy," he'd say, "I ran out of strong." In high school, he was an all-state wrestler at 103 pounds. In fact, he was a model child, except for the time when, after a little taste of liquor in his senior year, he nearly destroyed his room with his "Best Camper" paddle from Kanakuk Kamp, where all good Christian boys go.

In Dallas, I threw myself into my work, traveling more, striving for more international market share. I changed cars like I changed Armani suits and tired of each new toy I acquired as quickly as a toddler on Christmas morning.

Deborah, meanwhile, plugged into God. While I pursued the material, she plunged into the spiritual. While I dedicated my life to making money and spent a few minutes parked in a church pew on Sundays, she spent hours at Brian's House, a ministry to homeless babies with AIDS. When I stormed Europe impressing billionaires with my art savvy, she stormed heaven, praying for the needy. My passion was recognition and success. Her passion was to know God.

And so we pursued our separate loves. It didn't take long before our separate loves did not include each other.

— — —

Billy Graham has managed to maintain his integrity for decades by following a set of hard and fast rules designed to keep married men from doing something stupid. One of Billy's rules is: Never allow yourself to be alone with a woman who is not your wife.

I should have listened to Billy.

In 1988, while on a business trip, I found myself sitting in the Hard Rock Cafe in Beverly Hills, across from the kind of woman who seems to grow indigenously in California, right alongside the palm trees: willowy blonde, blue-eyed, a painter, and much younger than I.

If the subject had come up over lunch, I probably would have pinned my reason for being there on a loveless marriage. Deborah and I had faked it pretty well for about five years: the affluent Christian couple still so in love. Deborah, I learned later, was sure I loved art and money, but not sure I still loved her. I was sure she loved God and our children, and fairly certain she could just barely stand the sight of me.

But the subject of Deborah or the kids or the fact that I was married-filing-jointly never came up over lunch. Instead, there was chilled wine—white, and too much of it . . . a meaningful pause . . . in the eyes, the sparkle of invitation. Dancing toward the edge of the cliff and sizing up the distance to the bottom.

I would have liked to have thought I swept this woman into a hotel room with my wit and rugged good looks. The truth was, she was more interested in what I could do for her art career. It is a sorry fact of my history that if it hadn't been her, it would've been someone in Paris or Milan or New York City, anyone who gave me a second look, because I was looking, too—for a way out.

I remember for three or four years secretly wishing Deborah would divorce me because I didn't have the guts to divorce her and corrupt the

"Mr. Wonderful" image so many of our friends had layered over me like a holiday window cling.

In the end, I saw the artist only twice, once in California and once in New York, then confessed to Deborah—with a little help from my friends. I confided my conquest to a friend, who confided my confidence to his wife, who "encouraged" me to tell Deborah. If I didn't, she said, she would.

Calculating that it was better to rat myself out than look like a weasel, I called the artist from the office one day and told her I couldn't see her anymore. Then I went home and confessed to Deborah. My spin: Her disinterest had driven me into the arms of another woman, one who wanted me just the way I was—money and all.

"What!" she screamed, flying into a rage. "Nineteen years! Nineteen years! What were you thinking? How could you do this?"

Shoes, vases, and figurines flew through the air, some a direct hit. When nothing else presented itself as a weapon, Deborah pounded me with her bare fists until her arms wore out and hung limp at her sides.

The night spun by in a whirl of sleepless anger. The next morning we phoned our pastor, then drove to his office where we spent most of the day airing our garbage. In the end, we discovered that neither of us was quite ready to give up. We did still love each other, though in that vestigial way of couples who've worn each other out. We agreed to try to work things out.

Back at the house that night, we were sitting in our bedroom retreat, talking, when Deborah asked me something that nearly made me faint. "I want to talk to her. Will you give me her phone number?"

Deborah's resolve at that moment was like a student skydiver who, once at altitude, strides straight to the plane's open door and leaps without pausing to bat down the butterflies. She picked up the bedroom phone and punched each number as I recited it.

"This is Deborah Hall, Ron's wife," she said calmly into the phone.

I tried to imagine the shocked face on the other end of the line.

"I want you to know that I don't blame you for the affair with my husband," Deborah went on. "I know that I've not been the kind of wife Ron needed, and I take responsibility for that."

She paused, listening.

Then: "I want you to know that I forgive you," Deborah said. "I hope you find someone who will not only truly love you but honor you."

Her grace stunned me. But not nearly so much as what she said next: "I intend to work on being the best wife Ron could ever want, and if I do my job right, you will not be hearing from my husband again."

Deborah quietly placed the phone in its cradle, sighed with relief, and locked her eyes on mine. "You and I are now going to rewrite the future history of our marriage."

She wanted to spend a couple of months in counseling, she said, so we could figure out what was broken, how it got that way, and how to fix it. "If you'll do that," she said, "I'll forgive you. And I promise I will never bring this up, ever again."

It was a gracious offer, considering that I, and not Deborah, had been the traitor. Faster than you can say "divorce court," I said yes.

15

First time the train stopped, we was in Dallas. I'd never even been out-side Red River Parish; now here I was in a whole other state. The city was big and close. Intimidatin. Then the railroad police started messin with us, so me and that hobo fella hopped another boxcar outta there and rode the rails for a while. He showed me the ropes. After a while, I decided to see how I'd make out in Fort Worth. Stayed there a coupla years, then finally made it out to Los Angeles and stayed there another coupla years. Met a woman, stayed with her for a while. Me and the law didn't get along too well out there, though. Seemed like I was always in trouble for somethin or other, so I went on back to Fort Worth.

I tried to find work here and there, odd jobs, that kinda thing, but I learned purty quick there wadn't much call for cotton farmers in the city. Only reason I made out was 'cause Fort Worth was what the rail tramps called "hobo heaven." Said anybody that was passin through could always get "three hots and a cot" from some different outfits that was tryin to help. And there was plenty a' real nice Christian folks, too, who was willin to give you somethin when you ain't even askin, maybe a cup a' coffee or a dollar.

Now if you think the only way homeless folks gets money is by standin on the corner lookin pitiful, that ain't true. Me and my partner met another fella that taught us how to turn nothin into somethin. First thing we was taught was the "hamburger drop," a purty good trick for keepin a li'l money in our pockets.

First thing you had to do was get you a little grubstake, which usually meant scrapin up about a dollar. That don't take long if you go to the part of downtown where the smart people work, the kind that wear a coat and tie. Some of them gentlemen'd give you a whole dollar right outta the gate if you just make like you hungry enough. Some of em'd give it to you quick, too, so you'd hurry up and get outta their face so they wouldn't have to smell you too long. But other folks seemed like they really wanted to help—they'd look you in your eye and maybe even smile. I felt kinda bad hustlin a dollar off a person like that just so I could pull off the hamburger drop.

Anyhow, here's how it worked. After I'd get my dollar for that day, I'd go on down to the McDonald's and buy me a hamburger, take a coupla bites out of it, and wrap it back up. Then I'd pick me out one of them big, tall office buildins that's got a trash can on the sidewalk out front. When nobody was lookin, I'd stick that wrapped-up burger down in the can and wait.

Soon as I saw somebody comin, I'd pretend like I was diggin in the trash. Then I'd come up with that hamburger and commence to eatin it. For sure somebody always gon' stop and say, "Hey, don't eat that!"—and they gon' give you some money 'cause they think you eatin outta the garbage can. They feel real sorry for you, but they don't know it's your garbage that you done put in the can in the first place!

You can't fool all the same people all the time, so you got to change locations. And you got to be on the lookout for folks you done fooled already and let em get on down the road 'fore you start hustlin some other fella.

At the end of the day, me and my partner'd put our hamburger-drop money together and go to some joint and eat us a decent meal. And if we done *real* good that day, we might have enough money left over for a half-pint a' Jim Beam, what we called "antifreeze for the homeless."

Next time you walkin around in Fort Worth and you see some homeless folks, you might notice that some of em's filthy dirty and some of em ain't. That's 'cause some street people have done figured out ways to stay clean. Just 'cause you homeless don't mean you got to live like a pig. Me and my partner kept on the same clothes all the time, just wore em till they wore out. But we figured out how to keep from smellin. That same fella that taught us the hamburger drop also taught us how we could get a good bath: at the Fort Worth Water Gardens.

The Water Gardens is a city park with a big ole fountain in it look kinda like a little stadium with walls made like steps or seats. The water flows down the sides of the fountain and makes a great big pool at the bottom, almost like a swimmin pool, 'cept it ain't blue or nothin. There's lots a' trees all around it and back then, the workin folks would take their lunch and go down and sit in the shade around the edges, and listen to the water rush and sing.

There was lots of tourists, too, 'cause folks from outta town just loved to sit and watch that water dance down the walls. Me and my partner learned how to act like tourists. We'd wait till afternoon when there wadn't too many folks around, and we'd walk up to the Water Gardens with our shirts unbuttoned halfway, and some soap and a towel in our pockets. Then, when the coast was mostly clear, one of us would act like the other one was pushin him in the water. Then the one in the water pulled the other one in, laughin and jokin like we was just friends horsin around on vacation.

We wadn't supposed to be in that water, and we sure wadn't supposed to take our clothes off. So we soaped up under the water where nobody could see, soapin our clothes and our socks just like you would your body. When we'd get through washin up and rinsin off, we'd climb up on a high wall that was part of the park and sleep till the sun baked us dry. We'd laugh and laugh while we was in that water, but it wadn't no fun. We was like animals livin in the woods, just tryin to survive.

Over the years, I got a few jobs through something called the Labor Force. You ever go down to the city and seen a buncha raggedy-lookin men crowded on the sidewalk in the early mornin, then you mighta seen a place like the Labor Force. I was one of them men, showin up in the mornin hopin to get a job doin work nobody else want to do—like pickin up trash, cleanin out a ole warehouse, or sweepin up horse manure after a stock show.

I remember one time they took us way on over to Dallas to clean out the Cowboys stadium. They even let me look at the game for a while.

I wanted to work a regular job, but I couldn't read and couldn't write. I didn't look right neither 'cause I only had one set of clothes that was wore out all the time. And even if somebody was to look past all that, I didn't have no paperwork like a Social Security card or a birth certificate.

At the Labor Force, you didn't even have to tell em your name. Somebody just pull around in a truck and holler out somethin like, "We need ten men. Construction site needs cleanin." And the first ten fellas to climb on the truck got the job.

At the end of the day, we'd get $25 cash money, minus the $3 the Labor Force done advanced you for your lunch. Then they charge you $2 for drivin you to your job. So at the end of the day, you'd get maybe $20, not even enough to rent a room. Now let me ask you somethin. What you gon' do with $20 'cept buy yourself somethin to eat and maybe a six-pack a' somethin to help you forget you gon' sleep in a cardboard box again that night?

Sometimes it's drinkin or druggin that lands a man on the streets. And if he ain't drinkin or druggin already, most fellas like me start in once we get there. It ain't to have fun. It's to have less misery. To try and forget that no matter how many "partners in crime" we might hook up with on the street, we is still alone.

16

I ended my affair with the Beverly Hills painter only to begin a new one—this one with my wife. With counseling behind us, each of us moved several giant steps in the other's direction. I kept both hands in the art business but traveled less and spent more time with Deborah, Carson, and Regan. I also began to take spiritual matters more seriously. Deborah, meanwhile, continued her volunteer work and her pursuit of God, but committed time to the things that interested me.

Chief among those became Rocky Top, the 350-acre ranch we bought in 1990. Perched on a three-hundred-foot mesa overlooking a shimmering arc of the Brazos River, the ranch house became a refuge for our family. We decorated it cowboy-style, from the buffalo head over the stone fireplace to the autographed his-and-hers boots from Roy Rogers and Dale Evans to the herd-sized trestle table we parked in the kitchen, big enough to seat fifteen hungry hands. So authentic and picturesque were the architecture and decor that style magazines photographed the house for feature stories, movie directors paid to use it as a set, and Neiman Marcus began shooting its Christmas catalogs there.

But for Deborah, the kids, and I, Rocky Top was a place to escape the clamor of the city. Bald eagles soared and dived above the Brazos, their high keen startling the deer that frequented the river's edge. In a verdant pasture below the house, we kept twenty-eight longhorn cattle. (Every year, Deborah gave their babies terribly un-cowboyish names like Sophie and Sissy, and I let her.) And during the spring, lush thickets of bluebonnets covered the rolling chaparral like a violet quilt.

Carson and Regan were teenagers when we settled in at Rocky Top, and they spent their last few years before college importing carloads of friends, hunting, fishing, and exploring miles of winding trails on horseback.

At the ranch, Deborah and I cemented our relationship as best friends and ardent lovers, growing so close that we began to joke that we felt "velcroed at the hearts." The ranch also became our geographical anchor, a place that, wherever else we might move, we knew we would always call home.

As it turned out, we did move. In 1998, tired of the Park Cities, the Dallas rat race, and what Deborah would later describe as "twelve years of exile in the 'far east,'" we returned to Fort Worth. We moved into a French mansard-roofed rental home on a golf course and began building our new home on a secluded lot near a nature preserve on the Trinity River. Then we began to plan what we thought would be the last half of our lives.

We hadn't been in Fort Worth for more than a few days when Deborah spied an item in the *Star-Telegram* about homelessness in the city. The piece mentioned a place called the Union Gospel Mission. At the time, an insistent voice in Deborah's heart told her it was a place she might fit. Not long afterward, a letter arrived from Debbie Brown, an old friend, inviting us to join "Friends of the Union Gospel Mission," a circle of philanthropic donors. Deborah immediately told me that not only did she want to join, she also intended to inquire about volunteering at the mission itself.

"I was hoping you'd go with me," she said, smiling and tilting her head in a way so irresistible I sometimes thought she should register it for a patent.

The mission, on East Lancaster Street, was tucked deep in a nasty part of town. While it was true that the murder rate in Texas had been falling, I was sure that anyone still doing any murdering probably lived right around there.

I smiled back. "Sure I'll go."

But secretly, I hoped that once she actually rubbed shoulders with the kind of scuzzy derelicts that had robbed my gallery, Deborah would find it too scary, too *real*, to volunteer on East Lancaster. Then we could revert to doing our part by dropping off some old clothes or furniture—or, if she really found it tough to tear herself away, more money.

I should've known better, for other than yellow jackets and black-diamond ski slopes, Deborah feared only one thing.

17

Now, believe it or not, there used to be what you might call a "code of honor," or unity, in the hobo jungle. Down there, if one fella got hisself a can of Vienna Sausages and there was five other fellas around, then he gon' give each one of em a sausage. The same goes for his six-pack and his half-pint and his dope. 'Cause who knows whether somebody else might have somethin he wants a piece of the very next day?

One of the fellas in my circle had him a car he was livin in, a gold Ford Galaxy 500. Me and him got to be purty tight, so one time when he was runnin from the law and he had to get outta town for a spell, he asked me to watch out for his car. It sure wadn't no new car, but I liked it and it run purty good. I didn't drive it around much 'cause I never had drove nothin but a tractor. But he'd been stayin in it, so I figured I would, too.

That's when I got me an idea: There was enough room in there for more than just one fella to sleep. So I started rentin out two sleepin' spots in the backseat—$3 a night. Fellas said it beat sleepin on the sidewalk. I had me a regular Galaxy Hilton there for a while till the police showed up and hauled it off, said my little hotel had unpaid tickets and no insurance.

Regular folks that live in neighborhoods and go to work every day don't know nothin about no life like that. If you took a normal fella and dropped him off in the hobo jungle or under the bridge, he wouldn't know what to do. You got to be taught to live homeless. You ain't gon' put on no suit and no tie and think you gon' be pullin off the hamburger drop.

So I had me some partners for a while. But after a few winters went by, I began to pull away from the folks I'd been runnin with. Kinda slipped off into silence. I don't know why. Some kinda "mental adjustment," maybe. Or maybe I was just goin a little bit crazy. For a real long time, I didn't speak to nobody and didn't want nobody speakin to me. Got to where if I felt threatened, I'd attack. I took some money from a hamburger drop and bought me a .22 pistol. Thought I might need it for protection.

You get a spirit in you, a spirit makes you feel like nobody in the world cares nothin about you. Don't matter if you live or die. People with that spirit get mean, dangerous. They play by the rules of the jungle.

I earned respect with my fists. One time I was talkin on a public telephone, and this fella that was waitin to use it come up and hung up the phone while I was still talkin. I took that telephone and broke it on his head. He fell on the ground, hollerin and holdin his head, blood gushin out between his fingers. I just walked away.

Another time, while I was sleepin under the tracks, some gangstas from the projects crept up in the hobo jungle and started stealin what little bit the homeless folks had. They was young black fellas—actin the way some young fellas act, like can't nothin touch em long as they stick together and cuss you loud enough. It was dark and I was lyin inside my cardboard box awake when I heard em slither up, whisperin.

Now I can't use the kinda language I used that night, so let's just say I called em some names. I busted outta that box with a sawed-off piece a' steel pipe in my hand and started swingin: "You done tried to jack the wrong man! I'll *kill* you! You think I won't? I'll *kill* you!"

There was three of em. But when a crazy-lookin homeless man is swingin a pipe at ever head in sight and threatenin murder, three against one ain't no good gamble. They took off runnin and so did I: straight to the gold Ford Galaxy that my friend had done got back from the police. I jumped in and dug the key outta the seat cushion where I knowed he stashed it. Then I cranked up the Galaxy and headed for the projects to get me some revenge.

I couldn't see the thieves no more, but I knowed where they come from and the projects was just a few blocks away. I was drivin fast and purty soon I could see the brick buildings peekin up over the long, low dirt pile somebody'd put up along the street to keep cars from drivin up where the folks stayed. When I got to that dirt pile, I never even slowed down, just jumped the curb and punched the gas. That Galaxy zoomed up that dirt hill and went airborne just like you see them daredevils do on TV. I landed smack in the middle of the projects with the car smokin like a coal train.

I jumped out with the engine still runnin and started hollerin. "Bring it on! Bring it on! Come out! I'll *kill* you!" It was late, but there was still a few people in the big courtyard. Most of em ran in their houses, the mamas snatchin up their children and hustlin em indoors.

Didn't take long before lights started comin on. I knowed folks was callin the police on me, so I jumped back in the car and sped outta there. I had created a real problem and had to go hide out for a spell. The police come and took my friend's Galaxy again, but they didn't arrest him 'cause he swore somebody stole it. (I guess I had since I didn't tell him I was takin it.) Besides, he didn't match the eyewitness stories of the man folks said had crashed a flyin gold car into the middle of the projects.

If all that had a' happened these days, somebody prob'ly woulda pulled out a gun and tried to shoot me dead. But back then, not a single one of them boys would come out and face me. I guess they thought a man crazy enough to jump a car into a place with women and children around might be crazy enough to kill em. They was right. If I'd a' found em, I would have. 'Specially if I'd a' thought to grab my gun.

I had to lay low for a while after that so I hightailed it back to Lousiana to let the heat die down. Took my pistol with me. That's how I wound up in one of the worst hellholes ever invented by a white man.

— — —

I made it to Shreveport, but I didn't have no money. I had that .22, though, and I figured if I waved it around at somebody who did have some money, they might give me some of it. I ain't proud a' this one bit now, but I decided to rob a city bus. All I had to do was wait on a corner till a bus slowed down and stopped. When the door opened, I jumped up on the steps and showed the driver my pistol.

"Open that box and gimme that money!" I hollered. There was just a couple of folks on the bus and they ducked down in their seats real quick. One lady started cryin.

The driver's eyes got real big. "I can't open it," he said, his voice kinda shakin a little. "I don't have a key. You can't get the money out unless you break it."

I looked down at the money in the box then at the folks hunkerin down in the bus. I could hear that lady, still cryin. I looked back at the driver and saw he was looking at my gun. Then I got off the bus. I was mean and bad, but not mean and bad enough to shoot a man just 'cause he showed up for work on the wrong day. But now I had the law on my tail in Fort Worth *and* Shreveport, so I decided to turn myself in. I didn't tell the police my real name, though. Told em my name was Thomas Moore. But it wouldn't have mattered to the judge if my name was Abraham Lincoln. He found me guilty of armed robbery and sent me to Angola prison for twenty years.

It was May 1968. Now in case you ain't heard nothin 'bout Angola, it was hell, surrounded on three sides by a river. I didn't know this then, but in those days, it was the darkest, most vicious prison in America.

A few days after I got there, a prisoner I had met back at the Shreveport jail saw me and reached out like he was gon' shake my hand. Instead, he gave me a knife. "Put this under your pilla," he said. "You gon' need it."

I was back in the fields again, 'cept this time I really was a slave 'cause that's how they ran the prison—like a plantation. 'Cept it was prisoners workin crops all day in the swelterin sun. And there wadn't enough guards, so they turned some a' the inmates into guards, even gave em guns. They liked to point em at us while we worked. Lotta times the same fellas that was workin with me one day didn't come back the day after that. And nobody ever saw em again.

In those days, a man in Angola without a knife was either gon' wind up raped or dead. For the first few years I was there, at least forty men got stabbed to death and another bunch, hundreds of em, got cut up bad. I did what I had to do to protect myself.

I was on what you call two-for-one time. Judge locked me up for twenty years, but they let me out after ten. I was ashamed to go do somethin like try and live off Hershalee, so I went on back to Fort Worth. I knowed I wadn't gon' have no home or no job there, but I knowed how to get by. Word got around on the streets that I'd been in Angola and wadn't nobody to be messin with.

I didn't scare everybody, though. I slept in the doorway of that United Way over on Commerce Street for a whole lotta years. And every mornin for all that time, a lady who worked there brought me a sandwich. I never knowed her name and she never knowed mine. I wish I could thank her. Funny, though. That United Way buildin was right next door to a church, and for all them years, nobody at that church ever looked my way.

I had been sleepin there for a long time when the Fort Worth police put up no-loiterin signs all over the place and made me have to move my sleepin spot. I found out later some rich white folks was "revitalizin" downtown. Raggedy black fellas sleepin on the sidewalks wadn't part of the plan. The police told me I needed to be goin down to the Union Gospel Mission. After sleepin on the streets, I dunno, maybe fifteen, twenty years, I wadn't fixin to move indoors just like that. So I put my blankets on the concrete next to a old empty building across from the mission. Mr. Shisler, the manager of the mission, told me over and over I didn't need to be sleepin outside in the weather. After some years went by, I let him give me a bed. He let me clean up around the mission for my keep.

18

When Deborah was six years old, she started a fire club. To get in, her friends had to steal some matches from their mamas' kitchens and hand them over to Deborah so she could show them how they worked. During one such lesson, she almost burned down an oil-field camp in Premont, where she lived—a near disaster resulting in a leather-belt spanking from her daddy that kept her out of a bathing suit for weeks.

Another time, just to see what would happen, she collected a bucketful of bullfrogs and dumped them into the laps of three ladies who were playing bridge with her mama. What happened was shrieking ladies, upended iced tea, and another spanking.

So here we were in our fifties, with me hoping some bums in littered alleyways would scare her when the only things on earth she really feared were black ice, yellow jackets, and rattlesnakes. Not exactly your shrinking violet.

She did have one other fear, though: missing the call of God. And she felt called to work at the mission. I wish I could say I felt God had tapped me for the assignment, too, but I didn't. But I did feel called to be a good husband, so I went.

The Union Gospel Mission sits just beyond the beauty of the restored section of Fort Worth, a city that became a national model for downtown revitalization, thanks to the billionaires who loved it. In that part of town, soaring glass towers pulse with legal intrigue and high finance. Nearby, warmer-looking buildings refaced with brick and brownstone line sidewalks graced with raised iron flowerboxes, manicured trees, and—afterall, it's Texas—topiaries of longhorn cattle. A cultural district spans three city blocks, housing three world-class museums, the Kimbell, the Amon Carter, and the Modern. A mile east, cafés open onto cobblestone plazas where dazzling urbanites can sip lattes and mineral water, and watch cowboys amble by in their boots and spurs.

Travel farther east, though, and the colors and flora of restoration fade into hopelessness and despair. Drive under the I-30/I-35 interchange, pass beneath an impossible pretzel of freeways called the Mixmaster and through a tunnel that efficiently separates the haves from the unsightly have-nots, and there are no more plazas or monuments or flowerboxes and certainly no more dazzling urbanites. In their place: tumbledown buildings with busted-out glass. Walls scarred with urine stains and graffiti. Gutters choked with beer cans and yellowed newspapers. And vacant lots blanketed in johnsongrass tall enough to conceal a sea of empty vodka bottles and assorted drunks.

Driving out of that tunnel shocks most people into realizing they made a wrong turn. But on a sun-splashed Monday in the early spring of 1998, Deborah and I drove out there on purpose, she propelled by her passion to help the broken and I propelled by a love for my wife.

As we passed out of the dark tunnel onto East Lancaster Street, we witnessed a curious one-way migration, a streaming of people, like tributaries all flowing east into a single, larger river of souls. On our left, a string of shabby men staggered from the johnsongrass that covered a lot. To the right, a parade of women and children in dirty, mismatched clothes shambled along, dragging green garbage bags. One boy, about eight, wore only a man's undershirt and black socks.

"They're going to the mission!" Deborah said, beaming, as if the entire ragtag bunch was long-lost TCU alumni and she just couldn't wait to catch up. I managed some sort of agreeing noise and a thin smile. To me, they looked as if they'd somehow found a portal from the Middle Ages and squeaked through just in time to escape the plague.

When we reached the mission, I bumped our truck over the driveway dip where a brown-trousered fat man dangled a cigarette from his lips and stood guard at a rusted chain-link gate. I offered my friendliest east Texas grin. "We're here to volunteer," I told him.

He flashed back a toothless smile, and I swear his cigarette never moved, just clung to his bottom lip as though he'd tacked it there with a stapler.

I had pulled into the parking lot wondering how quickly I'd be able to pull out again, but Deborah suddenly spoke in a tone that you learn to recognize when you've loved someone for years, a tone that says, "Hear me on this."

"Ron, before we go in, I want to tell you something." She leaned back against her headrest, closed her eyes. "I picture this place differently than it is now. White flowerboxes lining the streets, trees and yellow flowers. Lots of yellow flowers like the pastures at Rocky Top in June."

Deborah opened her eyes and turned to me with an expectant smile: "Can't you just *see* that? No vagrants, no trash in the gutters, just a beautiful place where these people can know God loves them as much as He loves the people on the other side of that tunnel."

I smiled, kissed my fingertips, and laid them against her cheek. "Yes, I can see that." And I could. I just didn't mention that I thought she was getting a little ahead of herself.

She hesitated, then spoke again. "I had a dream about it."

"About this place?"

Yes," she said, gazing at me intently. "I saw this place changed. It was beautiful, like I was saying, with the flowers and everything. It was crystal clear, like I was standing right here and it was the future already."

— — —

Inside the mission, we met the director, Don Shisler. In his early fifties and stocky, with a short beard and close-cropped hair, he looked more like a banker or an accountant than a caretaker of the homeless—though I'm not sure what I thought one of those was supposed to look like. Don introduced us to Pam, the volunteer coordinator, who led us on a tour of the common areas, including the kitchen and the chapel.

Both were dirty and windowless, and reeked of body odor, old grease, and other not-quite-identifiable odors that made me want to turn and flee.

In the kitchen, we slid like roller skaters along the greasy floor, straight into the sweltering office of a chain-smoking live wire named "Chef Jim."

Jim Morgan was the kind of fellow who, like any self-respecting Baptist, passes up handshakes and goes straight to hugs. He first wrapped me in a backslapping embrace like an old college pal, then gave Deborah a kinder, gentler squeeze. Thin and graying, he looked sixty-five but might have been younger. He wore checked pants and a chef's tunic, surprisingly unstained.

Chef Jim gabbed with us enthusiastically about God, homeless folks, and to a lesser degree, food. Extremely articulate, he used words I'd never heard before, and he didn't fit my notion of a homeless person, which at the time was someone who was probably uneducated or at least not very smart for having gotten themselves in such a fix in the first place.

As it turned out, Chef Jim was a fellow TCU alumnus whose teenage son had died tragically, an event that landed his wife in a mental institution. Jim, by contrast, numbed his double-dose of grief with rivers of liquor and drugs, which cost him his job as head of catering at an international hotel chain, then his home. Now, he was at the mission plying his trade for room and board while attempting to rebuild his life.

Jim shared his story with self-deprecating humor and without an ounce of blame or self-pity. Then he encouraged us to come on down and dish up supper for the homeless once a week.

"Infect em with love!" he said.

He couldn't have used a more appropriate word, since infection was probably my greatest fear. Spending hours each week captive in a kitchen that smelled like rotten eggs boiled in Pine-Sol was bad enough. But I fervently did not want to be touched for fear of the germs and parasites I suspected floated in every particle of the air.

Chef Jim and Deborah chatted easily while I mentally balanced the ledger between pleasing my wife and contracting a terminal disease. I had to admit that his idea seemed like an easy way to start—serve the evening meal once a week, and we'd be in and out in three, four hours max. We could minister from behind the rusty steel serving counter, safely separated from the customers. And we could enter and leave through the rear kitchen door, thereby minimizing contact with those likely to hit us up for money. The whole arrangement seemed like a good way for us to fulfill Deborah's desire to help the homeless without our touching them or letting them touch us.

Her bright laugh pulled my attention back into the room. "I think that sounds great, Jim!" she was saying. "I don't see any reason why we can't start tomorrow. In fact, let's just say you can count on us to serve every Tuesday until you hear otherwise."

"Praise the Lord!" Chef Jim said, this time giving Deborah a great big Baptist hug. It did not sound great to me, but Deborah had not asked me what I thought. She never did do much by committee.

Driving home, she reflected aloud on how society generally regards the homeless as lazy and foolish, and maybe some were. But she felt there was so much more below that surface image: dysfunction and addiction, yes. But also gifts—like love, faith, and wisdom—that lay hidden like pearls waiting only to be discovered, polished, and set.

That night she dreamed about the mission again—and this time, about a man.

"It was like that verse in Ecclesiastes," she told me the next morning over breakfast. "A wise man who changes the city. I saw him."

She gazed at me warily, as if she was afraid I wouldn't believe her or that I might think she was losing her mind. But I knew she wasn't the dreams-and-visions, mumbo-jumbo type. I poured fresh coffee into her cup. "You saw the man in your dream?"

"Yes," she said cautiously. "I saw his face."

— — —

At first the daisy chain of wilted souls who shuffled by for their Tuesday handouts depressed me. The first in line were mamas with their children, most of whom wore stained, ill-fitting clothes and looked like someone had cut their hair with a kitchen knife. Next came a string of women ages eighteen to eighty-five, followed by the "old" men, many younger than I, but with creased and haggard faces that made them look ancient. After that, the younger men, some beaten and sullen, some hiding behind a loud, false cheer meant to mask their shame. These were the ones who wandered the streets all day, then slept at the mission.

Last to eat were the undiluted street people, shabby and pungent. It took me a while to get over their smell, which floated in their wake like the noxious cloud around a chemical plant. The odor seemed to stick to the hairs inside my nose. I swore I could see the hair on some of their heads rustling, jostled by hidden armies of squirming lice. A couple of the men had stumps protruding where an arm or a leg used to be. One long-haired fellow wore a necklace fashioned from several hundred cigarette butts tied together with string. He wore black plastic garbage bags tied to his belt loops. I didn't want to know what was in them.

On our first day, Deborah, surveying the street people, looked at me and said, "Let's call them 'God's people.'"

I was thinking they looked more like the extras in the movie *Mad Max Beyond Thunderdome*.

Everyone who ate at the mission earned their free meal only after going into the chapel to sit like dead men on hard benches while a white-haired and nearly blind preacher named Brother Bill roared about the saving power of Jesus and the unpleasant consequences reserved for the unredeemed. From the kitchen side of the chapel door—locked to prevent altar-call escapees—I could hear the hellfire-and-brimstone, tough-love message that I agree often cracks hard cases. But it seemed manipulative to me to make the hungry sit like good dogs for their supper. And it did not surprise me that even when Brother Bill split the air with one of his more rousing sermons, not a single soul ever burst through the chapel doors waving their hands and praising Jesus. At least not while we were there.

The men and women we served seemed pleasantly surprised to have a smiling couple with all their teeth serving them supper. I'm sure they thought Deborah was on amphetamines, or possibly running for mayor, as they had likely never seen anyone who smiled and asked after them as much as she did.

"I'm Deborah, and this is my husband, Ron," she'd say as though welcoming visitors into her home. "What's your name?" Often, she received blank stares. Some looked at her slack-jawed and goggle-eyed, as though she'd just landed in the parking lot on a spaceship from Mars.

Some fellows answered Deborah, though, and from that day on she was forever telling rough-looking characters with names like Butch and Killer, "Oh, what a pretty name!"

Of the hundreds we served on that first day, only a handful told us what people called them. Deborah wrote down their names: Melvin, Charley, Hal, David, Al, Jimmy—and Tiny, an affable fellow who stood six-foot-five, weighed 500 pounds, and wore Osh-Kosh overalls, fuzzy blue house slippers, and no shirt.

One man, who declined to share his name, did tell us exactly what he thought of our philanthropy. Black, pencil-slim, and looking wildly out of place, he wore a mauve sharkskin suit and a hustler's tie, both of which he had somehow managed to have sharply pressed. From beneath a cream-colored fedora, he surveyed his domain through dark glasses with a designer insignia stamped in gold. We later found out people called him "Mister."

That first Tuesday, Mister strode up to me with an aggressive, proprietary air, as though the mission dining hall was his and I was trespassing. "I don't know who you folks are," he growled around an unlit filter-tipped cigar, "but you think you're doin' us some kind of big favor. Well, tonight when you and your pretty little wife are home in your three-bedroom cottage watchin TV in your recliners thinkin you're better than us, you just think about this: You miss a coupla paychecks and your wife leaves you and you'll be homeless— just like us!"

Speaking for myself—on the "favor" part—he was more right than I cared to admit. I didn't know quite what to say, but when I opened my mouth, out came, "Thank you. Thank you for helping me see homelessness your way." Unmoved, Mister eyed me like an insect, chomped his cigar, and strode off in disgust.

The encounter unnerved me some, but also gave me a peek at how some of these folks felt. A thought nibbled at the edges of my brain: Maybe my mission wasn't to analyze them, like some sort of exotic specimens, but just to get to know them.

Meanwhile, no tally of disdain, strange glances, or silence seemed to bother Deborah. She wanted to *know* and truly serve these people, not merely feel good about herself. That first day, she fell in love with every one of them. At her urging, we memorized the names we learned that day and, that night, prayed for each one, even the obstreperous Mr. Mister, whose mind I suddenly found myself hoping to change.

— — —

After a couple of Tuesdays, we noticed that the only time these folks got in a hurry was when they jockeyed for position near the head of their designated section of the serving line. We found out the reason for this: They feared we might ladle out all the good stuff—meat, for example—leaving only soup or stale 7-Eleven sandwiches for those unlucky enough to have been seated at the front of the chapel, farthest from the door. When the stragglers wound up with such low-end fare, the looks on their faces told a sad story: As society's throwaways, they just accepted the fact that they survived on leftovers and discards.

It seemed to us such a simple thing to prepare a little more food so that the street people at the end of the line could eat as well as those who slept at the mission, so we asked Chef Jim for that favor and he agreed. From then on, it thrilled us to serve the street people the good stuff, like fried chicken, roast beef, and spaghetti and meatballs.

That was the first time I tried to do something to improve the lives of the people Deborah had dragged me along to serve. I hadn't yet touched any of them, but already they were touching me.

On our third Tuesday of serving, Deborah and I were in the dining hall helping Chef Jim prepare the extra food. Blind Brother Bill had just finished preaching on forgiveness and his congregants were filing in to eat, when we heard the crash of metal and a man roaring in anger near the chapel door.

Alarmed, we turned to see about twenty people scatter as a huge, angry black man hurled another chair across the dining hall floor.

"I'm gon' *kill* whoever done it!" he screamed. "I'm gon' *kill* whoever stole my shoes!" Then he sprayed the air with a volley of curses and advanced into the crowd, roundhousing his fists at anyone stupid enough to get in his way.

It looked for all the world like a gangland brawl was going to explode right there at the chapel door. As I scanned the room for mission personnel to save the day, Deborah leaned in and whispered excitedly in my ear.

"That's him!"

"What!" I said impatiently. "What are you talking about?"

"That's the man I saw in my dream! The one who changes the city. That's him!"

I turned and looked at Deborah as though she had truly gone over the edge. Across the room, a group of mission workers burst in and began pouring soothing words on the raging man's temper. Grudgingly, he allowed himself to be led away.

"That's him," Deborah said again, eyes sparkling. "I think you should try to make friends with him."

"Me!" My eyes widened in disbelief. "Did you not notice that the man you want me to make friends with just threatened to kill twenty people?"

She laid her hand on my shoulder and tilted her head with a smile. "I really think God's laid it on my heart that you need to reach out to him."

"Sorry," I said, trying hard to ignore the head tilt, "but I wasn't at that meeting where you heard from God."

━ ━ ━

I wasn't about to invite a killer out for tea. But we did start tracking the man Deborah said she had seen in her dream. He intrigued us both. Probably in his sixties, he looked younger and, somehow, older at the same time. He dressed in rags. A loner, the whites of his eyes had gone an eerie yellow. He never smiled and seldom spoke. Nor did we see anyone acknowledge him. But it wasn't as though others at the mission ostracized him; it was more like they kept a respectful distance, as one might give wide berth to a pit bull.

On Tuesdays, when the serving line had nearly dried up, he would suddenly appear out of nowhere. With a poker face and no eye contact, he'd indicate that he wanted two plates, claiming one was for an old man upstairs. It was a clear violation of the rules, but we weren't there to be the mission police. So we served him double and blessed him, to which he responded with a wall of silence. One Tuesday, someone in the kitchen told us they thought his name was Dallas.

Dallas always ate one plate in the dining hall, picking out a spot in a corner far from other human contact. If anyone dared to sit nearby, he got up and moved. While eating, he stared sternly into his plate, chewing slowly with his few good teeth. Never glancing left or right, he methodically scooped the food into his mouth until it was gone. Then he would vanish. I mean that—vanish. He had this strange knack: You rarely saw him come or go. It was more like he was there . . . and then he wasn't.

Often, driving up to the mission, we'd see Dallas standing alone in a parking lot across the street in the shadow of a Dumpster, his face a stone slate. A couple of times, I overheard people saying this loner was crazy and not to mess with him. Deborah wrote his name in her Bible, next to Ecclesiastes 9:15: "There was found in a certain city a poor man who was wise, and by his wisdom he saved the city."

Occasionally, Deborah reminded me that she had a feeling God wanted me to be Dallas's friend. But I wasn't looking for any new friends, and even if I had been, Dallas from Fort Worth did not fit the profile.

Still, only to please Deborah—God would have to wait—I began a gingerly pursuit of the man.

"Hey there, Dallas," I'd say whenever I saw him. "How're you doing today?"

Most of the time, he ignored me. But sometimes, his yellowing eyes skewered me with a look that said, "Leave. Me. Alone." Which I would have been only too happy to do had it not been for my wife.

After a couple of months of this, someone at the mission heard me call

Dallas "Dallas" and laughed at me like I was the town idiot. "His name ain't Dallas, fool. It's Denver."

Well, maybe that's why he looks disgusted every time I speak to him, I thought, suddenly hopeful.

"Hey, Denver!" I called the very next time I saw him out by the Dumpster. He never even looked at me. The man was about as approachable as an electric cattle fence.

19

Things was goin along just fine at the mission till that smilin white couple started servin in the dinin hall on Tuesdays. Ever week, that woman drew a bead on me in the serving line. She'd smile at me real big and ask me my name and how I was doin—you know: attackin me for no particular reason. I did my best to stay completely outta her way.

And I didn't tell her my name was Denver, neither, but some fool blowed my cover. After that, the woman would corner me and poke her skinny finger in my face and tell me I wadn't no bad fella.

"Denver, God has a calling on your life," she'd say.

I told her several times not to be messin with me 'cause I was a mean man.

"You are *not* a mean man, and I don't ever want to hear you say that!" she'd say.

She was gettin kinda smart with me. Ain't never been no woman done that before, and few men, either, without them gettin hurt. But she kept on attackin me until I thought to myself, *What'd I ever do to this woman that she won't leave me alone so I can go on about my business?*

It might seem like bein homeless don't take no skill, but I'm gon' tell you, to stay alive homeless folks has got to know who's who and what's what. Here's what the homeless in Fort Worth knowed about me: Stay outta my way, 'cause I would beat a man down, have him snorin 'fore he hit the ground.

But no matter how mean and bad I tried to act at the mission, I couldn't shake that woman loose. She was the first person I'd met in a long time that wadn't scared of me. Seemed like to me she had spiritual eyes: She could see right through my skin to who I was on the inside.

Lemme tell you what homeless people think about folks that help homeless people: When you homeless, you wonder *why* certain volunteers do what they do. What do they want? Everybody want somethin. For instance, when that couple come to the mission, I thought the man looked like the law. The way he dressed, the way he acted. Too high-class. His wife, too, at first. The way she acted, the way she treated people . . . she just looked too sophisticated. Wadn't the way she dressed. It was just something about the way she carried herself. And both of em was askin way too many questions.

While everbody else was fallin in love with em, I was what you call skeptical. I wadn't thinkin nothin evil. It was just that they didn't look like the type to come in and mess with the homeless. People like that may not feel it within themselves that they're better than you, but when you the one that's homeless, *you* feel like they feel like they're better than you.

But these folks was different. One reason was they didn't come just on holidays. Most people don't want the homeless close to em—think they're dirty, or got some kinda disease, or maybe they think that kind of troubled life gon' rub off on em. They come at Christmas and Easter and Thanksgivin and give you a little turkey and lukewarm gravy. Then they go home and gather round their own table and forget about you till the next time come around where they start feelin a little guilty 'cause they got so much to be thankful for.

On Tuesdays, I started waitin till there wadn't no line so I could get through real fast without talkin to that couple at all. But that didn't mean I wadn't watchin em.

20

It took a couple of months before I noticed a real change in my heart, a heart that was feeling like it had been run through the short cycle in a microwave—warm on the outside but still a little cool in the middle. I was fairly certain something had happened when I began waking up on Tuesday morning, Mission Day, and felt the same chill of excitement as when I woke up on Saturdays at Rocky Top. It wasn't a raising-the-dead caliber miracle or anything. But folks who knew me would have classified it as a minor one. At least.

My own take on the topic was that maybe—just maybe—God had also rung my number when He called Deborah. On days when nothing else pressed, I found myself dropping by the mission. Soon, the fellows in the hood started to recognize my dirty-green crew-cab truck, and when they saw me pop out of the tunnel on East Lancaster Street, they'd slip their paper-bag-wrapped liquor bottles behind their backs and wave at me like I was a neighbor coming home from work.

Sometimes I ventured into the streets, places where even in broad daylight, young women wandered by like death in blue jeans, offering sex for cigarettes. Or for a ride home to steal mama's TV and pawn it at Cash America. I hoped just to lend an ear, be an example. Sometimes, I stayed closer to the mission where some sunny afternoons, I'd sit on the curb in the shade of a vacant building and chat. One fellow told me he'd been married a thousand times to a thousand beautiful women—all of them as rich as Oprah. Of course, he said, all of them had also stolen every dime he'd ever made, so he asked me if I could spare a smoke.

If I hung around long enough and concentrated on spotting a fellow who didn't want to be spotted, I'd nearly always see Denver. But if I made a move toward him, he would move an equal distance away. The fact that I was now calling him by his real name seemed to do more harm than good. If anything, he seemed irritated, like he was mad that I now had it right.

The mission residents had by then dubbed Deborah "Mrs. Tuesday." They liked her a lot. But she became convinced that it would take more than "like"—and more than our ladling macaroni and meat loaf—to gain their trust. Without that, she realized, our efforts might mean a full belly on Tuesday nights, but little in the way of real change. Her goal was changed lives, healed hearts. Broken men and women rejoining the ranks of the clean and sober, moving out to places of their own, spending Sundays in the park with their families.

She began to rack her brain about ways to bring a little joy into their lives. Her first idea: Beauty Shop Night. Deborah and her best friend, Mary Ellen Davenport, would go to the mission loaded down with makeup kits, hairstyling tools, perfumes, soaps, and every manicure and pedicure accessory ever invented. And the homeless women would come. Deborah and Mary Ellen would comb the lice out of their hair, then wash and style it with blow-dryers and curling tools. If a woman wanted a pedicure, Deborah and Mary Ellen would wash her feet, use pumice stones to scrub away callouses layered on by ill-fitting shoes, and paint her toenails in a feminine shade of red or pink. They did facials and makeovers and gave the women little makeup kits to keep. Sometimes, on these nights, a homeless woman, catching a glimpse of herself in a mirror, would remember what she looked like before her life went off course and begin to cry.

Then Deborah dreamed up movie night. It sounded silly to me, but on the first night at least fifty men showed up to watch a movie about the Brooklyn Tabernacle choir. The next Wednesday, the dining hall was completely packed—150 people. The third week, something miraculous happened: Instead of heading for the exits when the video screen went blank, grown men, crusty and battle-hardened, began weeping and asking for prayer. God somehow managed to transform the dining hall into a confessional. It wasn't the movies that caused the metamorphosis. It was just the simple act of caring. The men began confiding in us things some of them had never told anyone—and truthfully some things I wish they'd never told us.

That spurred Deborah on to a new idea: birthday night. Once a month, we brought a giant, gorgeously frosted sheet cake and everyone, including "God's people," would be invited to eat some. Those with a birthday that month got two pieces. Some folks couldn't even remember what month they were born, but we weren't checking IDs. The cake was always a hit. So much so that people began having more and more birthdays it seemed— some every month. (During the twelve months we brought cake, some fellows at the mission aged twelve years.)

In the fall of 1998, the mailman delivered to our home an invitation that arrived with the junk mail but turned out to be a treasure. Our friend Tim Taylor was organizing "an outreach to the unreached"—that's fancy talk for evangelism—in a downtown theater that occupied the top floor of a landmark bar called the Caravan of Dreams.

Deborah and I had been to the Caravan, a smoky jazz and blues lounge owned by billionaire developer and Fort Worth renovator Ed Bass. But the bar had stayed hip while we had not, so it had been years since we'd dropped in. Still, Tim's invitation gave Deborah an idea: We could drive down to the mission and pack our cars with people who would enjoy a liquor-free night on the town. Given Jesus's habit of consorting with drinkers and gluttons, she didn't see the venue as a problem.

The next day, we whipped up a flyer announcing the free concert, drove down to the mission, and tacked it up on a bulletin board next to one offering to buy poor people's plasma.

The flyer didn't say what band was playing, but the Caravan was no hole in the wall. Anyone who'd been in Fort Worth awhile knew it occasionally featured a marquee performer. I'm sure the mission folks were hoping B. B. King might show up.

Rain slicked the pavement as we pulled up to the mission that evening, me in my Suburban and Deborah in her Land Cruiser. Still, we had customers:

about fifteen men and women standing on the shiny sidewalk dressed in their handout best.

Including Denver.

We were shocked to see him standing on the mission steps, solemn and rigid like the statue of a dictator. And he clearly meant to go with us: He was scrubbed so clean his ebony skin shone against a dark blue secondhand suit that almost fit. He stood alone, of course, at least twenty feet from anyone—which did not surprise us since the others always treated him like a bad dog on a long chain.

When I got out and opened the door to my Suburban, six men piled into the two backseats, leaving the front passenger seat vacant. No one wanted to sit near Denver, who had sourly observed the commotion of loading, yet had not made a move. For five solid minutes he stood there staring. I waited. Then, without a word, he stalked to the Suburban and slid into the front seat, inches from my elbow.

I had never been that close to him. I felt like Billy Crystal in the movie *City Slickers*, when he camps alone on the prairie with the menacing trail boss Curly, shivering as Curly sharpens his knife on a razor strop. To break the tension, I took a couple of stabs at trivial conversation, but Denver sat stock-still and silent, a sphinx riding shotgun.

As I eased down the street, the other fellows seemed happy to be riding in a car that wasn't marked "Fort Worth Police Department" on the sides. They wanted to know all about it, the monthly payments, and whether I knew any other rich people.

Deborah followed in her Land Cruiser with a carload of ladies. In five minutes, we were through the tunnel and at the Caravan. We both parked and our guests spilled out, chattering and laughing, glad to be dressed up and in the other Fort Worth. We all paraded in, up the stairs to the theater where 250 seats sloped toward a small stage.

Except for Denver. I was acutely aware he had not come in. Everyone was seated and the show was about to begin, but I got up and went back downstairs. I found him standing on the sidewalk puffing on a cigarette.

"The concert's about to start," I said. "Don't you want to come in?"

Smoke curled up around his dark head. I heard the spat-spat of rain off the eves. Denver said nothing. I posted myself just inside the Caravan door and waited. Finally, he walked past me and up the stairs, as if I were no more alive than a cigar-store Indian. I followed, and when he took an end seat on a row by himself, I sat down next to him.

Then I did something stupid: I smiled heartily and patted him on the knee. "Denver, I'm glad you came."

He didn't smile back, didn't even blink, just stood up and walked away. At first, I was afraid to turn around, but later, as the concert began, I saw him out of the corner of my eye, sitting on the back row, alone.

That tore it. *He's a nutcase*, I concluded, *not worth my trouble.* The man was definitely looking a gift-horse in the mouth.

Another thought nagged at me, though. Could it possibly be something he saw in me—something he didn't like? Maybe he felt like the target of a blow-dried white hunter searching for a trophy to show off to friends, one he bagged after a grueling four-month safari in the inner city. Meanwhile, if I caught him, what would I do with him? Maybe God and Deborah had gotten their signals crossed. Maybe I wasn't supposed to be his friend.

The concert lasted a little less than two hours. Afterward, as we skirted shallow rain puddles on the way back to the cars, our guests thanked us profusely. All except for Denver, who hung back as usual. But when all the others had piled back in the cars, he walked up to me and spoke the first words I had ever heard come out of his mouth outside the dining hall.

"I want to apologize to you," he said. "You and your wife been tryin to be nice to me for some time now, and I have purposely avoided you. I'm sorry."

Stunned, I didn't know what to say and didn't want to say too much for fear he'd bolt again. So all I said was, "That's okay."

"Next time you is at the mission, try and find me and let's have a cup a' coffee and chat a l'il bit."

"What about tomorrow morning?" was what came out when I opened my overeager yap. "I'll pick you up and we'll have breakfast together. How about me taking you to your favorite restaurant and I'll treat."

"I ain't got no favorite restaurant," he said, then added, "matter of fact, I don't think I ever been to no restaurant."

"Well, then I'll choose one and pick you up at 8:30. Same place I drop you off."

We climbed back into the Suburban and I sped back to the mission. I couldn't wait to tell Deborah the news.

Like I said, I'd been watchin Mr. and Mrs. Tuesday. They wadn't like the holiday volunteers. They'd come ever week and talk to the homeless folks, and not seem to be afraid of em. Talked to em like they was intelligent. I started to think Mr. and Mrs. Tuesday might be tryin to do some real good 'stead a just makin themselves feel better 'bout bein rich.

So when they started talkin somethin 'bout goin down to the Caravan of Dreams, that got me interested. There was a lot of folks at the mission that respected me. I thought if I went that might encourage some others to go, too. Besides that, I had lived downtown 'fore them millionaires started fixin it up. I hadn't seen a lot of them new buildings, and I thought I might like to go down there and check it out.

By that time, I had me a job workin in the clothing store at the mission. It wadn't nothin but a warehouse that seemed a hundred years old, with boxes a' clothes and shoes and such stacked up near as high as the lightbulbs hangin naked from the ceilin. When I heard about this trip to the Caravan, I grabbed the best suit that come through there that day. Picked it out special.

To tell you the truth, though, I was kinda hopin the cars would be full up, then I wouldn't have to go. You know how it is when you tryin to do the right thing even though you really don't wanna do it. Well, just my luck, God saved me a seat. All them men loaded theirselves into the big Suburban and which seat you think they left? The front one, right next to Mr. Tuesday. I just stood up on the steps, waitin and hopin somebody else'd come outta the mission, late and wantin to go to the Caravan 'stead a' me.

Well, that didn't happen, so I got in the car. Next thing I was hopin was that Mr. Tuesday wouldn't say nothin to me. But that was about like hopin the sun wouldn't come up, and of course he started right in. And then at the Caravan, not only would he not let me go on about my business, he had to haul off and put his hand on my knee! I guess he didn't know I'd knocked men out for less.

I didn't want him by me. I didn't want nobody by me. I wanted to be by myself. So I got up and burned off. That was just my way.

But after a while, I started feelin kinda bad about that. I'd been watchin Mr. and Mrs. Tuesday, and I knowed they was serious about helpin folks. It would've been kinda ugly of me not to tell em I appreciated it. So after the concert let out, I waited for everbody to get in the cars. Then I edged over to Mr. Tuesday and apologized.

He said that was okay. Then I said maybe we could have some coffee at the mission.

Lord-a-mercy, did *that* open up a can a' worms.

22

After the Caravan concert, I got back to the mission first. Exchanging thank-yous and good-nights, I dropped off the mission men curbside, speed-dialing Deborah's cell phone as I pulled away.

"You're not going to believe this!" I said when she picked up. "He talked to me!"

"Who?" she said. "I can barely hear you." I could hear the mission women still chattering in the background.

"Denver!"

"What!"

"Denver! He came up to me after the concert and apologized for running away from us all this time. And guess what? Tomorrow, I'm taking him out to breakfast!"

"I knew it!" Deborah said. "I knew you'd make friends with him!"

She was elated. Before we went to bed that night, we prayed together that God would show us how to reach Denver, how to let him know we cared about him. Still, before I left the next morning, I warned Deborah not to get her hopes up.

When I pulled up to the mission at 8:30 sharp, Denver was waiting for me on the steps. It was the second time I had seen him neatly dressed, and the second day in a row, this time in khaki trousers and a white shirt with a button-down collar he hadn't buttoned.

We exchanged greetings and drove with little small talk to the Cactus Flower Café, a little place I like on Throckmorton. Denver ordered eggs and grits and buttermilk, and when the waitress said they didn't have buttermilk,

I silently thanked God. When I was little, watching my dad gulp down the clabbered chunks made me gag.

The food came, followed by a lesson in patience. I was half done by the time Denver finished melting butter on his grits; I was mopping up egg yolk with my biscuit before he had taken his first bite. It took him a solid hour to eat two eggs and grits—I swear I wanted to snatch his fork away and feed him myself.

I did most of the talking, of course, asking about his family without getting too personal, a policy he reciprocated in his answers. In a quiet, country drawl, sometimes laughing and sometimes choosing his words with great caution, he sketched scenes of his past. I learned that he had been raised on a Louisiana plantation, that he'd never been to school a day in his life, and that somewhere in his late twenties—he wasn't quite sure when—he'd hopped a freight train with less than $20 in his pocket. He had been homeless, and in and out of scrapes with the law, ever since.

Suddenly, Denver dropped his head and became silent. "What is it?" I said, concerned I might have pushed too hard. He raised his head and stared into my eyes, his own like brown lasers locked on target. In my mind, I started counting to one hundred and was past eighty when he finally spoke.

"Mind if I ask you a personal question?" he said.

"Of course not. Ask me anything you want."

"I don't wanna make you mad, and you don't have to tell me nothin if you don't want to."

"Ask away," I said and braced myself.

Again, a long pause. Then, softly: "What's your name?"

"What's my name! That's what you wanted to ask me?"

"Yessir . . . ," he ventured, embarrassment creeping up his cheeks. "In the circle I live in, you don't ask nobody his name."

Suddenly, I flashed back to the slack-jawed stares we'd encountered on our first day at the mission. *You don't ask nobody his name . . .*

"Ron Hall!" I blurted, smiling.

"Mr. Ron," Denver replied, translating plantation-style.

"No, just Ron."

"No, it's *Mr.* Ron," he repeated firmly. "What's your wife's name?"

"Deborah."

"Miss Debbie," he said warmly. "I think she's an angel."

"Me, too," I said. "She just might be one."

His obvious affection for her touched me, especially because he had never really acknowledged her.

Now, I thought I knew why. If he opened up to her, he'd blow his cover and that would threaten his survival in the jungle where he was the lion and everyone feared him. I knew after listening to his story that he'd carved out a life for himself. Though meager and pathetic from the perspective of the more fortunate, it was a life he knew how to live. After more than thirty years, he was an expert at it. God may have been calling Denver, as Deborah had been telling him, but in Denver's view maybe God should've come knocking earlier.

By the time he'd finished his breakfast, my hair had grown an inch! I sensed he wasn't through talking, but I wasn't sure what else to say. Finally, he asked me a pointed question: "What you want from me?"

A direct hit, I thought, and decided to give him a completely unvarnished answer: "I just want to be your friend."

He raised his eyebrows in curious disbelief and a long moment of silence stretched between us.

"Let me think about it," he finally said.

I didn't feel rejected, which surprised me. Then again, I had never formally asked anyone to be my friend.

I paid the bill. Denver thanked me. As we rode back to the mission, he began to laugh. I didn't really get the joke, but his laugh turned into a roar so robust that tears appeared in the corners of his eyes and he began to choke like he'd swallowed a frog and couldn't catch his breath. After a block or so, I started laughing, too, at first because I was afraid not to, then naturally as his genuine mirth became contagious.

"Folks at the mission . . . ," he sputtered, still chuckling and wiping at his eyes. "Folks at the mission thinks you and your wife is from the CIA!"

"The CIA!"

"Yessir . . . the CIA!"

"Is that what you thought, too?"

"Yes . . . ," he said, finally able to collect himself. "Most folks that serve at the mission come once or twice and we never see em again. But you and your wife come ever week. And your wife always be askin everbody his name and his birthday . . . you know, gatherin information. Now just think about it: Why would anybody be wantin to know a homeless man's name and birthday, if they ain't the CIA?"

— — —

A week passed before I saw Denver again on a brilliant fall day, the sky a crisp blue. Sweater weather. Cruising down East Lancaster in the crew-cab, I spotted him standing stonelike by the Dumpster across the street from the mission. Gone was the pressed and proper cleaned-up man we had taken to the show; Denver had slipped back into his comfort zone as a vagrant.

I pulled to the curb and lowered the passenger-side window. "Hop in. Let's go get a cup of coffee."

I steered toward the Starbucks at University, a mall designed by Charles Hodges, an eminent Dallas–Fort Worth architect and a friend of mine. Instead of gargoyles along the eves, he'd installed replicas of the skulls of longhorn steers. Vintage Texas.

At first, Denver was quiet as we stood in line, and I found out later he was amazed that people would stand in line to pay two or three dollars for a cup of coffee that had to be ordered in a foreign language. On top of that, he got worried that the folks working the cash register were getting ready to mix it up with the folks brewing the coffee.

He elbowed me and whispered fiercely: "There's fixin to be a rumble!"

"A rumble?"

"Yeah, 'causa all that back-talkin they doin. One says 'decaf non-fat lat-tay,' and the other one hollers it back, and another one hollers 'frappay,' and somebody else hollers back 'frappay.' That's gang talk. That kind a' back-talkin get you killed on the streets!" He looked genuinely concerned.

I tried explaining the strange café language that seemed to have taken over the civilized world. Then we took our coffee outside and pulled up chairs at a tiny black patio table under a green umbrella. For a few minutes, I attempted to explain what an art dealer is to a man who had never heard of Picasso. When I launched off on a tangent about French impressionism, he appeared thoroughly unimpressed, then downright bored.

I finally figured out he wasn't listening and stopped my patter. Then things got quiet.

Denver was first to break the silence. "What's your name again?"

"Ron."

"And what's your wife's name?"

"Deborah."

"Mr. Ron and Miss Debbie," he said, allowing a smile to escape. "I'll try to remember."

Then his smile faded into seriousness, as if he'd had a rare light moment then someone had closed the blinds. He stared down at the steam rolling up from his coffee cup. "I been thinkin a lot about what you asked me."

I had no idea what he was talking about. "What did I ask you?"

"'Bout bein your friend."

My jaw dropped an inch. I'd forgotten that when I told him at the Cactus Flower Café that all I wanted from him was his friendship, he'd said he'd think about it. Now, I was shocked that anyone would spend a week pondering such a question. While the whole conversation had slipped my mind, Denver had clearly spent serious time preparing his answer.

He looked up from his coffee, fixing me with one eye, the other squinted like Clint Eastwood. "There's somethin I heard 'bout white folks that bothers me, and it has to do with fishin."

He was serious and I didn't dare laugh, but I did try to lighten the mood a bit. "I don't know if I'll be able to help you," I said, smiling. "I don't even own a tackle box."

Denver scowled, not amused. "I think you can."

He spoke slowly and deliberately, keeping me pinned with that eyeball, ignoring the Starbucks groupies coming and going on the patio around us.

"I heard that when white folks go fishin they do somethin called 'catch and release.'"

Catch and release? I nodded solemnly, suddenly nervous and curious at the same time.

"That really bothers me," Denver went on. "I just can't figure it out. 'Cause when colored folks go fishin, we really proud of what we catch, and we take it and show it off to everybody that'll look. Then we eat what we catch . . . in other words, we use it to *sustain* us. So it really bothers me that white folks would go to all that trouble to catch a fish, then when they done caught it, just throw it back in the water."

He paused again, and the silence between us stretched a full minute. Then: "Did you hear what I said?"

I nodded, afraid to speak, afraid to offend.

Denver looked away, searching the blue autumn sky, then locked onto me again with that drill-bit stare. "So, Mr. Ron, it occurred to me: If you is fishin for a friend you just gon' catch and release, then I ain't got no desire to be your friend."

The world seemed to halt in midstride and fall silent around us like one of those freeze-frame scenes on TV. I could hear my heart pounding and imagined Denver could see it popping my breast pocket up and down. I returned Denver's gaze with what I hoped was a receptive expression and hung on.

Suddenly his eyes gentled and he spoke more softly than before: "But if you is lookin for a *real* friend, then I'll be one. Forever."

23

I'm gon' tell you right now what I first thought about Mr. Ron askin me would I be his friend: I didn't like it. Why would he want to be my friend? That's what I was thinkin. What does he want? Everybody want somethin. Why don't he pick somebody else? Why *I* got to be his friend?

You got to understand that by that time, I had layers of street on me a mile thick. Some homeless folks got lotsa friends, but I hadn't ever let nobody get that close. It wadn't that I was worried about gettin hurt or nothin like that. Bein a friend is a heavy commitment. In a way, even more than a husband or a wife. And I was selfish. I could take care a' myself, and I didn't need nobody else's baggage. Besides that, friendship to me means more than just somebody to talk to, or run with, or hang with.

Bein friends is like being soldiers in the army. You live together; you fight together; you die together. I knowed Mr. Ron wadn't fixin to come up outta no bushes and help me fight.

But then I got to thinkin about him some more and thought maybe we might have somethin to offer each other. I could be his friend in a different way than he could be my friend. I knowed he wanted to help the homeless, and I could take him places he couldn't go by hisself. I didn't know what I might find in his circle or even that I had any business bein there, but I knowed he could help me find out whatever was down that road.

The way I looked at it, a fair exchange ain't no robbery, and a even swap ain't no swindle. He was gon' protect me in the country club, and I was gon' protect him in the hood. Even swap, straight down the line.

24

"If you is lookin for a *real* friend, then I'll be one. Forever."

As Denver's words echoed in my head, it occurred to me that I could not recall ever having heard any pronouncement on friendship more moving or profound than what I'd just heard from the mouth of a vagabond. Humbled, all I could do in return was make a simple, but sincere, promise: "Denver, if you'll be my friend, I promise not to catch and release."

He put out his hand and we shook. Then, like a sunrise, a grin lit Denver's face and we stood, facing each other, and hugged. In that moment, the fear and distrust that had hulked like an iceberg between us melted on the warm patio outside Starbucks.

Beginning that day, we became the new odd couple, Denver and I. A couple of times a week, I'd swing by the mission and pick him up, and we'd head out to a coffeehouse, a museum, or a café. Deborah, meanwhile, urged me on, praying deep roots for the friendship she'd prayed would bud in the first place. After our catch-and-release chat, Denver's sulking silence thawed into a gentle shyness. "Did you see how Denver said hi in the supper line?" she'd say, eyes shining. "I think you're really making progress."

No longer just Mr. and Mrs. Tuesday, Deborah and I began going to the mission even more often. She'd stay and work with the women and children while Denver and I went somewhere to hang out. If I planned to take him to a nice restaurant, I'd call ahead to the mission to give him time to slip into his preppie disguise. If we were going to Starbucks, though, he dressed to his own liking. Usually, that meant conspicuously poor—soiled shirt, but-

109

toned crooked; holey pants; and beaten-up leather shoes he wore like house-slides, his heels smashing down the backs.

It was at Starbucks that I learned about twentieth-century slavery. Not the slavery of auction blocks, of young blacks led away in ropes and chains. Instead, it was a slavery of debt-bondage, poverty, ignorance, and exploitation. A slavery in which the Man, of whom Denver's "Man" was only one among many, held all the cards and dealt them mostly from the bottom of the deck, the way his daddy had taught him, and his granddaddy before that.

More than half a century before Denver was born, Abraham Lincoln had formally declared that "all persons held as slaves within said designated States and parts of States are, and henceforward shall be, free." That was all well and fine, but white plantation owners did not go quietly into the night. First, Southern statehouses passed "Black Codes," laws that used legal tricks to keep black people slaves, forcing the federal government to break up the state legislatures and put the army in charge of the stubborn South. After state lawmakers promised to try to be good, planters and the people they once owned tried a new arrangement: sharecropping.

That turned out to be a devil's bargain. Not only did sharecropping spawn poverty and hopelessness among both blacks and poor whites, it also opened up an ugly, festering crack in the plantation South into which people like Denver Moore fell, some forever.

That fissure ran through Red River Parish, where Denver's Man was a shrewd dealer. Not wanting to lose his labor supply, he kept the aces to himself. He dealt the card of meager sustenance, but withheld the card of American progress. He dealt the card of backbreaking labor, but withheld the card of education—the get-out-of-jail-free card that would have liberated men like Denver. In the twentieth century, slaves were free to leave the plantation, but their debt and lack of education kept them shackled to the Man.

I listened to Denver's story with fifty-year-old ears that had been touched by the dream of Dr. Martin Luther King. Later, I found out that the Ku Klux Klan in Coushatta, Louisiana, a town in Red River Parish, had once plotted to assassinate Dr. King. The FBI had wanted to swoop in and foil the plot, but J. Edgar Hoover refused to let them.

The more I learned, the more I hated the Man and wanted to right the wrongs of Louisiana's modern-day slave masters. I sang Denver's story like a songbird to anyone who would listen. Then one day, a thought hit me like a right cross to the head: My own granddaddy had not been so much different from the Man. Fairer, yes. An honest and decent man in the Texas of his day. But the wages he paid were still no excuse for the pitiful way we treated the folks who worked his land.

Amazingly, though, Denver kept telling me that a man providing jobs has a right to earn a profit. Denver had lived in an unplumbed, two-room shack with no glass in the windows nearly until the time his country put men on the moon. But he still maintained that the Man wasn't really a bad fellow.

"He was just doin what he was raised up to do," Denver said. "Besides if everbody was rich, who gon' do the work?"

That kind of homespun, practical way of looking at things hooked me. After our catch-and-release conversation, I gave him my phone number and told him where we lived, breaking a cardinal rule for mission volunteers. The truth is, prior to my Starbucks fishing lesson, I never thought Denver and I would form a real friendship—at least not one carried on outside his neighborhood.

I hate to admit this now, but I had pictured myself more as a sort of indulgent benefactor: I would give him a little bit of my valuable time, which, had I not been so benevolent, I could have used to make a few more thousand dollars. And from time to time, I imagined, if Denver stayed cleaned up and sober, I'd take him on field trips from hobo-land to restaurants and malls, a kind of peep show where he could glimpse the fruit of responsible living and perhaps change his ways accordingly.

I was aware I might cause him some therapeutic torment over the fact that he would probably never own some of the high-end toys we had, like a horse trailer with sleeping quarters. He would certainly never own a ranch or a painting by Picasso. I was amazed when that didn't bother him a bit—especially not the Picasso part, after Denver saw some of his work.

One afternoon we visited three art museums—the Kimbell, the Amon Carter, and the Modern. At the Modern, he thought I was playing a joke on him. As we viewed one of Picasso's less, shall we say, *organized* works, Denver looked at me as if the museum curators were trying to pass off some kind of snake oil.

"You just kiddin me, right?" he said. "Folks ain't really callin this art, is they?"

I had decorated my own house with similar works and, as an art dealer, the modern masters were my niche. But as we strolled through the Modern that day, I tried to look through his eyes at the bold geometrics, splashed paints, and huge canvases dominated by "negative space." I had to admit: Some of it could be construed as junk.

The Kimbell was Denver's favorite. Old Master paintings drew him like magnets, especially those that were centuries old and depicted Christ. When we stopped in front of a large Matisse from the 1940s and I told him it cost $12 million, his mouth fell open.

"Well," he said, eyeing the work in dubious wonder, "I don't like it much, but I'm glad the museum bought it so somebody like me could see what a $12 million picture looks like." He paused, then added: "You think if the guards knowed I was homeless they'd let me in here?"

With the museums, the restaurants, and the malls, I was showing Denver a different way to live, a side of life in which people took time to appreciate fine things, where they talked about ideas, where raw yellowtail cost more than cooked catfish. But he remained absolutely convinced that his way of life was no worse than mine, only different, pointing out in the process certain inconsistencies: Why, he wondered, did rich people call it sushi while poor people called it bait?

I knew Denver was sincere when he told me that he would not want to trade places with me for even one day. His convictions became clear to me when I laid my key ring on the table between us at one of our earliest meetings for coffee.

Denver smiled a bit and sidled up to a cautious question. "I know it ain't none of my business, but does you own somethin that each one of them keys fits?"

I glanced at the keys; there were about ten of them. "I suppose," I replied, not really ever having thought about it.

"Are you sure you own them, or does they own you?"

That wisdom stuck to my brain like duct tape. The more I thought about it, the more I became convinced we'd enjoy life a whole lot more if we owned a whole lot less. In some ways, Denver became the professor and I the student as he shared his particular brand of spiritual insight and plain old country wisdom.

I also came to realize that though his thirty years on the streets had sewn a thick hide on the man, they had also forged in him staunch loyalty, a strong spirit, and a deep understanding of what beats in the heart of the downtrodden. Though wallowing in the sin and addictions of street life, he claimed in his solitude to have heard from God. His brain had filed away everything he had seen over the years, and it seemed he had just been waiting for someone willing to listen. I was privileged to be the first to lend an ear.

8

25

Me and Mr. Ron started spending a fair amount of time together, me takin him out into the hood to show him what's what, and him takin me to museums and restaurants and cafés and such. I learned a lot on those trips—like the difference between a taco and a enchilada. The taco is the crunchy thing, and the enchilada is that long thing that kinda flops down beside the taco. (I usually just eat the inside a' the taco, though, 'cause I ain't got that many good teeth.) I also found out the difference between a restaurant and a café: A restaurant is where they roll your fork and your knife up in a fancy towel that you use for a napkin. In a café you just have a regular ole paper napkin and ain't nothin rolled up in it usually.

First time Mr. Ron took me to a restaurant, I couldn't find no fork for the longest time till I saw him unroll the dark red towel he had on his side of the table. He caught me gawkin and told me the towel was a napkin, which I thought was crazy 'cause who gon' wash em all?

Me and Miss Debbie started talkin a li'l more, too. I didn't burn off when I saw her no more, and when she asked me how I was doin', I'd say fine. She was always real nice to me, asked me about my life and what was I gon' do that day and did I need her to bring me anything. I'd see her down at the Lot, and I'd help out her and Sister Bettie and Miss Debbie's friend, Miss Mary Ellen.

I met Sister Bettie before I met Miss Debbie. She ain't no nun or nothin like that. We call her "Sister" 'cause she's a real spiritual woman.

I don't know how old Sister Bettie was when I met her, but right this minute she got a crown a' hair just as white as a cloud on a summer day, and twinklin eyes as blue as the sky them clouds go sailin in. When she's talkin to you, she'll lay a hand on your arm like she's knowed you all your life, like maybe you was her own child. And even if she keeps her hand there awhile, it don't bother you none. You just feel happy God saw fit to drop a lady like that into this world.

Sister Bettie lives at the mission, but it ain't 'cause she don't have nowhere else to go. A long time back, she lived in a regular neighborhood. But after her husband died, Sister Bettie felt the Lord tuggin on her heart, tellin her to spend the rest a' her life servin the homeless. She sold her home and everything she had except for a little bitty Toyota truck, and she asked the folks at the Union Gospel Mission could she set up housekeepin down there.

It didn't take long 'fore most a' the homeless folks in Fort Worth knowed Sister Bettie. She'd go to restaurants to ask em for their leftovers, and stores to ask em for socks and blankets and toothpaste and such. Then she'd haul her old bones up and down the nastiest streets, offerin help to men so mean they'd as soon tear your head off as look at you. That didn't scare Sister Bettie none 'cause she believed God's angels camped all around her and wadn't gon' let nothin bad happen to her. And if it did, she said, that would be God's will.

She never carried no purse with her, just whatever she had to give out that day and her Bible. After a while, it got so it didn't matter what Sister Bettie believed about God's angels: Even the meanest man on the street wouldn't dare lay a hand on her, 'cause he'd get beat down if he did. To this day, that woman could walk naked on the railroad in the hobo jungle at midnight and be as safe as if she was tucked in her own bed.

After I'd been at the mission awhile, I started helpin Sister Bettie with some things. We never did have no conversation, but if she needed somethin, she knew she could ask me and I'd do it. Like I helped keep her little truck runnin, changed the oil and the fan belt, that kinda thing.

I also started helpin her at the Lot, a place street folks calls "Under the Tree." It's over on Annie Street in one a' the worst neighborhoods in the city, spillin over with crackheads and criminals and ragged, empty-eyed folks livin so low they're surprised ever time they open their eyes and find out they done lived through another day.

Don't get me wrong. Wadn't like I was clean and sober all the time, nei-ther. Just 'cause me and Mr. Ron was friends don't mean I turned into no overnight saint. We might a' been goin out to fancy places in the daytime. But at night I'd still go out to the hobo jungle and pass around the Jim Beam with the fellas.

I tried not to drink too much on Tuesday nights, though, 'cause I liked to help Sister Bettie out the next day. Ever Wednesday, she fed 200 or 250 folks at the Lot and it was always some kinda miracle, like that loaves-and-fishes story in the Bible. Nobody really knows where all the food come from, but ever week you can smell it two blocks away: big, steamin pots a' beef stew full a' carrots and peas and potatoes. Baskets a' fried chicken. Fresh-cooked pintos and kettles of chili. All of it's home-cooked. Seems like folks just show up with it outta nowhere.

One day somewhere along the way, Sister Bettie found out I could sing and she asked me would I come down and sing at the Lot. First, I was a little worried about it, but when Sister Bettie asks you to help out, ain't too much you can do but help out.

26

In Sister Bettie, Deborah sensed someone who would lead her into a new spiritual dimension, a level of service more fearless, more sacrificial than what she could perform inside the walls of the mission. She wanted to share the experience with her best friend Mary Ellen Davenport, whom Deborah called a "prayer warrior," which is to say, she'd stop and offer to pray with anyone about anything for as long as they would let her.

Plucky is a silly-sounding word, but *Webster's* defines it as "spirited" and "brave." It should've included a picture of Mary Ellen. A registered nurse, she and her husband, Alan, a physician, became our friends in 1980 when we threw a July 4 pool party at the Williamsburg-style home we'd moved into in Fort Worth two years earlier. We'd invited our friends, the Hawkins, who asked if they could bring their friends, the Davenports.

Alan and Mary Ellen had recently moved back to Fort Worth from Galveston, where Alan had completed his medical residency. We didn't know them personally, but Deborah knew *of* them. She had heard that Mary Ellen had had a difficult pregnancy with triplets, and she had been praying for her by name.

But when the Davenports pulled up to our address on the day of the party and Mary Ellen spotted our sweeping porch, tall white columns, and a three-car garage that looked bigger than their whole house, she threw a fit.

"I'm not going in there!" she told Alan.

"Why not?" he asked.

"Why not? My gosh, just look at their house! They're millionaires—what could we possibly have in common with them?"

So the Davenports sat in the car with the air-conditioning blasting and debated whether to stay. Soon the triplets, by then fifteen months old, and Jay Mac, their three-year-old, were wailing. Decked out in swimsuits and floaties, their dials were tuned to "SWIM," and they didn't like the sound of the conversation up front. In the end, Mary Ellen lost the battle, and I remember them walking into our backyard for the first time, Alan grinning nervously and the smile pasted on Mary Ellen's face as fake as a Rembrandt painted in Chihuahua.

But Deborah rescued the afternoon. "I'm so glad to finally meet you!" she said, greeting Mary Ellen with a warm smile. "I've been praying for you and your family for *months*." Then Deborah, the "millionaire's" wife, offered to babysit the triplets so that the Davenports could get organized in their new home. At that, Mary Ellen threw down her weapons. Gracefully, she accepted the offer, launching a close family friendship that would last decades.

From Mary Ellen, Deborah learned boldness. Deborah had never been bold, just persistent. Mary Ellen was bold *and* persistent. So when Deborah invited her friend to join her in volunteering at the mission, Denver's misery was "doubled," he later said, since that meant two white ladies were pestering him instead of just one.

At Sister Bettie's urging, Deborah and Mary Ellen began teaching and singing a day each week at the mission's women's and children's chapel service. But it was Sister Bettie's service at the Lot that drew Deborah like a magnet.

The Lot itself is a lush little refuge, dotted with red crepe myrtles, rough-hewn benches, and a cross made of railroad ties topped with a crown of thorns someone fashioned from barbed wire. The area *surrounding* the Lot, however, is a model for urban decay: rusted chain link, buildings boarded up and condemned, adjoining lots clotted with johnsongrass that hid bodies that barely oozed life. Next door to the Lot, Sister Bettie's free-lunch customers stumble out of Lois's Lounge, a dark little den where they blot out their waking lives by drinking cheap liquor purchased with panhandled funds. I'm not judging them: It's just a simple fact that in America drugs and booze cost money, but food is free to anyone willing to snooze through a gospel message.

Scores of them do, dragging themselves to the Lot each week, some riding rusting wheelchairs pushed by others who can barely stand, others carried on the backs of men more sober than themselves. Often, following an afternoon there, Deborah would return home in tears, her heart broken by encounters with drug addicts and alcoholics, people busy paying a very high price for very low living.

Before we ever connected with him, we sometimes glimpsed Denver there, standing across the street, stock-still and trying to blend in with a telephone pole. I asked Sister Bettie about him. "What, specifically, is his problem?"

"Denver?" she replied in that soft way of hers, smiling. "Oh, he's very helpful. Keeps my little truck running. And he can sing beautifully!"

From time to time, she said, she could coax him into doing so at the Lot, or at the chapel service where she taught on Thursdays. "With Denver, you must ask him only at the moment you want him, because with any warning, he'll slip away and disappear."

Though we'd become friends, Denver hadn't entirely abandoned his vanishing act. Now, he felt guilty facing people on the street, many of whom he had, at one time or another, threatened to kill. They feared the old Denver, but the one that was emerging scared even him. So he would often disappear when asked to do "Christian" things, like sing for Sister Bettie. Deborah and I served as constant reminders to him that change was under way—change he could have lived just fine without.

Meanwhile, following hard after what she felt was her call to serve, Deborah blossomed. In twenty-nine years of marriage, I had never seen her happier. I can also attest that as a couple we had never been more deeply in love. The peace forged in counseling and the early years at Rocky Top had mellowed into an upbeat contentment.

We might've gotten there a lot faster if I'd been willing to recognize the truth of an old saying: "If Mama ain't happy, ain't nobody happy." But we got there. And from the summit of our relationship, Deborah exported a fresh and contagious joy to the Lot. There, under the giant and ancient elm that shaded the benches, she always found some pearls hidden below the amber sea of crushed beer bottles and syringes.

The pearl she found one day glistened in the smile of a grizzled street veteran who lived under a railroad trestle in a cardboard box shaped like a casket. This man ate from garbage cans, an unpleasant truth you knew automatically if you had a nose. His beard was matted with dried vomit and the remnants of his last few meals, and he reeked so strongly of booze that it seemed he might explode if someone got too close and struck a match.

Here was a man whose life seemed disposable. Yet he found a reason to smile. Drawn to him, Deborah offered him a plate of home-cooked food and a prayer. Then, truly puzzled, she asked him, "Why are you so happy?"

"I woke up!" he replied, eyes twinkling in his haggard face, "and that's reason enough to be happy!"

Deborah rushed home to tell me what he'd said, as though she'd been given a treasure that needed to be deposited immediately in my memory bank. From that day on, three words—"We woke up!"—were the first to come out of our mouths, a tiny prayer of thanksgiving for something we'd always taken for granted, but that a derelict had had the wisdom to see as a blessing fundamental to all others.

We greeted each other that way every morning, never suspecting that each morning would soon be a precious gift we could count on one hand.

27

It wadn't long 'fore Miss Debbie and Miss Mary Ellen started askin me would I sing in their chapel service. I would, if they was smart enough to catch me. I'd sing some spirituals I brung with me in my heart from the plantation. Other times, I'd sing some songs I made up on my own. Like I said, I know plenty a' Scripture.

It didn't take long, though, 'fore Miss Debbie started gettin bossy again. She got a burr under her saddle 'bout somethin she called a "retreat." Said her and a bunch of her Christian friends was goin up to the woods to "hear from the Lord."

"I've been praying about it, Denver," she'd say whenever she seen me, "and I believe God's telling me that you should go with us."

I asked some of the fellas round the mission if they knowed what a retreat was and not a one of em had any idea, 'cept Mr. Shisler. He said a retreat was some religious thing where you go off someplace lonesome and talk and pray and cry all weekend. I knowed for sure I didn't want nothin to do with that. But Miss Debbie wouldn't let up. I just shined her on, though, 'cause wadn't no way in the world I was fixin to drive up in no woods with no carload a' white women.

Well, then I guess she put Mr. Ron on the case. One day at Starbucks, he started in, talkin 'bout "retreat" this and "retreat" that. Said it wadn't gon' be just women. Men was gon' be there, too.

"Think about all the nice folks you'll meet," he said. "And all that free food!"

"Not from Jump Street!" I said. "I ain't goin! I ain't goin *nowhere* to *no* retreat to meet *nobody*! And I 'specially ain't goin to no retreat with no white lady that's somebody else's *wife*!"

Just so we'd be clear on the whole thing, I eyeballed him like he was crazy.

I ain't real sure what he told Miss Debbie after that, but the very next time I went through the servin line, she blowed out from behind that counter like a streak a' lightnin. And here come that skinny finger in my face again. "Denver, you *are* going with me to the retreat, and I don't want to hear you say anything else about it!"

Now here I is, six feet, 230 pounds, a mean sixty-two-year-old black man, and this skinny little white lady thinks she can make me mind. Not even Big Mama talked to me like that. There was fixin to be a problem—a big problem.

Finally, the day come for the retreat and Miss Debbie drives down to the mission lookin for me. I was doin my best to hide out, but some helpful fellas spotted me and told her where I was at. She convinced me to at least come on out to the car and see who all was goin. I didn't want to be ugly to her 'cause we was gettin to be friends and all. So I walked on out in front of the mission.

I looked in Miss Debbie's Land Cruiser and sure 'nough, there was *four* other white ladies sittin inside. In my life, I had bad enough luck with just *one* white lady. And here was four, all smilin and wavin at me. "Come *on*, Denver! We want you to go with us!"

Right about then, one of the street fellas sittin on the mission steps started sing-songin like a little girl: "Yeah, *Denver*, you go right on!" and busted out laughin.

Then his friend piped up and started singin': "Swing low . . . sweet chariot, comin for to carry me home . . ." And they both busted up.

I didn't think it was funny. But I had to make up my mind. There was all them white ladies in the car tryin to be so nice to me, and there was them fellas sittin on the steps singin me a funeral song. I guess I knowed I was takin my life in my hands when I got in that car, 'cause it was a cold day in January, but I was sweatin like a hog in August.

28

While I'd been getting to know Denver, my art business percolated prof-
itably, with clients seeking out my partners and me, instead of the other
way around. We worked with an elite group of clients who were interested
only in the finest works. Even so, in the fall of 1998, I received the kind of
call of which art dealers' fantasies are made.

The call came after Denver and I had begun making the rounds of museums. I had just dropped him off near the mission when my cell phone rang.
The man on the line headed a large Canadian real estate development firm
that had purchased a thirty-six-story bank building in downtown Fort Worth.
Fortunately for the Canadians, the deal included "Eagle," a forty-foot sculpture by the twentieth-century master Alexander Calder, one of only sixteen
monumental stabile sculptures the artist executed in his lifetime.

At that moment, Eagle was firmly nested eighteen inches deep in the
concrete plaza outside the bank building, a spot that dominated the heart of
the city. The citizens of Fort Worth had long considered the master sculpture public domain, a symbol of the city's place in the world of art and culture. The new Canadian owners, however, weren't so sentimental; the man
on the phone said they wanted me to sell it.

My heart raced as I thought of the possibility of making this seven-
figure deal—likely to be the biggest of my career at that time or ever—especially since a Calder sculpture of that category would almost certainly never
be for sale again. At the same time, I realized that if I did sell it, I risked
being run out of town. I knew that to be a fact because the prior owner, a
bank in crisis, had asked me to explore a sale only a couple of years earlier,

123

but had ultimately backed down, bowing to citizen pressure so formidable that even local museums had declined to buy the Calder and left it in the city instead. But the Canadians, the man on the phone said, wanted a deal that was clean, fast, and silent. And, as it happened, I had a buyer.

We developed a plan shrouded in secrecy that included code names, as well as "The Phoenix," a Delaware corporation my partners and I set up just to handle this very special transaction. We hired two eighteen-wheel transport trucks, along with crews and drivers who would jackhammer and disassemble the twelve-ton sculpture under cover of darkness. I joked that if word leaked, the workmen might need to wear body armor. But maybe I was only half-joking: So great was the need for absolute secrecy that the plan included the proviso that the crews would not be told where they were taking "Eagle" until they crossed the Texas border into Oklahoma.

We set the date for the move: April 10. Months passed as my partners and I hammered out the details. Meanwhile, I worked on my relationship with Denver. In late December, I'd started trying to talk him into going to the mountain retreat with Debbie. But by January, I'd pretty much given up on that idea. Deborah and Mary Ellen were still going, but I wasn't there to see them off since the retreat coincided with the Palm Beach Art Fair.

That's where I was when my cell phone rang just as I was attempting to sell a Matisse drawing to a fancy couple wearing matching pink slacks. It was Deborah, calling to tell me that she'd convinced Denver to go to the retreat. Our son, Carson, by then twenty-two and aiming toward a career dealing in art, had joined me on the trip, so I excused myself and let him take over. In light of Denver's "Jump Street" speech, I couldn't believe he'd actually gotten in Deborah's car—or, even more amazingly, that he had stayed at the retreat the whole weekend.

The highlight, Deborah chattered over the phone, was the last day when Denver—urged on by all the white ladies—sang. Reluctantly, he sat down at the piano in the worship area and belted out a song he made up as he went. His audience gave him a standing ovation.

"I wish you had been there," Deborah said.

"I wish I had, too." On the other hand, I thought, if I had been, maybe

Denver and I would have been off fishing when God wanted Denver to be singing. "On second thought," I said, "I think everyone was exactly where we needed to be."

I couldn't wait to hear Denver's take on the retreat—the horrors of hanging with white ladies and all that. But that Tuesday when we went down to the mission, I learned that no one had seen him since Deborah had dropped him off on Sunday. And the next day, still no Denver. That night at home, Deborah and I had started to feel like a family member had gone missing when the phone rang. It was Denver—calling from a hospital.

"I'm okay," he said. "But when I got home from the retreat, I was hurtin so bad, I walked to the hospital and checked myself in."

I dropped everything and took off. The Harris Hospital is a good two miles southwest of the mission. I sped there, making a quick stop at Whataburger to pick up Denver's favorite milk shake, vanilla. Inside Harris, I remembered the floor but forgot the room number, so I walked down the long hall, peeking into each room as I went. Finally, I saw his name, handprinted on a card, slipped into a slot on a closed door.

A pretty blonde nurse stood nearby, jotting notes on a chart. "Can I help you?"

"Well, I just spent the last ten minutes looking for my friend's room, but I guess I just found it," I said, nodding toward Denver's name card.

"He won't be in *there*," she said, lowering her voice confidentially: "The man in there is black and homeless."

I grinned. "Then I'm obviously in the right place."

Embarrassed, she skirted off, probably hoping I wouldn't tell her boss. I pushed my way through the door. "Hey there, Denver! All those white ladies put you in the hospital?"

Denver, by now able to laugh, told me about his long walk to the hospital through the hood. "Don't tell Miss Debbie, but out there at the religious resort, I just kept eatin all that free food, but I just didn't feel right 'bout usin the Man's bathroom, so I didn't go the whole time I was up there. So here I am, tryin to get unplugged!"

We both howled. When we finally settled down, he got serious. "Miss

Debbie knowed what she was doin takin me up to that retreat." He didn't
confide any details and I didn't press.

A couple of weeks later, when his innards were ready, I took Denver to the
Mexican restaurant where he had first learned to identify the parts of a com-
bination plate. He ordered his usual—taco, enchilada, rice, and beans—but he
pushed it all around on his plate, more interested in talking than eating.

"Miss Debbie knowed what she was doin—takin me outta the street
environment I was in so I would have time to think about my life," he said.
"You know, you got to get the devil out the house 'fore you can clean it up!
And that's what happened to me up in them woods. I had time to clear my
head and shake loose of some old demons and think about what God might
have in mind for the last part of my life."

Then Denver got quiet again. Finally, he parked his fork tines in his
refrieds, wiped his hands on his napkin, and put it back in his lap. "Mr. Ron,
I got somethin important to tell you. The work Miss Debbie is doin at the
mission is very important. She is becomin precious to God."

Denver's brow wrinkled and his head dropped. Then with that dark
glower that always preceded his most serious pronouncements, he said
something that still rings in my ears today: "When you is precious to God,
you become important to Satan. Watch your back, Mr. Ron. Somethin bad
gettin ready to happen to Miss Debbie. The thief comes in the night."

29

Certain days in life, you remember the headlines.

November 22, 1963: JFK assassinated. Easy to remember since I had a front-row seat.

July 20, 1969: Neil Armstrong took one small step for man and one giant leap for mankind as Deborah and I, newly engaged, made out on the couch in my apartment at TCU.

April 1, 1999: I remember the headlines from that day less for the events themselves than for the fact that April Fools' Day was the fulcrum that flung our lives down a path we could not have foreseen.

Per our usual coffee-in-the-kitchen routine, it was the Bible for Deborah that morning, the *Star-Telegram* for me. Albanian refugees were pouring out of Kosovo, the paper said . . . former Catwoman Eartha Kitt was still lounge-singing at age seventy-two . . . Texas Governor George W. Bush had pulled in $6 million in less than a month for his likely presidential campaign.

After coffee, Deborah took off for her exercise class, then to her annual physical. She was military about that yearly visit—she checked in, got the "you are in fantastic health for a woman half your age" report from the doctor, then made her appointment for the following year on her way out the door. Weddings, parties, and travel plans all were scheduled *around* that physical.

I headed out for my office in Dallas, looking forward to a lunch date with our daughter, Regan. She had been working for me in the gallery. With an art history degree from the University of Texas and a certificate of completion from Christie's Fine Arts course in New York City, it seemed like a natural fit. But she hated it.

Even in high school, Regan had felt more comfortable around the disadvantaged than the privileged. She often would whip up a batch of sandwiches and, we were mortified to find out later, take them *alone* to the bums living under the bridges in downtown Dallas.

During the Christie's course, she discovered she did not enjoy the art business—the pampered clients, the self-involved dealers, the pretentious power lunches. But maybe it was just that way in New York City, she thought. So she kept mum, came home, and stuck it out at our Dallas gallery for a while. Carson, meanwhile, was a senior at TCU, and Deborah was enjoying having all her chicks back in the nest.

But Regan's discontent grew daily. So we met for lunch that day at Yamaguchi Sushi and, in a corner booth over raw tuna topped with jalapeño slices, got down to the serious business of charting another course for her life. As we discussed options, grad school and ministry among them, my cell phone rang. It was Deborah.

"Craig felt something in my abdomen," she said, her voice thin and strained. The doctor, a personal friend named Craig Dearden, wanted to do a sonogram in his office then send her to the hospital for X-rays. "Would you come back to Fort Worth and meet me at All Saints?"

"Absolutely," I said. "I'll be there in half an hour. And don't worry, okay? You're the healthiest person I know."

I hated to cut short lunch with Regan, but we agreed to reschedule the next day, and I told her I'd call as soon as I talked with Craig. When I arrived at All Saints, I found Deborah in the radiology waiting room. Mary Ellen was already there. So was Alan, an All Saints physician and former chief of staff.

I scooped Deborah into a long hug. Her shoulders felt tense, but she gradually relaxed. I pulled back and looked into her eyes. "You okay?"

She nodded, trying on a weak smile.

Deborah got X-rays, but also a CAT scan. When the films were ready, we sat in an examining room, lights dimmed, X-ray illuminator glowing. Another doctor, John Burk, clipped the first film to the illuminator. At first, the amorphous image, milky white on gray, meant nothing to me.

"This is Deborah's liver," Dr. Burk explained, drawing an invisible circle around a shape on the screen.

Then I saw them: shadows. Her liver was completely covered with them.

As we stared at the film, several more doctors filtered into the room, their white coats and serious faces vaguely blue in the dim light. A couple of them experimented with sounding upbeat.

"These spots are a little troubling, but it's nothing to worry about yet," said one.

"It's possible they're birthmarks," said another. "I've seen that before."

But none of them looked us in the eye. The word *cancer* floated through my mind like a poisonous gas, but I didn't dare utter it.

"We've scheduled a colonoscopy for tomorrow morning," Craig said. They would withhold judgment until then.

At home that night, we settled into bed, and Deborah shared with me the story of Joshua and Caleb, two of twelve men Moses sent to spy out the Promised Land and bring back a report for the children of Israel.

We lay facing each other, heads on white-cased pillows. "When the spies came back, they brought good news and bad news," Deborah said, her voice lilting softly like a storyteller. "The good news was that the land *did* flow with milk and honey, just as God had promised. The bad news was that the land was inhabited by giants." The Israelites wept with fear, she went on, all except for Joshua and Caleb, who said, "If the Lord is pleased with us, He will give us the land. Do not be afraid."

Deborah fell silent for a few minutes, then raised her eyes to mine. "Ron, I'm afraid."

I pulled her to me and held her. We prayed about the colonoscopy. That the Lord would be pleased with us, that the doctors would bring back a good report.

— — —

Stars hung like ice in a black sky when we pulled into the All Saints parking lot the next morning. Word of Deborah's pending diagnosis had spread among our friends, and we were surprised and touched to find about twenty of them clustered in the day surgery waiting room, praying.

As the doctors wheeled Deborah away and she made her pale face brave, we prayed for a good report. I posted myself outside the door of the endoscopy room—as close to Deborah as they'd let me get—and paced the cold tile floors. I alternated between prayer and mild panic, between "the peace of God that surpasses all understanding" and bubbling nausea. An eon ticked by, then an epoch. Sand through an hourglass a grain at a time.

Finally, through the square of wired safety glass, I saw nurses wheeling Deborah into recovery and rushed to join her. Through heavily lidded eyes, she looked up at me, her bottom lip protruding slightly in a way it did only when she was truly sad. She mouthed the word *cancer*, her lips attempting a half-smile to cushion the blow.

Then tiny tears appeared in the corners of her eyes and spilled down her pale cheeks and I remembered her words from the night before: *giants in the Promised Land.*

30

It was Miss Mary Ellen that told me about Miss Debbie. She come down to the mission alone to lead that Bible study Sister Bettie let em have, and when I seen Miss Debbie wadn't with her, I asked her where was she at.

Miss Mary Ellen put her hand on my shoulder. "I have some bad news, Denver. Miss Debbie went to the doctor and . . . it's serious. She has cancer."

When Miss Mary Ellen said "cancer," I couldn't hardly believe it. Didn't look like a thing in the world was wrong with Miss Debbie. Here she was, comin down to the mission two or three times ever week, feedin down at the Lot, leadin a Bible study. Seemed so perfect in her health.

The first thing I knowed was that God was gon' heal Miss Debbie. The second thing I knowed was that I was afraid. What if He didn't heal her? In my life, I had already lost most a' the people that was important to me—Big Mama and Uncle James and Aunt Etha. Miss Debbie was the first person that had loved me unconditionally in over thirty years. Here I'd let her get close and, sure 'nough, looked like maybe God was gettin ready to take her, too.

I got scared my life was gon' be changed forever. Then I started worryin how was everbody else at the mission gon' take it when they heard?

I ain't gon' sugarcoat it: They took it purty hard. There's a lot of folks come down to the mission and volunteer, but most of em was not faithful like Miss Debbie. But that wadn't all. It was the way she treated the homeless that made them accept her as their friend. She never asked em no questions, like how come you is in here? Where you been? How many times you been in jail? How come you done all them bad things in your life? She just loved em, no strings attached.

That's the way she loved me, too. The Word says God don't give us credit for lovin the folks we want to love anyway. No, He gives us credit for loving the unlovable. The perfect love of God don't come with no conditions, and that's the kind of love Miss Debbie showed the folks at the mission.

After we heard about Miss Debbie, me and Chef Jim got to be purty tight. We never had no special prayer group before, but ever mornin me and Chef Jim would meet up in the kitchen and pray for Miss Debbie and her family. And there was other folks prayin, too.

You know, if you ain't poor, you might think it's the folks in them big ole fine brick churches that's doin all the givin and the carin and the prayin. I wish you coulda seen all them little circles a' homeless folks with their heads bowed and their eyes closed, whisperin what was on their hearts. Seemed like they didn't have nothin to give, but they was givin what they had, takin the time to knock on God's front door and ask Him to heal this woman that had loved them.

31

Deborah's doctors scheduled another surgery for three days later. Deborah, Carson, Regan, and I retreated to Rocky Top to pray and think things through as a family. Maybe "retreated" isn't the right word, at least not in my case, for the ranch became my war room.

We would probably spend a year in this battle, I told Deborah, then celebrate our victory, maybe even with a parade like soldiers returning from war, or the Apollo 13 astronauts rumbling safely back to earth after a space flight that seemed doomed. On the road from here to there, we knew that pain, tears, and fear waited like assassins. But pain makes life fuller, richer. And I remembered what Denver's aunt Etha told him: "Good medicine always tastes bad."

I was confident that the right medicine was out there, and it became my mission to find it. As of that day, supported by my partners, I basically hung an out-of-business sign on my Dallas gallery. It was only days before hired crews were to sweep into Fort Worth to remove the Calder sculpture in the most lucrative coup of my career. But my partners agreed to handle the final operation, and I asked them not to fill me in on the details. It meant nothing now. I was in the army again, this time a field general in the war on cancer.

Our friends Roy Gene and Pame Evans joined us at Rocky Top. An investor, horseman, and the scion of a prominent Dallas family, Roy Gene had built his ranch house one bluff over from ours, overlooking the same crescent of the Brazos and the green valley beyond. We had spent nearly every weekend at the ranch with them for the past eight years.

They hadn't planned to come down that weekend, but drove the one hundred miles just to come and love on Deborah for a while and encourage her to fight hard. Roy Gene, as another friend once described him, is a little like John Wayne: a big, comforting presence who speaks slowly, softly, and uses few words, but always good ones. Pame is a cancer survivor, a woman of many words who uses them to heal, like salve on a wound.

Conflicting emotions layered those days at Rocky Top. Our optimism and confident prayers for healing were real. But like rain falling from a sunny sky, Deborah and I sensed without discussing it aloud that her prospects for a long life were grim. A few years earlier, we had lost our friend John Truleson to colon cancer of the liver. After multiple rounds of debilitating chemotherapy, he died, withered to a shadow and racked with pain.

Those memories were fresh on both our minds. "Ron, if the cancer has spread outside my colon and those spots we saw aren't birthmarks, I don't want to fight it," she told me on our second day at Rocky Top.

"We don't have to make that decision now," I said.

But in fact, the decision had already been made. This was the woman who feared nothing but rattlesnakes and yellow jackets. Who had stared a dead marriage and another woman in the eye and fought to keep her man. Who tamed Denver Moore, the meanest junkyard dog in one of the nastiest ghettos in Texas.

She would fight. She just didn't know it yet.

And yet for all the courage I knew she had, she had shown this glimmer of fear. Oh, how I loved her then. Fiercely. The passion you feel down in your guts where no one else can see and only you know its frightening force. I could remember that there were times in our nearly three decades of marriage that I had loved her less than at that moment, and guilt pierced my heart like a spike. Though she had always given unconditionally, I had often not been willing to do so in return. *She has deserved better than she's gotten from me*, I thought, and nearly drowned in a wave of regret thirty years deep.

Then I resolved to love her as she had never been loved before.

— — —

On the day of the surgery, we drove to All Saints Hospital unsure of our future but with a full tank of faith. A team of surgeons, led by Dr. Paul Senter, planned to remove most of her colon and any other cancer they found that they deemed safe to remove. During the five-hour surgery, about fifty friends gathered in the waiting room.

Five hours after surgical technicians wheeled my wife away, Dr. Senter returned. Unsmiling and battle-weary, he asked to speak to me and the children, alone.

"I'll be honest with you," he said, after we'd moved to a small office. "It's not good."

The cancer had pushed outward from her colon, invading her entire abdominal cavity, wrapping itself around her liver like a shroud.

"She needs more surgery," he said.

I asked for no prognosis, no time-left-to-live, as only God knows the number of our days. Still, God had apparently been busy with other matters. Our most passionate prayers had not triggered a good report after the colonoscopy. Our prayers for healing at Rocky Top had not beaten back the lethal invader doctors had discovered inside my wife. Wounded and nearly blind with fear, I clung to the Scriptures:

"Ask and you shall receive . . ."

"Pray without ceasing . . ."

"I will do whatever you ask for in My name . . ."

Grimly, I shut out another verse, this one from the book of Job: "The Lord giveth and the Lord taketh away."

— — —

After the surgery, I sat shell-shocked beside Deborah's bed. Tubes bristled from her face and arms, probing her sleep, snaking back to boxes that blinked a maddening medical code I couldn't understand. My insides felt crushed, as though we'd been injured in some apocalyptic accident. Numb and silent, I waited for her to wake. I did not move my eyes from hers. I wondered what she might be feeling. I wondered if either of us would survive.

That Deborah would get cancer made no more sense than a drive-by shooting. She was the most health-conscious person I had ever known. She didn't eat junk food or smoke. She stayed fit and took vitamins. There was no history of cancer in her family. Zero risk factors.

What Denver had said three weeks earlier haunted me: *Those precious to God become important to Satan. Watch your back, Mr. Ron! Somethin bad fixin to happen to Miss Debbie.*

Just before midnight she stirred. I stood and leaned over her bed, my face pressed close to hers. Her eyes opened, drowsy with narcotics. "Is it in my liver?"

"Yes." I paused and looked down at her, trying vainly to drive sadness from my face. "But there's still hope."

She closed her eyes again, and the moment I had dreaded for hours passed quickly without a single tear. My own dry eyes didn't surprise me— I had never really learned how to cry. But now life had presented a reason to learn, and I yearned for a river of tears, a biblical flood. Maybe my broken heart would teach my eyes what to do.

32

After four days, Deborah's hospital room looked like a florist's shop. But when mountains of roses, daisies, and bluebonnets began spilling into the hallway, the hospital administrator decreed they would have to go. Deborah insisted we take them to the mission. We already had a little experience with this. Earlier that year, she had taken bouquets there to decorate the tables in the dining hall. But Don Shisler and Chef Jim nixed the idea, concerned that some parts of the arrangements, like the wires holding the flowers erect, could be used as weapons.

Hard for us to imagine, but then we were naive when it came to flower weapons. Anyway, thinking mission management might make an exception this time, Carson and I hauled two truckloads of concealed pistils down to East Lancaster Street. When we walked in the front door, an unusual sight struck me: six or seven men holding hands in a circle.

Tino, a bald-headed Telly Savalas look-alike, caught my eye. "We're praying for Miss Debbie. We love her and we want her back."

Overwhelmed, Carson and I joined the circle and prayed with these men who seemed on the outside to have nothing to give but had been giving, without our knowing it, the most precious gift of all: compassion.

Afterward, we scattered flowers everywhere—the chapel, the dining hall, the ladies' dorm—an explosion of color brightening cinder block and institutional tile. It reminded me of that first day we pulled up to the mission, and Deborah had daydreamed about daisies and picket fences.

We hadn't seen Denver since the cancer diagnosis, and I was concerned he might be feeling he'd been caught and released. In the hallway to the kitchen, we ran into Chef Jim. I asked him if he'd seen Denver that day.

"He's probably sleeping," he said.

"Sleeping!" I blurted. *Lazy*, I thought. It was already midafternoon.

Jim raised an eyebrow. "You don't know?"

"Know what?"

"Well, when Denver heard about Miss Debbie, he told me she had a lot of friends that would be praying for her all day. But he figured she needed someone to pray all night, and he would be the one to do it."

My eyes widened as he went on. "So he goes outside at midnight, sits down next to the Dumpster, and prays for Miss Debbie and your family. When I get up and come down here at three in the morning to get breakfast going, he comes in for a cup of coffee and we pray here in the kitchen for her until about four. Then he goes back outside and prays till sunup."

Ashamed, I realized again how deep grew the roots of my own prejudice, of my arrogant snap judgments of the poor.

33

I guess I coulda prayed in my bed, but I felt like I was keepin watch, and I didn't want to fall asleep like Jesus's disciples in the garden. And I coulda prayed in the chapel, but I didn't want nobody comin round breakin my concentration. I knowed wadn't nobody gon' come around the Dumpster, so that's where I kept watch over Miss Debbie ever night, what they call a "vigil."

I sat on the ground with my back propped up against the brick wall of an old building where the Dumpster was at and looked up into the dark sky and talked to God about her. I asked Him a lot to heal her, and I also asked Him why. Why have You afflicted this woman who has been nothin but a faithful servant to You? Someone who is doin what You said, visitin the sick, feedin the hungry, invitin the stranger in? How come You bring this heartache to her family and cut off the love she be givin to the homeless?

It didn't make no sense to me. But after a while, God explained it. A lotta times while I was out there, I'd see a shootin star burn across the black sky, bright one minute and gone the next. Ever time I seen one, seemed like it was gon' fall all the way to the ground, and I couldn't understand why I never could see where it went. After I seen a lot of em act that way, I felt like God was givin me a message 'bout Miss Debbie.

The Word says God put ever star in the heavens and even give ever one of em a name. If one of em was gon' fall out the sky, that was up to Him, too. Maybe we can't see where it's gon' wind up, but He can.

That's when I knew that even though it didn't make no sense to me, God had put Miss Debbie in my life like a bright star, and God knew where she was gon' wind up. And I found out that sometimes we just have to accept the things we don't understand. So I just tried to accept that Miss Debbie was sick and kept on prayin out there by that Dumpster. I felt like it was the most important job I ever had, and I wadn't gon' quit.

34

Deborah's hospital stay lasted a week. Seven days after that, the rental house we'd been staying in sold, but our new home on the Trinity River wouldn't be ready for several more weeks. A month earlier, that might have thrown Deborah. But she was way past worrying about something as mundane as a roof over our heads. If she couldn't beat the cancer, there would be no need for a house here on earth.

Still, we needed one for the meantime, so the Davenports opened their home to us. For the next two months, nine of us lived together—the four adults, the Davenports' four kids, and Deborah's sister Daphene, who became her near-constant companion. Mary Ellen and Alan had been our best friends for nineteen years, but while we lived with them we grew even closer—so close we even washed our underwear in the same load.

Meanwhile, their home came to resemble the world headquarters for Meals on Wheels. Church friends brought home-cooked meals every day, sometimes for as many as seventeen people, when Carson, Regan, and all the kids' boyfriends and girlfriends were factored in. Many who wanted to bring food never got to—the line was too long.

Less than a month had passed since Dr. Dearden first found lumps in Deborah's abdomen. But already pain had become a formidable enemy. It raged like wildfire through her belly, forcing her out of bed at night to pace, sit upright, soak in a hot bath, anything to change her focus. It seemed surreal to us: How could the pain flare from being nonexistent to a bonfire in so short a time?

We asked Alan, who had treated cancer patients. He compared cancer to hornets. "You can stand next to a hive, even get hornets all over you and not get stung. But poke a stick in the hive and stir it up, and the hornets can fly into a rage and kill you."

The surgeries had seemed to stir the tumors in Deborah's abdomen into a venomous fury. But she hated taking pain medications. For one thing, she feared addiction. Also, she had dozens of visitors and loathed the idea of receiving them drugged up and slurring. And so, sleep became an elusive dream as we battled the enemy of pain.

Four weeks after her first surgery, we drove to Baylor University Medical Center to see Dr. Robert Goldstein, a world-renowned liver specialist. After an MRI, we met with the doctor in his office. It was a space curiously absent of diplomas and other credentials, filled instead with pictures of the gray-haired, ponytailed doctor and his pretty wife posing on Harley-Davidsons.

Facing us across his desk, Dr. Goldstein wasted no words. "I'm sorry. The MRI results aren't good."

Deborah and I sat next to each other, in a pair of side chairs. "What do you mean?" she asked.

He laid it on the line. "Most people in your condition live no more than a year."

In the millisecond it took for his last few words to register in her brain, Deborah fainted. She actually fell out of her chair onto the floor. Dr. Goldstein dashed into the hall waving his arms like an accident bystander trying to flag down help. I dropped to my knees and lifted her limp body so that her head lay in my lap. A nurse came in, the doctor close behind, and covered Deborah's face and arms with cool, damp cloths.

Moments later, she came to, pale and shaking, and I helped her get back into her chair. Then I put one arm around her shoulders and with my other, held her hand. I gazed at Dr. Goldstein for a moment, knowing he was a walking repository of the latest information on colon cancer. There had to be options.

"What's your recommendation?" I asked him.

"Nothing," he said.

Then he looked at Deborah. "The cancer is too extensive. If you were my wife, I would send you home and tell you to enjoy your family as best you can, and hope a cure can be found within the next few months."

Deborah looked deeply into Dr. Goldstein's eyes. "Do you believe in God?"

"I believe in medicine," he said.

Accordingly, he ticked off treatment options then shot them down like skeet: Chemotherapy—wouldn't work. Liver resectioning—too many tumors on both lobes. Ablation, or burning the cancer off the liver—tumors too large.

His words hit like hammer blows, crushing our hope. I could feel my heart pounding, breaking. Our hands clasped tight, Deborah and I stood.

"Thank you for your opinion, Dr. Goldstein," I said through lips that felt like wax. We walked out of his office and out to the car where we sat, mute and paralyzed. Finally, Deborah spoke into the roaring silence.

"Let's praise God," she said.

For what? I thought without saying it.

"Let's forget what he said about only living one year, and let's just trust God," she told me. "Dr. Goldstein is just a doctor. We serve the living God, who knows our number of days. I intend to fulfill each one of mine."

～ ～ ～

Despite the hope-crushing meeting with Dr. Goldstein, Deborah and I weren't going down without a fight. Shortly after moving in with the Davenports, she commenced a grueling course of chemotherapies at a grim-looking oncology clinic in Fort Worth. The chemo lab was gray and dimly lit, with twenty blue recliners laid out on linoleum tile in two ranks of ten, usually full with cancer warriors, pale and gaunt.

Deborah lay there, soldierlike, for three or four hours at a stretch, as poison dripped into her veins. She said the chemicals felt like heavy metal flowing into her body; she could taste iron and copper. No screens or dividers created private spaces for suffering. So, as I sat with her, talking softly, stroking her hair, people around us vomited into trays provided for the purpose. Sometimes Mary Ellen or other friends would come and sit with her, read to her.

We usually didn't make it far from the clinic before Deborah was overcome with a wave of nausea or diarrhea. I'd pull the car over and help her through it. Apart from her pain, the indignity of being unable to control her body was tough going for a woman who had never looked tousled, even when she got out of bed in the morning.

The medicine took her down quickly, slashing her weight to one hundred pounds. Still, she was determined to eradicate the enemy and insisted on trying different kinds of chemo treatments, sometimes in the same week, hoping to incinerate the cancer with the medical equivalent of napalm. At home, whenever she could lift her head off the pillow, she slipped on her Reeboks and we would walk together. The kids and I couldn't get her to stop, even when she ran out of strong.

35

It was Deborah who first brought up the idea of getting Denver a driver's license, in the fall of 1998. She felt bad that her cancer—and how it consumed our time—was hampering Denver from being more a part of our lives. If he had a license, she reasoned, he could more freely join in the things we were doing, without being dependent on our hunting him down in the hood.

When we broached the subject with Denver, he responded in typical fashion: "Let me think about it," he said.

A few weeks later, we talked it around over coffee at the mission. "I like the idea of bein able to drive, Mr. Ron," he said. "But I got to tell you, I ain't exactly clean."

"Clean?"

"I got a record."

It seemed Denver had done a little scouting down at the Department of Public Safety. When the clerk typed his name into the computer, up popped a list of problems: a disorderly charge in Louisiana, a few unpaid tickets related to his car-motel business, and—this was the deal-breaker—a citation for marijuana possession bestowed on him in Baton Rouge during some years he spent riding the rails. With the pot charge on his record, there could be no driver's license.

Denver wanted to clear his name, so we agreed he had to travel to Baton Rouge and subject himself to the laws of Napoleon. It is an odd fact of American history that some laws in the Bayou State haven't been rewritten since the little Corsican still owned the place.

It was December 1998, and we picked a sorry night for a road trip. A freezing rain had shut down highways all over Texas. But Denver wanted his past behind him, so I drove him down to the Greyhound station. He figured there might be a few drunks on the bus, but fewer than at the mission, which was always packed to the rafters during lousy weather.

Denver wagered that a couple of hundred dollars in the hand of the right Louisiana lawman might fix his legal problem. "That's just the way it is down there," he said. So I gave him $200 to pay the fine.

After a long, slippery trip on the Greyhound—"That dawg slid like a hog on ice!" Denver told me later—he rolled into Baton Rouge. The day was about like the night before, with the kind of icy wind that makes your toes ache and your nose run. Denver pushed through the doors at the police station, stamped the cold out of his feet, and tried to explain that he wanted to turn himself in for a ten-year-old marijuana charge.

The police just laughed at him.

He hunted down a payphone and called to tell me he wasn't having any luck. "They think I'm crazy, Mr. Ron," he said with a chuckle. "They think I'm just tryin' to get arrested so I can have a warm place to sleep. I can't find nobody to take my money under the table—*or on the top!*"

If I couldn't help Denver get fined or arrested, I figured I'd have to use the good-ole-boy system. I called a fellow I knew, a young mover and shaker in Louisiana who'd grown up playing Hot Wheels with the governor's son. Deborah had taught him in the first grade. I figured he would know someone who'd either arrest Denver or set him free. He did, and just like that, Denver's record was clean. As Denver told me before he headed down to Baton Rouge in the first place: Things are different down there.

And so, the way was clear for Denver to get his driver's license. That meant passing a written test—no big deal for someone who can read. But, unable to study the Department of Public Safety manual on his own, Denver opted instead for tutoring. A couple of fellows at the mission worked with him for weeks until he knew all the questions and most of the answers. When he declared himself ready, I took him down to the DPS.

After an oral exam, Denver emerged from the DPS office laughing, raising his hand for a big high five. Next came the driving test. He had driven a tractor and even a couple of cars, but had never parallel-parked. I drove my new car, a silver-green Infinity Q45, out to the big parking lot next to the Lakeworth High School football stadium and let him slide into the driver's seat. Then, for a couple of hours, Denver practiced parallel parking between the phone booth and the concession stand before the Lakeworth marching band took over the parking lot and ran us off.

Finally, in September 1999, ten months after his trip to Louisiana to try to get arrested, Denver got his license. (The lady who gave Denver his road test said she really liked his Q45 and wondered aloud how much his monthly payments were.) He thanked me again and again, until I finally had to tell him to quit. He took nothing for granted and declared the license one of a great many blessings God had lately sent his way, Deborah and I among them.

In practical terms, Denver's getting his license was a validation: Without one, so many things are out of reach—not only driving, but other things that make a person feel like a person, like just being able to prove who you are. Soon after he got his license, Denver used it to prove more than that.

— — —

Regan had finally found a job she was sure she'd love, as a cook for Young Life, a Christian youth camp. It was half the pay and twice the hours she worked at the gallery, but it was ministry work and it was in Colorado, set against the majestic Rockies, where a lot of twenty-five-year-olds feel called to suffer for the Lord.

Deborah felt strongly that Regan shouldn't hover around home, waiting to see how the cancer would progress. We encouraged her to take the job. So she packed her bags and headed west to the Crooked Creek Ranch in Winter Park, Colorado. But at twenty-five, Regan had more than luggage, having had apartments in both New York and Dallas.

Jokingly, I said to Denver one day, "Now that you've got a driver's license, would you like to drive Regan's things to Colorado?"

When I mentioned the route wound through the capital city of Denver, his smile stretched wider than an eight-lane interstate. "I always wanted to see the city I was named after," he said.

Now I'd opened my trap and couldn't take it back. So over the next three days, we hammered out a plan. I pulled out a road atlas and traced the route to Winter Park with colored marking pens. But Denver couldn't read the words in the atlas, so on plain paper, I drew a rough map with pictures of highway signs, and showed him what the one going to Colorado looked like. Denver was thoroughly convinced he could follow a map—and he convinced me as well.

So on a brilliant October day, we loaded my nearly new F-350 crew-cab pickup with everything Regan owned—TVs, stereos, clothes, furniture. We set a meeting time for him and Regan, 6:00 p.m. the following day at the Safeway grocery store in Winter Park. And after a final one-hour cram session, I sent him on his way, armed with $700 cash, a simple little hand-drawn map with checkpoints, phone numbers to call if he got in trouble, and a $30,000 truck with a free and clear title.

As he eased down the driveway, I ran alongside the truck, repeating, "Two-eighty-seven! Two-eighty-seven!" If he made the turn onto Highway 287, he'd be on his way to Colorado. If he missed it, he'd wind up in the hinterlands of Oklahoma where, I had tried to convince him, humans spoke an entirely different language.

I tried to convince myself I knew what I was doing, but the plain facts were that Denver was heading out on a two-thousand-mile round-trip, navigating interstates, back roads, and mountain passes—the highest in Colorado—using a driver's license that had arrived in the mail only the week before. What was he thinking? Better yet, what was I thinking?

As he pulled away with the money, my truck, and everything Regan owned, Denver wiped his forehead with the towel that he usually carried, grinning a little semi-grin that I couldn't quite decode.

The angel on my right shoulder whispered that it meant, "Thank you, Mr. Ron, for trustin me."

The devil on my left cackled, "No, it means 'Adiós, sucker!'"

36

I ain't no thief and I ain't no liar, but Mr. Ron didn't know that. It just didn't make no sense to me why he gon' trust me to take all his daughter's stuff way off yonder to Colorado. Now I ain't the most intelligent man, but I can figure things out purty good, so I wadn't worried 'bout gettin there. But for the life of me, I couldn't figure out why a rich white man would give me his four-by-four, $700 cash, and all his daughter's possessions, and expect a broke, homeless man that can't read or write to go nearly a thousand miles to somewhere he ain't never been, deliver the goods—and bring back the truck!

It just didn't make no sense. I knowed he was a smart man that maybe thinks he knows what he's doin. But bein smart don't mean he'll ever see his truck again—that takes faith.

I expect I never had no more than $20 or $30 of my own at one time, 'cept for once when Mr. Ron slipped me a hundred. Then he gives me *$700 cash* and a *$30,000 truck* fulla TVs, furniture, and stereos. I just couldn't let the man down.

He drawed me a map, thinkin I could read it, and explained the best he could what signs to look for and how to get there. After we finished loadin the truck, he pointed me in the gen'l direction of Colorado. Then, when I was pullin out, he kept runnin by the truck, hollerin, "Two-eighty-seven! Two-eighty-seven!"

Now, I'm gon' be honest with you: With all his talkin and pointin and hollerin, I was real nervous and couldn't remember everthing he told me. But I did remember him sayin if I miss 287, I'm gon' wind up in Oklahoma.

And the way I'm gon' know it is I'd cross a big bridge over a big river and the sign'd say "OKLAHOMA," and the river'd say "RED."

And that's exactly what happened. I knowed I had a problem so I stopped at a gas station and told a fella I was lookin for Highway 287 to Colorado. He told me a different way to get there, and I was a little worried about that 'cause he didn't look too smart. I took outta there again and was drivin purty slow 'cause I was afraid all Mr. Ron's daughter's stuff gon' blow out the back. I figured he'd rather me be gettin there late with the goods than on time with a empty truck.

Part of the $700 he give me was for a motel room, but I slept in the truck 'cause ain't nobody ever trusted me before with that much stuff, and wadn't no way in the world I was gon' take a chance on somebody stealin it.

Things was goin purty good. The folks in the gas stations kept me goin in the right direction. Now, when I got into Colorado, I started seein mountains away off, and I was thinkin how purty they was. But I figured Mr. Ron's daughter's camp musta been *around* on the other side of them mountains, 'cause for sure ain't nobody gon' drive up over em in a truck. The more I kept on drivin, the bigger them mountains got. I could see snow on top of em, but I couldn't see where they ended so I started worryin about how I was gon' get around em. Next thing I knew I was smack up next to em with the road headin straight up!

I stopped at another gas station and asked a lady how I was s'posed to get to Winter Park. She looked at me and pointed *up* the mountain. And when I asked her where the Crooked Creek Ranch was, she pointed to the top.

"The road is narrow," she said. "Once you head up there, there's no turning around."

That caused me and myself to have a little talk. *I'm a strong fella*, I thought. *Ain't no reason to be scared.* So I got back in the truck and headed up the mountain. Real slow.

The drive was mighty purty, the sky spreadin out from the mountain blue as a lake, and the trees all red and orange and yella like they was on fire. 'Bout halfway up the mountain, I decided to do me a little sightseein, so I pulled over to take a look over the edge and see how far could I see.

That was a mistake.

I couldn't see no bottom. The edge of that road dropped off into the biggest nothin I ever saw in my life. I got back in the truck right quick and squeezed that steerin wheel so tight I thought it was gon' break off in my hands, and I started pourin sweat even though it was freezin outside. I didn't go no more than about five miles an hour the rest of the way and by the time I got to Winter Park, I had about a hundred cars stacked up behind me like a freight train.

37

When Denver failed to make the meeting with Regan, my faith slipped off the mountain. First I thought of calling the highway patrol to report an accident. But I changed my mind as I imagined the dispatcher breaking into a belly laugh when I told what I'd done. Besides, Denver was supposed to have crossed three states, and I had no idea where to tell the authorities to look for him.

It ate at me that Denver had all my numbers but that I had not heard from him in two days. I remembered how wide his eyes got when I handed over the $700—it must have seemed to him a small fortune. I flashed back to a lecture I'd gotten from Don Shisler about the fate of a buck in the hands of a bum. Maybe the temptation had been too great.

Maybe he'd taken the money, the truck, and Regan's stuff and set up housekeeping in Mexico. Or Canada. He'd always said he wanted to see Canada.

I hated to tell Deborah that Denver was missing, but I knew she could hear, each time Regan and I touched base on the telephone, that our voices had climbed the octaves from concern to worry to panic. So I went into the bedroom and told her.

Her response was vintage Deborah: "Well, why don't you stop worrying and let's start praying for Denver's safety?"

I knelt beside the bed, and we held hands and prayed. We'd been like that for only a few minutes when the phone rang. It was Regan: "He's here!"

38

Late the next day, the doorbell rang and there stood Denver, wearing the biggest grin I'd ever seen in my life. In the driveway sat the truck, washed and waxed.

We sat down at the kitchen table and he told the tale of his trip. Finally, he said, "Mr. Ron, you got more faith than any man I ever knowed. Things got a li'l shaky, but I just couldn't let you down." Then he handed me a ball of wadded-up cash—about $400.

"How come there's so much left over?" I asked.

"'Cause I slept in the truck the whole time and ate at McDonald's and 7-Eleven."

I hadn't expected there would be any money left after expenses, so I said, "You keep it for doing such a good job."

"No, sir," he said quietly. "I ain't for hire. I did that to bless you and your family. Money can't buy no blessins."

Humbled, I stood there and looked at him, not sure if I'd ever received a more gracious gift in my life. I couldn't let him go away empty-handed, though, so I told him to take it and use it to do some good for someone else.

The trip turned out to be life-changing for both of us—for him, having proved he was trustworthy, and for me, having learned to trust. Two weeks later, I sent Denver to Baton Rouge in a Ryder truck loaded with paintings and sculptures valued at more than $1 million. According to my client there, Denver guarded the contents of that truck like it was the gold in Fort Knox.

39

Between May and November, it seemed we wore ruts in the road between the suburbs and the chemo clinic. Mercifully, surrounding Thanksgiving, Deborah had a two-week respite from all chemotherapy.

We always celebrated that holiday at Rocky Top. On Thanksgiving morning, I rose before daylight to hunt deer. Saw a nice buck, just wasn't in the mood to kill him. Deborah, meanwhile, prepared a grand feast for about twenty-five friends and family, including Denver, who by this time fell into the latter category. The chemo was working to shrink the tumors, and during the break from it, Deborah had regained a few pounds and a flush of color. Had our guests not known her condition, they wouldn't even have suspected she was ill.

By December, the chemotherapy had shrunk the tumors enough to make Deborah a candidate for liver surgery. On December 21, she had fourteen tumors burned off—removed by ablation—and after the four-hour operation, we had our miracle.

"Cancer free!" exclaimed her surgeon, who had scoped her entire body cavity for cancer during the procedure and could find no trace.

Deborah burst out laughing and crying at the same time, and I nearly burned up my cell phone spreading the good news. We considered it our Christmas present from God.

40

Our joy was short-lived. Like an enemy that seemed vanquished but had only been lying in wait, the cancer flanked us. By the end of January, it was back with a vengeance. By March, Deborah's doctors were weighing another liver surgery, but felt it too risky only three months after the ablation. More chemo didn't knock the tumors back, but instead seemed to feed them. They rose like an evil regiment, and fighting back was like throwing rocks at an advancing platoon of tanks.

By that time, Denver was spreading his wings, tooling around town in a car he called "manna" because, he said, it fell from heaven. (Actually, Alan Davenport gave it to him.) He often stopped by to visit, and every time I saw him it was like going to the bank and clipping bond coupons: I was growing richer, collecting dividends from his wisdom. Seldom was there any idle chitchat. He always got right to the point—my lesson for the day.

One day he stopped by and, as usual, got down to it. He looked straight into my eyes and said, "Mr. Ron, what did God say when He finished making the world and all that is in it?"

Knowing Denver wasn't much for trick questions, I gave him a straight answer: "He said, 'It is good.'"

Denver's face lit up in a smile. "Exactly."

Launching into a sermon, he assured me that God didn't make cancer because cancer is not good, and he cautioned me not to blame God for something He didn't make. The theology lesson helped, for a little while.

Spring arrived and with it the rites of Rocky Top. Ill but determined to enjoy the season, Deborah watched expectantly for the first budding of our bluebonnets, then for the birth of our longhorn calves. She named two of them Freckles and Bubbles, and I didn't roll my eyes. We watched the eagles feast on spawning sand bass and marveled at the savage midair battles they sometimes waged over a catch. At night, stars frosted the sky like jewels and moonlight rippled on the Brazos, fish arcing in the cool glow. The only sound for miles was wind shimmering in the post oaks and the low, lonely whistle of distant trains.

Denver went with us to the ranch. I had invited him to the Cowboy Spring Gathering, an annual event where about two hundred people camped together at the Rio Vista, our friends Rob and Holly Farrell's ranch, right across the river from Rocky Top. We'd met there for more than twenty years to pitch teepees, ride and rope, enjoy chuckwagon cooking, and read cowboy poetry around campfires.

"I heard cowboys don't like black folks," Denver said when I invited him. "You sure you want me to go?"

"Of course I want you to go," I said, but I still practically had to rope and drag him.

Denver pitched his teepee reluctantly that first night, and the next morning I found him sleeping in the backseat of a car. It wasn't that he minded sleeping outdoors having done so for decades in downtown Fort Worth. But there weren't many rattlesnakes there.

Soon, though, he found his cowboy legs and began feeling comfortable among us all. He didn't ride, but he did want to have his picture taken on a horse so he could show his buddies in the hood. If we had had one, we could've used a forklift to get his 230-pound butt in the saddle.

The campfires and camaraderie worked magic on Denver as he began to know what it was like to be accepted and loved by a group of white guys on horseback with ropes in their hands. Exactly the kind of people he had feared all his life.

— — —

Back in Fort Worth, Deborah continued to shed pounds, her skin growing slack on her tiny frame. Still, she fought.

"Do you know what I'm going to do today?" she asked me brightly one March morning. "I'm going *shopping*."

She felt like her old self, she said. I suspected she just ached to feel normal again, but I didn't say so. She hadn't driven a car in a year. I stood by the window, watched her pull away in her Land Cruiser, and worried the whole time she was gone—burned to follow her, actually, but stayed put. When I heard her purr back into the garage about an hour later, I scrambled outside to help her unload.

But there were no packages. Eyes red and swollen, tears streaming down her cheeks, she looked at me, her throat working.

"Am I 'terminal'?" she asked finally, seeming to hold the word at a distance like a distasteful science specimen.

Terminal is a harsh word when used in the context of death and not one we'd ever uttered aloud. But according to *Webster's*, it's also a place people pass through on their way to somewhere else. Deborah knew her "somewhere else" was heaven. She was just hoping the train was delayed.

I scooped a tear off her cheek and tried to slip around her question. "We're all terminal," I said, smiling gently. "None of us makes it out of here alive."

"No, tell me straight up. Am I terminal? Is that what people are saying?"

At the mall, she told me, she had run into an old college friend who'd heard about the cancer. Very sweet and concerned, not meaning to upset Deborah, the friend had said, "I just heard you were terminal."

Unwilling to appear shaken, Deborah replied, "No one has told me that."

Then, fighting to remain calm, she made a dignified escape, only collapsing when she reached the safety of her car. She cried out loud all the way home, she told me. It was the last time she ever left the house alone.

In April, doctors performed a second surgery on Deborah's liver and warned that her body couldn't take another such invasion for at least nine months to a year. Still, the following Sunday, she insisted on going to church, where we met Denver. But during the prayer time before the service, she fell ill and asked me to take her to the home of our friends Scott and Janina Walker. Janina was home recovering from surgery of her own; maybe they could do each other some good.

After church, Denver stopped by the Walkers to visit. He stayed for lunch then excused himself. "I have to go check on Mr. Ballantine," he said. Curious, Scott asked if he could go, too.

I had known Mr. Ballantine when he stayed at the mission. Sometime before Deborah and I started serving there, Denver told us, he had watched a car screech up to the curb on East Lancaster. The driver shoved an elderly man out of the passenger-side door, pitched a beat-up Tourister suitcase out behind him, and roared away. Abandoned on the curb, the old man staggered like a drunken sailor on shore leave and fired off a salvo of slurry curses. But to Denver, he also looked . . . scared. At the time, Denver had still been an island, a stone-faced loner who didn't poke about in other people's business. But something—he thinks now maybe it was how helpless the man looked—plucked a string in his heart.

Denver walked up to the man and offered to help him get into the mission. In return, the man cursed him and called him a nigger.

Denver helped anyway, learning in the process that the fellow's name was Ballantine, that he was a mean old drunk who'd earned his family's contempt, and that he hated black people. He hated Christians even more, considered them a pack of mewling, insipid hypocrites. That's why, free meal or not, he would rather have starved than endure a chapel sermon. Others might have let him. Instead, for about two years, Denver ordered two plates of food in the serving line and took one upstairs to Mr. Ballantine. Foul-tempered, cantankerous, and utterly remorseless, Mr. Ballantine continued to address his benefactor as "nigger."

The next year a hoodlum jumped Mr. Ballantine outside the mission and demanded his Social Security check. Rather than give in, the old man submitted to a vicious beating that left him a cripple. Unequipped to care for an invalid, Don Shisler had no choice but to find space for Mr. Ballantine in a government-funded nursing center. There, minimum-wage orderlies tended to the basics, but the truth was Mr. Ballantine, at eighty-five, found himself hobbled, helpless, and completely alone. Except for Denver. After the old man's relocation, Denver regularly walked the two miles through the hood to take Mr. Ballantine some non-nursing-home food or a few cigarettes.

One day, Denver asked me to drive him there. In some ways, I wish he hadn't, since the trip stripped off my do-gooder veneer to reveal a squeamish man whose charity, at the time, had definite limits.

When we entered Mr. Ballantine's room at the nursing home, the smell hit me first—the stench of age, dead skin, and bodily fluids. The old man lay on his bed in a puddle of urine, naked except for a neon orange ski jacket. His ghostly chicken-bone legs sprawled across a sheet that had once been white but now was dingy gray, streaked with brown and ocher stains. Around him lay strewn trash and trays of half-eaten food . . . scrambled eggs, crusted hard-yellow . . . shriveled meats . . . petrified sandwiches. On a couple of trays, school-lunch-size milk cartons, tipped over, the puddles congealed into stinking clabber.

In a single, sweeping glance, Denver sized up the room, then me, wobbling and on the verge of vomit. "Mr. Ron just come to say hi," he told Mr. Ballantine. "He got to be goin now."

I bolted, leaving Denver alone to clean up Mr. Ballantine and his nasty room. I didn't offer to help, or even to stay and pray. Feeling guilty, but not guilty enough to change, I jumped in my car and wept as I drove away— for Mr. Ballantine, homeless and decrepit, who would stew in his own excrement if not for Denver; and I wept for myself, because I didn't have the courage to stay. It was easy for someone like me to serve a few meals, write a few checks, and get my name and picture in the paper for showing up at some glitzy benefit. But Denver served invisibly, loved without fanfare. The tables had turned, and I now feared that it was he who would catch-and-release me, a person who lacked true compassion, who perhaps wasn't a catch worth keeping.

I gained a new and more profound respect for Denver that day, my perception of him changing like puzzle pieces slowly clicking into place. He wasn't showing off, only sharing with me a secret part of his life. Had his secrets included pitching dice in an alley with a hoard of drunken bums, I wouldn't have been put off. But I was shocked that they included not only praying through the night for my wife, but also nursing this man who never said thank you and continued to call him "nigger."

For the first time, it struck me that when Denver said he'd be my friend for life, he meant it—for better or for worse. The hell of it was, Mr. Ballantine never wanted a friend, especially a black one. But once Denver committed, he stuck. It reminded me of what Jesus told His disciples: "Greater love has no man than this, that he lay down his life for his friends."

42

When Mr. Scott asked me could he go with me to see Mr. Ballantine after lunch that day, I said yes. But I wondered if he was gon' do like Mr. Ron done the first time he saw the man. I was thinkin prob'ly not, 'cause I'd started goin down to the nursing home purty regular to help keep Mr. Ballantine's room from gettin so nasty.

When me and Mr. Scott got there that day, he was real nice to Mr. Ballantine. He told the man his name and talked a li'l bit 'bout this and that, the weather, and what have you. Then he said, "Mr. Ballantine, I'd like to bless you with a few necessities. Is there anything I can bring you . . . anything you need?"

Mr. Ballantine said what he always said, "Yeah. I could use some cigarettes and Ensure."

So me and Mr. Scott took off for the drugstore. But when it come time to buy Mr. Ballantine his blessins, he wanted to get the Ensure, but not the cigarettes.

"I just don't feel right about it, Denver," he said. "It's like I'm helping him kill himself."

Well, that made me have to eyeball him. "You *asked* the man how you could bless him, and he told you he wanted two things—cigarettes and Ensure. Now you tryin to judge him instead of blessin him by blessin him with only half the things he asked for. You saw the man. Now tell me the truth: How much worse you think he gon' be after smokin? Cigarettes is the only pleasure he got left."

Mr. Scott said I had a point. He bought the Ensure and a carton of Mr.

Ballantine's favorite smokes, then headed on home while I delivered the blessins. You ain't gon' believe what happened next.

— — —

When I went back to Mr. Ballantine's room, he asked me who paid for the cigarettes and I told him Mr. Scott.

"How am I going to pay him back?'" he asked me.

I said, "You don't."

"Why would that man buy me cigarettes when he doesn't even know me?"

"'Cause he's a Christian."

"Well, I still don't understand. And anyway, you know I hate Christians."

I didn't say nothin for a minute, just sat there in a ole orange plastic chair and watched Mr. Ballantine lyin there in his bed. Then I said to him, "I'm a Christian."

I wish you coulda seen the look on his face. It didn't take but a minute for him to start apologizin for cussin Christians all the time I'd knowed him. Then I guess it hit him that while I'd been takin care of him—it was about three years by then—he'd still been callin me names.

"Denver, I'm sorry for all those times I called you a nigger," he said.

"That's okay."

Then I took a chance and told Mr. Ballantine that I'd been takin care of him all that time, 'cause I knowed God loved him. "God's got a special place prepared for you if you just confess your sins and accept the love of Jesus."

I ain't gon' kid you, he was skeptical. Same time, though, he said he didn't think I'd lie to him. "But even if you aren't lying," he said, "I've lived too long and sinned too much for God to forgive me."

He laid there in that bed and lit up one a' Mr. Scott's cigarettes, starin up at the ceilin, smokin and thinkin. I just kept quiet. Then all of a sudden he piped up again. "On the other hand, I'm too damn old for much more sinning. Maybe that'll count for something!"

Well, Mr. Ballantine stopped callin me "nigger" that day. And wadn't too long after that I wheeled him through the doors at McKinney Bible

Church—the same place Mr. Ron and Miss Debbie used to go to church at. We sat together on the back row, and it was the first time Mr. Ballantine had ever set foot inside a church. He was eighty-five years old.

After the service let out, he looked at me and smiled.

"Real nice," he said.

42

A little over a year had passed since Deborah's anxious cell-phone call to the sushi restaurant sent our lives careening off-course. During the worst of times, doctors professed no hope, and she lay in our bed, curling her emaciated frame like a fetus, vomiting, fighting through searing pain. But the hotter the fires burned, the more beautiful she became to me. She always tried to shift the focus from herself, and when she could walk upright, found the strength to visit and pray for sick friends, particularly those she met in the cryptlike chemo lab.

If she believed she was dying, she hadn't told me. Instead, we talked about living. About our dreams for our children, our marriage, our city. She paged through Martha Stewart magazines, cutting out pictures of wedding cakes and flower arrangements for Regan's and Carson's weddings. Neither was engaged, but we dreamed about it anyway, chatting over coffee, murmuring after lights-out about whom they might marry, the grandchildren we would have, the sweet patter of baby feet at Rocky Top at Christmastime. We talked about everything important in living life, but we did not talk about death, for we thought that would be giving quarter to the enemy.

The second surgery brought a fresh burst of hope. For the second time in four months, doctors pronounced Deborah "cancer free." A month later, we jetted to New York City to fulfill a promise she'd made: to be with Carson on Mother's Day.

Deborah still ached from the brutality of the surgery, but we planned on doing all the things we would have done had there been no pain. On Friday, we went to lunch with Carson and my partner, Michael Altman, at Bella Blue, an Italian restaurant. We ordered the house specialty, *lobster fra diavolo*, and chatted over drinks. But just as the food arrived, Deborah winced sharply and pinned me with a desperate look that said, "Get me out of here!"

Daphene's apartment was just a few blocks away. I hustled her out of the restaurant, and we walked maybe half a block before Deborah nearly collapsed. Clutching at her belly, she couldn't take another step. As I tried to flag down a cab, terror fell over her face like a cloud blotting out the sun: "Call the doctor!" she whispered fiercely. "Something bad is happening."

I fumbled out my cell phone and punched wrong numbers in a panic. Finally, I managed to dial right and reached Deborah's oncologist. "Not to worry," he said mildly after hearing that my wife seemed near death on a New York City sidewalk. "I'll see you when you get back on Monday."

Not to worry? I called a friend, a Texas surgeon, who guessed at the source of the pain: a possible hernia, caused by the latest ablation. Ride it out till Monday, he said.

— — —

Back in Texas, CAT scans and other tests revealed more cancer. In more places. The news strafed us like bullets.

Faith, said Paul the Apostle, is the assurance of things hoped for, the conviction of things not seen. I clung to faith like a ropeless climber to the side of a cliff—faith that the God who said He loved me would not rip out my heart, steal my wife, my children's mother. Maybe this sounds stupid, arrogant even, but with all the bad press He'd been getting, I felt now might be a good time for God to buff up His reputation with a miracle—and there's no miracle like a good healing. We'd go on *Oprah* and spread the news. I told Him so.

Deborah and I would have loved to have done nothing at this point—no chemo, no surgery, no experimental drugs. We knew and believed the Scriptures:

"All things work together for the good of them that love God . . ."

"Wait upon the Lord . . ."

"Be still and know that He is God . . ."

But I wasn't willing to be still and wait, and I don't think Deborah was either.

43

Dozens of friends, many of them doctors, scoured the Web and medical literature, hoping to find a cure. We learned of a brand-new chemotherapy drug called CPT-11. The FDA had rushed to approve it after clinical trials showcased its effectiveness against metastasized colorectal cancer. To try it, we traveled 250 miles to the Cancer Therapy and Research Center in San Antonio. I rigged my Suburban so that Deborah could lie on a soft pallet for the whole five-hundred-mile roundtrip, her feet facing the tailgate, her head on the pillow-topped console where I could stroke her hair while I drove. I made arrangements for us to stay at the Hyatt Hill Country resort, hoping a sumptuous suite with a sweeping view of San Antonio's rolling country-side might take the focus off our circumstances. It didn't. Nor did the peppy mariachi band singing through their noses in the hotel courtyard seem the appropriate soundtrack for beating back death.

But Deborah had been born in San Antonio and on our second day there, before her first scheduled treatment, she began to reminisce as I drove out of the hospital parking lot, her head on the console beside me. "Daphene and I were the first Rh-positive twins born in the Nix Hospital with an Rh-negative mother. We both had to have blood transfusions," she said to the ceiling. "That was risky back then. Now I'm back again for another risky treatment."

Tears welled in her eyes then. "I don't want to die here."

"You're not going to die here," I said, smoothing her hair. But the truth was that the specter of death had begun to gnaw at the edges of my hope.

The next day, we found the rat-infested second-story apartment on Fabulous Drive that we had shared for three weeks in 1970. We had moved there for a job I'd accepted selling stocks via cold calls on straight commission. Lured by $100,000 in potential annual salary, I did receive one paycheck before the company went broke—for thirteen dollars and eighty-seven cents. Deborah and I ate thirteen-cent bean rolls for three weeks until the money ran out and we hightailed it back to Fort Worth. Now, thirty years later, we had returned, hoping this second gamble in San Antonio would pay off better than the first.

It didn't. For Deborah, CPT-11 was a disaster. A veteran of scores of chemotherapy treatments, as soon as this one invaded her veins, Deborah's eyes locked onto mine: "Please tell them to stop!" she cried. The nurses quickly reduced the flow, but burning cramps still rolled through her guts.

Still, we kept up the treatments for weeks. The CPT-11 treatments ravaged Deborah, stripping her down to a gaunt and hollow-eyed waif. During this time, I would often see Denver, sitting outside our home in prayer.

On July 14, 2000, we celebrated her fifty-fifth birthday. At the end of that month, Carson flew out from New York and drove with us to Colorado to visit Regan at Crooked Creek Ranch, Deborah lying in the rear seat, which we'd converted into a bed. But the trip was cut short when the altitude began, literally, to suffocate Deborah. The chemo had so depleted her red blood cell count that her heart had to race to pump oxygenated blood. We rushed her down the mountain at hair-raising speeds, dodging deer and rabbits on the way to the hospital. We were able to return to Crooked Creek, but only so long as Deborah remained tethered to an oxygen bottle.

After we returned to Texas, she caught me off-guard one day. "I've called Pastor Ken," she said, "and asked him to come over to discuss my memorial service."

— — —

On the Saturday before Labor Day, Regan realized it was time to come home. She called Carson, who hopped the next flight from New York to Colorado, helped her pack, and drove her to Fort Worth.

I, too, sensed time was growing short, like shadows nearing noon. Dr.

Senter, Deborah's first surgeon, confirmed my suspicions on October 8. Deborah's condition had deteriorated to critical, and I rushed her to the hospital. She had begged me not to take her to the hospital, afraid she would never come out.

"I don't want to die there," she said, tears welling. Then she broke down: "I don't want to die at all."

After a stint in the ER, the hospital staff admitted Deborah to a private room. Trying to collect myself, I paced the hall outside until I ran into Dr. Senter, who asked me if I would come to his office for a personal talk—not as a doctor, but as a friend.

"Deborah is very sick," he began. "The last patient I knew of in her condition lived only three or four days."

I wasn't surprised. Deborah's waking hours had dissolved into a blur of writhing agony. But I didn't want to believe him. That death was so near didn't square with our prayers, our faith.

"You should start calling family and friends that she would want to see before . . ." He paused and rearranged his words: "Ron, the clock can't be turned back. I'm sorry."

He walked me to the door and gave me a hug, something doctors don't do enough of. Then I wandered out of his office, down the antiseptic hallway, fumbling with my cell phone as I went. Who to call? . . . Carson, yes, of course, Carson . . . and Regan . . . and Daphene. I walked across a street to a parking lot. I don't know whether cars passed. I got into my car. I closed the door, laid my head on the steering wheel, and wept. At some point, I realized I was screaming.

44

Carson called me and told me what the doctors told Mr. Ron, so I went on down to the hospital and stood outside Miss Debbie's door and prayed. Ever now and then, I'd peek through the window and I could see folks in there . . . Carson, Regan, Miss Mary Ellen, some nurses. I could see Mr. Ron, too, sometimes sittin beside Miss Debbie's bed, a lotta times with his head in his hands. I could tell he was hurtin real bad, but there was somethin else in his face that bothered me some: He was mad. And I knowed Who he was mad at.

Ever once in a while, somebody'd come out of the room. I'd hug em and they'd go on home. Got to be around midnight by the time everbody was gone. Purty soon after that, Mr. Ron come out in the hall, and I asked him if I could talk to him alone.

I knowed what he was goin through. It was just like when I was standin there watchin that house burn down and my grandmother was in there. I also knowed that if Miss Debbie died, he was gon' have to live through it, just like I lived through it with Big Mama, BB, and Uncle James.

There's somethin I learned when I was homeless: Our limitation is God's opportunity. When you get all the way to the end of your rope and there ain't nothin you can do, that's when God takes over. I remember one time I was hunkered down in the hobo jungle with some folks. We was talkin 'bout life, and this fella was talkin, said, "People think they're in control, but they ain't. The truth is, that which must befall thee must befall thee. And that which must pass thee by must past thee by."

You'd be surprised what you can learn talkin to homeless people. I

learned to accept life for what it is. With Miss Debbie, we had done got to
the point where we had to leave it up to God. Sometimes to touch us, God
touches someone that's close to us. This is what opens our eyes to the fact
there is a higher power than ourselves, whether we call it God or not.

You know already Mr. Ron's a talker, but he didn't say a word to me out
in that hallway . . . just wandered over in a corner and stood there starin
down at the floor. I got kinda firm with him. "Mr. Ron, raise your head up
and look at me!"

He snapped his head up like somebody'd jerked it, and I could see
through his eyes that little pieces of his heart was breakin off while we was
standin there.

"I know you is hurtin and questionin God," I told him. "I'm hurtin, too.
And you is probably wonderin why a saint like Miss Debbie is in that room
sufferin when all them street bums she ministered to seem to be gettin
along just fine. Well, let me tell you somethin: God calls some good ones
like Miss Debbie home so He can accomplish His purposes down here on
the earth."

Mr. Ron just stared at me. That's when I noticed his eyes was all red and
swoll up. His throat was just a-workin, like he was fixin to break down on
me, but I went right on anyway, 'cause I felt like if I didn't, he was gon' turn
his back on God.

"I ain't sayin God can't use the bums and the addicts to work His will
down here—He's God, and He can sure 'nough do anything He wants. I'm
just tellin you He sometimes needs to call the good ones home to bring
glory to His name. And I can tell you something else—I don't care what no
doctors say, Miss Debbie ain't goin nowhere till she finished the work here
on earth that God gave her to do. You can take *that* to the bank."

45

When I found Denver in the hallway, I was still walking in a stupor, so I didn't remember everything he said. But I did remember his words about Deborah's not dying, that I could take that to the bank. I recall being dimly encouraged that a bank still existed somewhere that would accept deposits of what pitiful little remained of my faith.

Back in the room, Carson and Regan slept fitfully in Naugahyde hospital recliners. I finessed my way through an obstacle course of IV lines and pulled Deborah close. Soon I could feel her warm tears sliding into the narrow valley between our faces. "Ronnie, I don't want to die," she said, whispering so the children couldn't hear.

Grief crippled my vocal cords, and for a full minute I couldn't speak. When I did, all I could say was, "I don't want you to die either."

The next morning, doctors suggested a last-ditch colonscopy. In her frail condition, the risks included death. But we agreed to keep walking through every open door until all were locked and impassable.

Mary Ellen was there. The medical staff prepped Deborah and took her away. Hours later, we saw surgical technicians wheel her into recovery and raced to join her. The surgeons filed in, looking grim, and I wondered bizarrely if they teach appropriate facial decorum in medical school. Back in her room a couple of hours later, a doctor named Redrow came to give us a more thorough summation.

Before he could speak, Deborah smiled weakly and greeted him. "I'm so-o-o hungry. When can I have something to eat?"

Dr. Redrow looked at her sadly. "You can't eat."

Deborah smiled again, used to postsurgical protocols. "Right, but when *can* I eat?"

He gazed at her steadily. "You can't."

She looked at him, processing words that refused to be processed. "You mean I'll never get to eat again?" In disbelief, she flashed me a look that begged me to ask him the question differently so that the answer might be different. I knew it wouldn't be. Though I hadn't told her yet, I'd already learned that the tumors, overwhelming and inoperable, had grown inward around her remaining colon, sealing it like a vault. Digestion of anything solid was biologically impossible. Ice chips and small sips of water were all she could have.

In measured, quiet tones, Dr. Redrow explained. When he finished, she asked him, "How long can I live on ice chips and water?"

"Days . . . maybe a couple of weeks."

He expressed his sorrow, businesslike, and left just as Alan arrived. The room grew still and quiet. Then Deborah let a question slip into the silence: "How do you live the rest of your life in just a few days?"

46

On October 14, eleven days before our thirty-first wedding anniversary, we brought Deborah home. As I drove through the warm autumn day, she seemed to notice every detail—the sun's brilliance, the cool breeze on her face, the fiery fall colors just beginning to show.

Later that day, we sat in the master bedroom with Regan and Carson, poring over memory albums that chronicled our family's thirty-one years. The kids and I had often over the years made fun of Deborah as she sat for hours creating those books, stacks of them, painstakingly pasting in treasured photographs. But she hadn't made them for then; she had made them for such a time as this, and by turning their plastic-covered pages, we were able to travel back in time.

We laughed at pictures of our wedding: Here, a shot of her grand-mother sitting with her legs a little too far apart and her girdle showing. There, a shot of friends toasting with bottles of champagne. (Two weeks after we married, Deborah's father had sent us a bill for the champagne, with a note explaining that he never intended to pay for our friends to get drunk.)

We paged through hundreds of shots of the kids: Pictures of us holding Regan for the first time sparked the thousandth retelling of how we'd honked the horn of our 1970 Chevy all the way home from Harris Hospital. And shots of Carson as a tiny baby had Regan insisting again that she'd got-ten to pick him out of several other choices at the Gladney Home nursery. We thought then that he looked a little bit like a turtle and we hadn't changed our minds. In the space of a few hours, our kids grew up and we grew gray through thirty volumes of photos. And we remembered, laughing and crying, just the four of us on the big, four-poster bed.

A couple of days later, Deborah seemed to turn her attention to housekeeping, to final details. Not with sadness, but with the joy of a traveler lightening her load before a trip to a place she'd always wanted to go, Deborah began giving away nearly everything she had. On the same big bed, we sat for hours with Regan and Carson, and Deborah talked about the things she wanted each one to have. I brought her jewelry box and she laid out all her necklaces, rings, and brooches, told the story behind each piece, then gave it all to Regan, except for a strand of pearls she gave to Carson, a gift for his future bride.

Apart from the cowboy memorabilia we'd gathered from junk stores to decorate the ranch, Deborah never was much of a collector. But she had accumulated a small collection of antique perfume bottles. She loved the colors and shapes and the notion that they'd once held a fragrance whose essence you could still catch if you removed the top. One by one, over two days, Deborah summoned her closest friends, told each what they'd meant to her, and gave them one of her treasured bottles. The first one went to Mary Ellen, who'd been with Deborah every day of her illness.

Late in the afternoon, on the day she finished giving the bottles away, I walked into the bedroom to find Deborah propped up with several pillows behind her back, smiling cheerfully, somehow expectantly. I sat down beside her. She wore a soft green pajama top, and the edge of the sheet was folded back and smooth across her waist. I marveled: She was even dying in pristine fashion. I slipped in under the sheet beside her and snuggled up close, careful to run my hands over the folded edge to brush away the wrinkles.

"I want to have a meeting with you and Carson and Regan," she said.

"About what?"

"You'll see. Just ask them to come in."

Having just slid in, I slid out of the bed again and called the kids. Minutes later, as we all sat on the big bed, Deborah addressed Carson and Regan with the tone of an affable but busy CEO handling emergency business that couldn't wait. "Your father has been a wonderful husband and father, and I want you to know that I am releasing him to find someone, date, and even marry."

Her words triggered actual pain in my body, as though my blood had suddenly turned hot.

"No . . . please," I interrupted.

She continued talking to the kids as if I hadn't spoken. "I know it's going to be hard for you, but I'm asking you to honor his decisions and let him be happy again."

Carson and Regan stared at her, openmouthed and silent. Suddenly, trying to breeze away the heaviness in the room, Deborah smiled broadly: "Of course, you two are also free to marry whomever you choose."

Regan smiled and cracked wise. "*Thanks*, Mom."

The meeting lasted less than five minutes, but seemed so much more a "final detail" than any discussion we'd had to that point. An acknowledgment that though we had journeyed together for more than thirty years, one of us was preparing to step off the path.

Carson, then Regan, crawled higher on the bed and kissed Deborah on the cheek. Then they slipped out, seeming to sense their mother had more to say. They were right. She asked me to help her into the wheelchair that the hospice people had parked by the bed. She wanted to go to the garden near the waterfall that architects had designed into the landscape behind our house. She'd rarely been able to enjoy it since we moved in.

I pushed her chair near the edge of the shallow reflecting pool and pulled up a lawn chair next to her. Though she'd been in command in the bedroom, she suddenly seemed more subdued. She spoke, but even the soft splash of water spilling into the pool was enough to steal the sound of her voice.

I asked her to repeat herself and leaned so close that her lips brushed my ear. "Even her," she said.

I knew immediately what she meant. True to her promise of eleven years before, the one she made the day after learning of my infidelity, she had never once mentioned the Beverly Hills artist.

"No," I said. "I don't want to go there."

"Yes," she whispered resolutely. "It was a *good* thing, a thing that turned out good for *us*. Look at the last eleven years . . . if she hadn't happened, our life together would never have been as wonderful as it has been. And now you have my permission to go back to her."

I told her I didn't even want to think of those things. I was still praying that God would heal her, I said, and added, "I'm still hoping God will take me first."

47

October 25

We had prayed to be able to celebrate our thirty-first anniversary together. Now, watching her cling to life, her breathing hitched and shallow, I wasn't sure she would live to see it. But she did. As daylight peeked through the crack in our bedroom drapes, I whispered in her ear: "Debbie, we woke up." But she could not answer. Five days earlier, she had fallen silent.

So I talked for both of us. Read to her from Proverbs 31 about the "excellent wife" . . . reminisced about the first time I saw her . . . walked through memories of our first few dates to football games, when I was too frightened to kiss her and serenaded her with "Mack the Knife" instead. She lay still on the bed, at less than eighty pounds barely raising the sheet. I gently slid my arm under her head and touched her face with my fingertips.

"Blink if you can hear me," I whispered. She did and tears trickled like tiny streams.

In the afternoon, the hospice doctor came, and after a quick examination called me out of the room to tell me that Deborah would not live through the day. I chose not to believe him. I chose to believe that God would not be so cruel as to take her on our anniversary.

The next day would have marked a week of total silence, but Deborah began to stir and moan. That afternoon, the kids and I, and Mary Ellen, were sitting with her, when she suddenly cried out, "Ron! Get me some wings!"

It wasn't a request, but a command, and it startled me into laughter.

Unable to move for nearly two weeks, she now began reaching her hands toward the ceiling—right, left, right, left—as if she were climbing a ladder. Fearing she'd yank her IV tubes out, all four of us tried to restrain her, but she struggled mightily, fighting to go up, up. She really was no more than a living skeleton; it was an extraordinary display of strength.

Day passed, then a long, thrashing night as we all stayed with her. "Jesus! Jesus!" Deborah cried as sunlight crept into the room. "Can you see them? They're flying!"

"What are you seeing?" I asked.

"Angels!" she said. "There they are!" And she would point to one part of the room, then quickly to another. We followed her motions expectantly, hoping to see angels ourselves. Her climbing and crying out continued for twenty-three hours. Then, as suddenly as she had broken her silence, she fell silent again. Ice gripped my heart as I thought she might have died.

But after about two minutes, she spoke again in a loud, clear voice: "Jesus! How are you?"

Another minute of silence and then resolutely: "No, I think I'll stay here!"

It was 2:00 a.m. Regan and I stared at each other, astonished. Had we just witnessed a visitation? I pressed my ear against Deborah's soft cotton gown; her heart was still beating strong. I kissed her cheek.

"It's okay to go with Jesus," I said. "Regan, Carson, and I will join you in heaven soon."

"And Mary Ellen . . . ," she whispered faintly.

"Yes, and Mary Ellen," I said, thrilled to know she had fully comprehended the moment.

＿ ＿ ＿

Early the next morning, Denver showed up on our doorstep in dirty, ragged clothes, smelling like cigarettes.

"Come on in," I said, opening the door wide. "Want some coffee?"

"I didn't come for no visit," he said. "I come to deliver a word from the Lord."

He was agitated and looked like he'd been up all night. He took a seat at the kitchen table, leaned forward and eyed me. "Last night, I was drivin up on the interstate, Mr. Ron, when I felt the need to pull over and pray. So I pull over on the side of the road up on that hill that look over the city, and that's when God spoke to my heart. God says Miss Debbie's spirit is cryin out to be with the Lord and showed me visions of angels comin into her room to take her home. But the saints on earth was holdin on to her body 'cause her work here ain't finished yet."

He told me he had seen Jesus and angels and lightning. He also told me what time he'd seen this "vision": precisely the same time it had happened in our home.

—   —   —

It had now been more than three weeks since Deborah had eaten. Her skin clung thinly to her limbs like gauze, hugged her cheekbones, crept into her eye sockets. How many times had various doctors predicted she would not live through the day? And yet a "foolish" old homeless man had been far more accurate than the learned medicine men.

The next morning Denver knocked at the kitchen door again. We sat at the kitchen table, stirred our coffee. He dropped his head and paused a long moment, unhurriedly collecting his thoughts like shells on a beach. Then: "God gives each person on the earth a set of keys, keys to live this life down here on the earth. Now in this set, there is one key you can use to unlock prison doors and set captives free."

Denver turned his head just slightly so that the right side of his face was closer to me than the left. He leaned in with his right shoulder and narrowed his eyes even farther. "Mr. Ron, I was captive in the devil's prison. That was easy for Miss Debbie to see. But I got to tell you: Many folks had seen me behind the bars in that prison for more than thirty years, and they just walked on by. Kept their keys in their pocket and left me locked up. Now I ain't tryin to run them other folks down, 'cause I was not a nice fella—dangerous—and prob'ly just as happy to stay in prison. But Miss

Debbie was different—she seen me behind them bars and reached way down in her pocket and pulled out the keys God gave her and used one to *unlock the prison door and set me free*."

Denver pounded home those last words like eight separate nails, then sat back in his chair, sipped his coffee. He put the mug down. "She's the onlyest person that ever loved me enough not to give up on me, and I praise God that today I can sit here in your home a changed man—a *free* man."

48

November 1

A week past our anniversary, the hospice doctor and nurses were beyond amazement that Deborah was still alive. They had stopped making predictions and instead discussed how the books on dying should be altered, or at least footnoted, to include the possible outcomes of people like Deborah, who, when death came calling, summoned the strength to reschedule and politely close the door.

For months, we had been in a long Texas drought, but now dark skies brought cold, sluicing rains. I imagined that the angels were crying. *But why?* I thought bitterly. It seemed God was getting His way. I remembered what Denver had said, that He needed to take home some good folks to work His will on earth. I thought that was a crappy plan.

That morning, Deborah lay in our bed, still and spectral. But at noon, her body began to tremble, then convulse. Within seconds, violent seizures began ripping through her torso and limbs. Her face contorted in pain. I jumped into the bed and tried to hold on as she shook and thrashed, pleading silently with God to stop torturing her. Alan, Mary, the kids, and the hospice people watched in growing horror.

After two hours, I leaped out of the bed and literally shook my fist at heaven. "Stop it, God! Please!"

For two more hours, Deborah writhed on the bed like a live power line. After what seemed like a frantic consultation, the hospice people decided to give her phenobarbital. The dose was enormous; it would probably stop the pain, but it might kill her. The hospice doctor asked if I was willing to administer the drugs. I consented without hesitation. I would've done anything to stop her suffering. Still, I wondered if I was signing her death warrant.

As the drugs began to flow, her tremors subsided, closing off what might have been a glimpse into hell. Without a doubt, I was now ready to see her safely to her eternal home. And I thought she must be ready to go, too.

November 2

Early in the morning, the doorbell rang. When I opened the door, I saw Denver standing there, ragged, looking again like a vagrant who had not slept. But his eyes were different this time—blank and hollow, almost as if he were in shock. I hugged him, but he only stood there, as though he was too exhausted to respond. He kept his head low and for a couple of minutes, wouldn't look me in the eye.

"I didn't come for no coffee or no visit," he said as we took seats at the kitchen table again. "I come to deliver a word from the Lord."

By this time, my towering faith had crumbled. The experts had failed. I had failed. And God, it appeared, was on the verge of failing, too. The God who promised that whatever we asked for in faith would be done in heaven had not delivered.

But I also knew it was Denver who had first predicted that a thief would come for Deborah. And when the doctors said Deborah wouldn't last another day, Denver said she would and he was right. Denver knew about the angels before anyone had told him what had happened in our bedroom. Somehow, in a way I couldn't understand, this simple man was dialed into God. So when this time he said he had a word from the Lord, I decided I needed a witness. I bounded up the stairs and summoned Carson. As soon as we returned to the kitchen together, Denver fixed us with his eye, narrow and intense.

"Mr. Ron, I've been out on a hill overlookin the city all night long, and I heard from the Lord. He said Miss Debbie's body is cryin out for paradise, but the saints here on earth still has a chain around her and won't let her go. So the Lord told me to come and break the chain."

I didn't speak, but flashed back to Deborah's violent seizures, her crying out. Was she crying out for paradise? And I wondered what "the chain" could be and who were the saints? Later, I learned that thirty of Deborah's friends had gathered in our yard the evening before and, linking hands, encircled our home to pray that God would heal her. Denver continued: "The Lord also told me to tell Miss Debbie that she could lay down her torch, and the Lord told me to pick it up. So, Mr. Ron, out of obedience to God, I'm here to break the chain, and I gon' ask you and Carson to pray with me to break it."

After nineteen months of praying for a miracle, it seemed strange now to be praying for God to take Deborah. But as I began, new promises from Scripture came to my lips unbidden. "Father," I prayed, "help us as a family to fully give Deborah over to You. Help us trust that You have ordained from the beginning the number of our days and that You won't take Deborah until she has completed the number You have ordained for her."

When we finished, Denver drilled me with a stare, and surprised us with words that seemed to contradict his prayer. "Still, Miss Debbie ain't goin nowhere till her work on earth is through."

Then tears spilled from his eyes. I had never seen him weep. His tears flowed into the lines in his face like rivers of grief, and it hit me again how much he loved Deborah. I marveled at the intricate tapestry of God's providence. Deborah, led by God to deliver mercy and compassion, had rescued this wreck of a man who, when she fell ill, in turn became her chief intercessor. For nineteen months, he prayed through the night until dawn and delivered the word of God to our door like a kind of heavenly paperboy. I was embarrassed that I once thought myself superior to him, stooping to sprinkle my wealth and wisdom into his lowly life.

49

I'd shed plenty a' tears when I was prayin out by the Dumpster, but I hadn't ever cried in front a' Mr. Ron before. I couldn't help it, though. I knowed everythin that could be done for Miss Debbie had been done. The doctors had done all they could do. Mr. Ron had done all he could do. And God had laid it on my heart that it was time for Miss Debbie to go on home to be with Him. But grief had still grabbed ahold of me and them tears spilled out 'fore I knew what hit me.

I tried to catch em with the backs of my fingers, and I could see Mr. Ron and Carson sittin there starin at me, a little bit surprised. Then they both looked down and started stirrin their coffee. That's when I got up and headed down the hall toward Miss Debbie's room. I didn't plan to do that. Seemed like the Lord just tugged at me and I felt like that's what I was s'posed to do.

The bedroom door was standin open and there Miss Debbie was, layin on her back in the middle of the big bed, thin and weak-lookin under the sheet. The curtains was open and the mornin light was gray, comin in through the rain that drizzled down the glass.

Her eyes was closed and her face had mainly wasted away till she didn't look much like herself, 'cept for still bein beautiful. I stood there for a spell just watchin her breathe.

"How you doin, Miss Debbie?" I said after a little while. But she stayed still, her chest risin and fallin in the quiet. Now, I'd been in to see her several times, and Mr. Ron or Miss Mary Ellen or somebody'd always be there, just 'cause there wadn't hardly ever a second when somebody wadn't right by her side. Since we'd just prayed that prayer of lettin Miss Debbie's soul sail on off to glory, I was kinda surprised Carson and Mr. Ron didn't follow me back to the room. I figured they'd want to be there in case we needed to pray the same thing right here with her. But they didn't come. Me and Miss Debbie was alone. Lookin back, I think maybe the Lord opened that little window in time to do His business.

I was standin on the left side a' the bed, with her head by my right hand and her feet by my left hand. The sheet covering her thin body rose and fell, rose and fell, just a bare little bit. With her face turned up toward heaven the way it was, she couldn't see me and I wadn't even sure she could hear me. And I wanted to be sure she heard what I had come to say. So I put my right knee on the bed. Then I slipped my hand up under her head and raised it off the pillow just a little bit, and turned her head to my face.

"Miss Debbie," I said.

She opened her eyes wide, starin straight at me.

I knowed she could hear me then, so I went right on. "I can understand how important it is to you that we keep on reachin out to the homeless. Now you done did all you could do. And God has put it on my heart to tell you that if you lay down the torch, I'll pick it up and keep your ministry to the homeless goin."

She didn't move or say nothin, but her eyes started to shine up with tears. My heart started poundin, achin in my chest like it was too big for my body.

"So you can go on home now, Miss Debbie," I said. "Go on home in peace."

Her tears spilled over then and my heart stretched until I thought it would tear in two. I kept holdin her head up, so she could see me. Then I said the last words I ever spoke to her: "Farewell. I'll see you on the other side."

I laid her head back down on the pillow and she let her eyes slip closed. And I knowed that she knowed we'd never see each other again. Not in this life.

50

November 3

I no longer slept. I lay with Deborah through the night. She lay beside me, gaunt, her eyes fixed open, mouth slack, lifted heavenward as if on the verge of a question. Her chest rose and fell sporadically, sometimes in short, quick hitches, sometimes not at all. I watched red minutes tick by on the digital clock, eating up what remained of the life we had built. As dawn crept into the room, thunder rumbled. I could hear rain showering down the eaves, streaming through the gutters.

My New York partner, Michael, had called and asked if he could come see Deborah, and was on his way down. I had tried to discourage him and others from coming during these last weeks. Deborah had wasted away so that she barely raised the sheet that covered her. Her eyes had faded and seemed cruelly suspended in sockets of protruding bone. I wanted everyone to remember her as the beautiful, elegant woman they'd always known.

But Michael pressed, and since we were godparents to his son Jack, I said yes. Jewish by birth, he was not a particularly religious man. He knew we were Christians and had witnessed our own trek of faith. We'd talked about Jesus as Messiah, but that didn't mesh with his own religious upbringing. Ours were philosophical discussions—friendly, never heated.

When Michael pulled up to the house at around 10:00 a.m., Mary Ellen and I were in the bedroom with Deborah, singing along to a CD of Christian songs, some of Deborah's favorites. I went out to greet Michael, then he, Carson, and I went back to the bedroom. The moment Michael stepped through the door, the song "We Are Standing on Holy Ground" began to play: *"We are standing on holy ground and I know that there are angels all around."*

As the song washed through the room, Michael looked at Deborah, then at Mary Ellen. "We *are* on holy ground," he whispered. Then, as though someone had kicked the backs of his legs, he fell to his knees and wept. Frozen in place, Carson, Mary Ellen, and I traded glances. In the twenty years I had known him, I had never seen Michael cry. When the song ended, he collected himself. Pulling out a picture of Jack, he moved to the edge of the bed and placed it in Deborah's palm, gently folding her fingers around it.

"Will you watch over him from heaven?" he said. "Be his guardian angel?" The moment later became a mystery. No one ever saw that picture of Jack again.

Michael thanked Deborah for all the prayers he knew she had prayed for him. She didn't move or speak. He stayed about twenty minutes. When I walked him down through the living room, he seemed dazed.

"There was a power or a presence in that room that was not of this world," he said. "All the times you spoke to me about an encounter with God . . . I just had one. I don't think I'll ever be the same."

That was all we said. He ran through sheets of slanting rain and ducked into his car. Michael had always held faith at arm's distance. Denver's words echoed in my mind: "Miss Debbie ain't goin nowhere till her work on earth is done."

Is it done now? I wondered.

I bounded down the hall and told Deborah about Michael. Though she remained silent, I knew that she knew. Her pulse had dropped to a whisper, and her breathing to an irregular series of shallow gasps. I lay down, wrapped my arms around her, and waited for the angels.

52

"Come quick! She's stopped breathing!"

It was Daphene. She'd come running upstairs in a panic. I had left Deborah's room less than fifteen minutes earlier, ushered away by Carson and Regan, who insisted that I get a couple of hours of sleep. At about 10:00 p.m., I had traced Deborah's face with my fingertips and kissed her forehead, afraid to leave for fear I'd never see her alive again, and gone upstairs.

Daphene took my place, prepared to keep watch all night. But at 10:15, she burst into the guest room where I had lain down. For nineteen months I had hardly let Deborah out of my sight. For the previous three weeks, I had seldom left her side. I had been there for thirty-one years and seven days of living. But it was Daphene, who had entered the world with her fifty-five years before, who saw her sister safely home.

The hospice nurse was standing over Deborah when I entered the room. I crawled up on the bed beside my wife. Her eyes were still open. I closed them. Quietly, I asked the nurse to remove the tubes and IVs that had bound her for a month. Then I asked the nurse to give us a few minutes alone, during which I held my dead wife and wept, begging God to raise her as Christ had raised Lazarus.

When He didn't—and I truly believed He could—my heart exploded.

Within minutes, a nondescript-looking man who introduced himself as the medical examiner appeared in our bedroom to pronounce her dead, as if I didn't know. Then, two men who had arrived in an unmarked white cargo van appeared to take her body away. Dressed in navy blue shirts and trousers, they looked for all the world like washing-machine repairmen. I had hoped they would look like angels, but they didn't. And I'd hoped they wouldn't look like morticians, but they did.

That night, Daphene brought two tiny white pills that Alan said would help me sleep. As I lay in bed, my mind drifted to Rocky Top, and questions needled my heart. Silly things, like who would give our baby longhorns their names? And who would pick the peaches in July and make the cobbler that scented the house with cinnamon? The last thoughts to cross my mind caused me to cry myself to sleep: that Deborah would not see Carson and Regan get married, that she would not meet our grandchildren, or watch them ride calves at Rocky Top after I roped them on Christmas morning like my granddaddy had done for me.

I guessed I could still do it. Maybe God would let her see.

52

Three days later, we buried Deborah in a simple pine casket on a lonely hill at Rocky Top—just the way she wanted it. The weather, though, at first seemed a slap in the face. The kids and I had driven out to the ranch that morning in a flashing thunderstorm. As winds from the cusp of winter blew cold sheets of rain across the highway, bitterness seethed in my heart. Maybe I was under some kind of divine punishment, but Deborah certainly didn't deserve this.

The burial site was the highest point on Rocky Top. A small clearing guarded by wizened oaks, it had always been one of Deborah's favorite nooks on the ranch. She especially loved the spot where an enormous flat boulder rested like a bench in the shade of a leaning oak, forming a natural gazebo perfect for prayer or simple solitude.

When Carson, Regan, and I drove up the hill, Roy Gene, Pame, and other friends were spreading hay to soak up the huge puddles that formed in the drenching rain. They had also uncovered the grave, a sight that unnerved me. I don't know what I had been expecting. I knew we weren't burying Deborah in a traditional cemetery, where headstones and epitaphs somehow affirm the civility of the final rite. But with cruel clarity, it hit me that her final resting place was nothing but a dark hole in desolate ground where wild animals foraged at night. A wave of nausea rolled through my guts, and I nearly collapsed under the reality of what we were about to do.

Mercifully, the weather broke. Like a minor miracle, the skies cleared and the cold north bluster reversed itself, replaced with a warm southern breeze that breathed over the hilltop, drying out the ground in less than an hour.

Denver arrived, along with about a hundred friends and family. Like country folks, we sat around Deborah's grave on hay bales. Someone had saddled Rocky, her palomino, and left him tied nearby. For the next hour and a half, we honored my wife. We sang old-time spirituals and country hymns, accompanied by two cowboy friends playing acoustic guitars Warm sunlight filtered through the oaks, casting circles of gold on Deborah's pine casket, so that the simple box she'd asked for appeared covered in shimmering medallions.

In no special order, folks stood up and shared Deborah stories. Unsurprisingly, Denver remained silent. I ended with a poem I had written for her on our anniversary. Pame walked through the crowd with a bucket of bluebonnet seeds and I watched as each mourner scooped out a handful and scattered it on the moist ground. Then the kids and I got into the Suburban and drove away, leading a procession of cars down the dirt road to the ranch house. Denver and the other pallbearers stayed at the site to lower Deborah into the earth with ropes. As I left my wife on the hilltop, I tried not to think about the shovels I had seen leaning behind a tree.

53

When we let Miss Debbie down into the ground, I knowed it wadn't nothin but her earthly body. But I still felt my heart sinkin right down into that hole. I knowed God had a plan and a reason why He took her. But I still didn't understand why He gon' cut off such a beautiful life while the whole world was crawlin with criminals and fellas like me that ain't never done nobody much good.

After we got her casket down into the grave, me and Mr. Roy Gene and some other fellas picked up them shovels and started in. I hated the sound when that dirt thumped on the wooden coffin and showered down around it like an evil rain. Even though I knowed Miss Debbie's spirit was with the Lord, I tried real hard not to think about what was inside that box. I was glad when all I could hear was dirt hittin dirt and not hittin that casket no more.

After we was finished, there was a fresh pile a' red earth where the hole used to be. One a' Miss Debbie and Mr. Ron's friends had made a big cross outta cedar wood with the bark still on it, lashed it together with rawhide. Somebody used a shovel and pounded it in the earth up by her head.

And that was it. The place didn't look no different than no other place on the ranch, 'cept for that big red scar on the ground.

After everbody went on to the house, I stayed up there with her, sittin on a bale a' hay. Sometimes I talked to God, askin Him why. Even though I'd had a word or two from Him about His purposes, and even though I'd delivered them words to Mr. Ron like He asked me to, that didn't mean I had to like it. And I told Him I didn't like it. That's the good thing 'bout God. Since

He can see right through your heart anyway, you can go on and tell Him what you really think.

Since I knowed wadn't nobody gon' hear me, I talked to Miss Debbie, too. Out loud.

"You was the onlyest person that looked past my skin and past my meanness and saw that there was somebody on the inside worth savin. I don't know how, but you knowed that most a' the time when I acted like a bad fella, it was just so folks wouldn't get too close. I didn't want nobody close to me. It wadn't worth the trouble. Besides that, I had done lost enough people in my life, and I didn't want to lose nobody else."

Well, it was too late for that. But I didn't regret lettin Miss Debbie get close. Instead, I thanked God for her life and the simple fact that she loved me enough to stand up to me. That got me to cryin. I cried and cried out loud and told Miss Debbie that was the most important thing she taught me: "Ever man should have the courage to stand up and face the enemy," I said, "'cause ever person that looks like a enemy on the outside ain't necessarily one on the inside. We all has more in common than we think. You stood up with courage and faced me when I was dangerous, and it changed my life. You loved me for who I was on the inside, the person God meant for me to be, the one that had just gotten lost for a while on some ugly roads in life."

I don't know how long I sat up there on that hay bale. But it was mornin when we buried Miss Debbie and night when I finally got through talkin to her and went on home.

54

The next morning, we held a memorial service at church, under strict orders from Deborah that it was to be a celebration. Denver planned to follow us there in his car and arrived in our driveway looking stylish in a dark pinstriped suit and tie. I got out of my car and gave him a long hug. I'd heard from a friend who had attended the burial service that when she left Rocky Top at twilight, she had seen Denver, still sitting by Deborah's grave.

The church parking lot was already packed when we pulled in, and I had to find a parking spot like everyone else. Deborah had not wanted limos or anything else that would make it look like a funeral. Inside, nearly a thousand people had gathered, and for the next two hours, Deborah's close friends and family shared memories of a life well-lived. Sister Bettie was among those who stood to speak.

Slender and soft-spoken, she walked to the podium and told briefly of how God had led Deborah to the mission, and how they had become sisters in Christ with a common goal to change the city. Then she looked down at Denver, who was seated in the front row, just in front of Regan, Carson, Daphene, and me. "Now, Brother Denver has a few words to say."

Denver pulled out his handkerchief and mopped his head. Then he rose from his seat and walked slowly to the dais. I glanced at Carson and Regan, and we shared a smile as Denver's ponderous gait made the climb up to the podium seem like a mountain trek.

Normally soft-spoken, Denver this day needed no microphone. In a rousing voice that grew louder and stronger with each word, he delivered a message about courage, hope, and the love of a woman.

"God has blessed me that someone would come to me that was concerned about me and not interested in whatever bad places I had come from. Ever since I'd known her, Miss Debbie offered for me to come to church here, but wadn't no way I was comin *here!*" Denver said, smiling as the mostly white congregation laughed. "So she came and got me and brought me. I tried to stall at the door, but she said, 'Come on in,' and she walked in here with me just as proud. She was a real lady."

As Denver told the tale of the white ladies and the retreat, laughter rang, and when he told how God had prompted him to pick up Miss Debbie's torch, people cried. Regan and Carson, their own tears flowing, squeezed my hands, thrilled to witness this answered prayer and so proud of their mom, whose legacy was sealed by the powerful testimony of a man who'd survived some of the worst America has to offer, and trouble of his own making, a man whom we now considered a member of our family.

As Denver left the podium, I saw Roy Gene and our friend Rob Farrell stand and begin clapping. Then the entire congregation stood, and applause thundered through the church. For nineteen months we had prayed for and expected a miracle. Suddenly I realized I was staring one right in the face. A face that didn't try to hide from me anymore. A face with eyes that were no longer angry and yellow, but clear and a powerful brown. A face that beamed a joyful smile when it seemed once to have forgotten how.

As Denver lumbered down from the dais, the applause continued. Regan, Carson, and I stood, tears streaming, and when he reached us, gathered him into our arms.

55

Never one to leave details to chance, Deborah had told us that after she died, she wanted Carson, Regan, and I to take a trip somewhere—just the three of us. We were to leave right after her memorial service, she said, stay at least one week, and not talk about anything sad. She had issued these orders a month ago, on her last day in the hospital. That day, the four of us sat in her room and yakked about where we should go.

"Italy," I suggested. "We can stay with Julio and Pilar in Florence. We'll eat pasta, drink wine, and laugh over memories."

"Too far," Regan said, ever practical. "I want to float the Rio Grande and hike in Big Bend."

Deborah liked that and Carson agreed, so it was decided: desolate Big Bend National Park in far west Texas. Per Deborah's instructions, we packed the car the day after the service and were literally walking out the door when the phone rang. It was Don Shisler.

"Ron, can you come down to the mission right away?"

"Not really. The kids and I were just leaving for a week in Big Bend."

"But this can't wait. Can you stay by the phone for a minute? I'm going to have Bob Crow call you right back."

Bob was a mission board member. I said I'd wait. Within a minute, Bob was on the phone explaining what he described as "the most powerful move of God in the 112 years of the Union Gospel Mission."

Here's what happened: Immediately after Deborah's memorial service, a couple named John and Nancy Snyder approached Bob, saying they wanted to make a major gift and assist in raising additional funds to build a new

Union Gospel Mission. The existing mission was aging and beyond repair, and it was Sister Bettie's powerful testimony and Denver's story of how Deborah's love for him had changed his life that had stirred their hearts.

That news alone stunned me, but what Bob said next made my knees wobble: "Ron, they want to build a new chapel for the mission and name it the 'Deborah Hall Memorial Chapel.'"

My throat closed and tears surged. I could barely squeeze out the words "We'll talk it over during our trip" before hanging up.

Carson and Regan were elated about the gifts for the new mission, and we left for Big Bend with high spirits mercifully buoying our heavy hearts. We debated the chapel-naming issue as we barreled down the road in the Suburban, loaded down with boots and backpacks. All of us were positive Deborah wouldn't want her name emblazoned on anything any more than she'd wanted the red Rolls-Royce boasting from our driveway.

If mission donors wanted to name the new chapel after someone, it should be Sister Bettie, we all agreed at first. Then from the backseat Carson threw in a monkey wrench. "Isn't it usually the people writing the checks who get to name the place their money is going to build?"

We chewed on that for a minute, Regan staring out the window at the chaparral whipping by. "You know, Dad," she said finally, "they didn't ask us to name the chapel, just to give our blessing to the name they already picked out." We tabled the subject for the duration of the trip.

At Big Bend, the Rio Grande meanders through the shimmering arroyos of the Chihuahuan desert, the jagged peaks of the Chisos Mountains towering above. We hiked the rimrocks and floated down the chilly river through narrow canyon cuts, sheer volcanic walls soaring over our heads into a vault of blue. It was a simple escape, clean and austere, a monastery of sky and stone.

The week passed slowly, blessedly free of the noise of living. I thought about Deborah, jumbled images flashing randomly through my mind as though someone had reshuffled our lives into some kind of anachronistic slide show. Deborah holding baby Carson. Deborah frail and dying. Deborah saying, "I do." Deborah laughing on a ski slope. Serving meat loaf at the mission. Baking with Regan.

I thought about Denver, again random pictures. Denver's words at the memorial service. My putting my hand on his knee at the Caravan. Denver with Mr. Ballantine. Denver praying by the Dumpster for Deborah. There would be, I knew, no catch-and-release.

When our time at Big Bend was up, we were ready to come home. And the moment we emerged from the desert into cell-phone range, I found I had a message from Don Shisler.

56

While they was gone to the river, I prayed for Mr. Ron and Carson and Regan, that God would bring them a time of healin. There's somethin special about a river, somethin spiritual that I believe goes all the way back to the river Jordan. Wadn't no kinda trip gon' make Mr. Ron and his kids feel better about losin Miss Debbie. But I prayed they would have a time of refreshin out there where there ain't nothin but what God has made.

I knowed when they come back, I was gon' have to get dressed up again. Mr. Shisler had done invited me to come to somethin he called "National Philanthropy Day." He'd already invited Mr. Ron, said he left him a message on his cell phone to remind him. Miss Debbie was one of the folks they was gon' honor. I wadn't too happy to be puttin on a suit for the third time in a month, but I was all for participatin in anything that would let folks know what kinda woman the Lord had called home.

The mornin after he got back from the river, Mr. Ron come by the mission to pick me up. I had on a suit I had got at the mission store that seemed like it was brand-new. When Mr. Ron saw it, he smiled and said I looked like a million bucks, so I figured I done purty good.

They was holdin this National Philanthropy Day ceremony at the Worthington, a rich folks' hotel on Main Street. When we walked into the lobby, there was about a million people crowdin around, waitin to go in through some big ole fancy doors that Mr. Ron said went into the ballroom where they was havin this shindig. We hadn't been there but a few minutes when people I never seen in my life started comin up to me.

This one lady wearin a pearl necklace and a hat says to me, "I heard you speak at Deborah's memorial service. What a *wonderful* story!"

"Denver, I want to shake your hand," said a tall, skinny fella with a diamond stickin outta his necktie. "I'm so glad to hear how you turned your life around!"

On and on it went like that, with strangers comin up to me and callin me by my given name. I started to sweat. Mr. Ron just smiled and said maybe he should be my agent. When them ballroom doors finally did swing open, I thanked the Lord and hoped nobody'd be congratulatin me no more.

Now Mr. Ron had taken me to some fancy places, but that ballroom was prob'ly the biggest, fanciest one yet. Looked like somebody'd hauled in all the silver and crystal in Texas and laid it all out on round tables draped with dark red tablecloths. I sat down beside Mr. Ron and tried to act like I belonged there, but I couldn't help starin up at the chandeliers.

Mr. Ron saw me grinnin. "What are you thinking about?" he said.

"I been seein this hotel from the outside for twenty years," I said. "But I never figured I'd ever be on the inside."

When I was still on the streets, I told him, I used to come down to the Worthington on the coldest nights and slip in behind the hotel where they had some of them big fans that blow hot air onto the sidewalk. I'd sleep on top of the grates to keep warm. One of the security guards took a likin to me. Just to be nice, he used to come by every now and then and kick me a little to make sure I hadn't froze to death. Sometimes he'd even bring me some hot coffee.

"He never did run me off," I told Mr. Ron. "Long as I didn't make my bed till after midnight and was gone by six in the mornin, he let me stay."

"Did you never even walk in the lobby here? I think all hotel lobbies are open to the public."

I looked Mr. Ron in the eye. "Homeless folks ain't no public," I said.

I guess I was public now, though, 'cause I saw my name on the "Invited Guests" list. When the food come, I took my cloth napkin and put it on my lap. And I kept a eye on Mr. Ron to make sure I was usin the right fork. I had learned by then that rich white folks got a lotta rules 'bout forks. I still ain't figured out why they got to use three or four different ones and make a lotta extra work for the folks in the kitchen.

We'd about finished eatin when Mr. Ron brought up the subject of namin the new mission chapel after Miss Debbie. "We've decided against it," he said. "We don't think she would've wanted to draw attention to herself that way."

I got real serious with him then. "Mr. Ron, Miss Debbie is in heaven, and this is not 'bout Miss Debbie anyway. It's about God. Are you gon' get in the way of God when He's on the move?"

Mr. Ron shook his head, kinda hangdog. "No. I guess not."

"Then just get out the way and let God do His thing!"

57

Denver Moore made his way through the glittering crowd of the wealthiest people in Fort Worth and, with grace and dignity, accepted a philanthropy award on Deborah's behalf. He received a standing ovation.

The next day, I met with the mission board and told them why our family didn't want to name the chapel after Deborah. But I also passed along Denver's counsel and so, of course, it was decided: The new worship space would be called the Deborah Hall Memorial Chapel. Meanwhile, the fundraising drive for New Beginnings, the new mission facility, was officially under way. Within two days of Deborah's memorial service, while we had been floating on the river in Big Bend, the Snyders and our friends, Tom and Patricia Chambers, had donated $350,000 to the mission in her honor.

That board meeting seemed to mark an end to the grace that had sustained me through Deborah's burial and memorial service, through Big Bend and the banquet. It also proved to be the last civilized stop before life spit me out on an unmarked trail. I was fifty-five, graying at the temples, with half my heart lying in the ground at Rocky Top. How to survive? How to move forward? I felt trapped in a whiteout snowstorm with no guide and fresh out of supplies. The intensity of my fear surprised me.

For weeks, I wandered through the house like a ghost in a graveyard. I haunted Deborah's closet, opening the drawers and cabinets, touching her scarves, her stockings, burying my face in her clothes, trying to breathe in her scent. Sometimes I closed the closet door behind me and sat there in the dark, holding the last photograph ever taken of us together.

I combed through files and photo albums and made a scrapbook of my favorite pictures of her and letters she'd written. For several days and nights, I sat on our bed in a daze, slowly turning the pages, reliving moments: the spring I fell in love with her and delivered lemon drops in a tiny brown paper bag to her at the school where she taught . . . the summer we got engaged, swimming in the lake, kissing underwater for so long we'd pop up sputtering for air, giggling that we'd nearly drowned . . . our autumn honeymoon in Vail, so poor we had to share a room with another couple . . . sunny days with the children in the park . . . winters building cowboy snowmen and exploring Indian caves at Rocky Top.

I abandoned my Bible and read hers, not for words of comfort from God, with whom I was barely on speaking terms, but for Deborah's words— thousands of them, scribbled in the margins of 2,094 pages. She had chronicled our valleys and mountaintops, struggles and victories—in marriage, raising the kids, journeying with friends. Her words—not our money, jewels, antiques, or paintings by twentieth-century masters—were our family treasure: the outpouring of Deborah's heart, written in her own hand.

My own heart felt shriveled and black, and my body shriveled with it. Nearly six feet tall, I weighed only 135 pounds. Friends told me I looked worse than terrible. I was glad. Thought it was proper. Mary Ellen asked me if I had a death wish. In a way, I suppose I did: I was wishing for someone who was dead.

My fear gave way to anger, and I had plenty to go around. But as I fired arrows of blame—at the doctors, the pharmaceutical industry, cancer researchers—clearly the bull's-eye was God. It was He who had ripped a gaping and irreparable hole in my heart. Without a gun or mask, He robbed me of my wife and stole my children's mother and my grandchildren's grandmother. I had trusted Him, and He had failed me.

How do you forgive that?

— — —

Thanksgiving came, a day to be endured, not celebrated. In a house that on Deborah's favorite holiday had looked like the Pilgrims' feast, Denver and my parents were our only guests. I got up early, put a scrawny turkey in the oven, and walked out to the back deck nursing a cup of coffee. As the sunrise gradually lit the valley, I watched bucks chasing does near the river. Every year until this one, I'd hunted deer on Thanksgiving morning. But death seemed too personal now.

I drove up to sit with Deborah. I sat down on the big rock under the leaning oak, sinking deeper into misery as its bloodred leaves drifted to the ground around me. The white roses on Deborah's grave had turned brown. Only an ugly mesh of chicken wire shielded her resting place from wild animals.

My heart stung as I asked myself how I could have left her here like this, with no wall or gates to protect her. Denver had told me he wanted to help me turn this place into a family cemetery, so we planned to do it together.

In mid-December, he and I convened at Rocky Top to begin our labor of love, transforming the stark, lonely hill where Deborah lay into a safe harbor of rest. The evening before we started the work, we piled logs in the big stone fireplace and stretched out in leather chairs to warm our feet. Firelight glowed against Denver's dark skin as we reminisced about Deborah.

"Remember when she threw me that birthday party, Mr. Ron?"

"Sure do! At the Red, Hot & Blue."

Denver was turning sixty-three, and Deborah had planned a little surprise party. After church, we'd taken him to the Red, Hot & Blue, a barbecue restaurant where Denver and I had often dropped in to eat pulled-pig sandwiches with collard greens and sweet potatoes on the side. Scott and Janina and their kids showed up to honor the birthday man.

"Denver," Deborah said after we ordered, "tell us about your favorite birthday party."

He looked down at the table and thought a few moments, then looked back at Deborah. "Well, I reckon this is my favorite birthday party, 'cause it's the onlyest one I ever had."

"What about as a child?" Deborah said, surprised.

"No, ma'am. On the plantation, we never celebrated no birthdays. I really never knowed when mine was till I was grown and my sister told me." Then he brightened. "So this birthday party is sure 'nough my favorite."

Deborah had brought a little cake, chocolate with white frosting. She lit the candles and we sang "Happy Birthday," the kids' voices chirping high while Denver smiled shyly.

He smiled now at the memory, stretching his feet toward the crackling fire. "That sure made me feel good. And the barbecue and the cake was mighty good, too."

"But you had a heck of a time wrestling with that barbecue," I said, remembering how showers of saliva squirted through his few good teeth onto the red-checkered tablecloth every time he took a bite.

"I sure 'nough did," he said, chuckling at the memory. He'd had such a tough time eating his birthday lunch that the next day I'd called Glen Petta, a dentist who had met Denver at the retreat. At the time, he'd offered to make Denver a set of teeth free of charge. When I called Glen, he was happy to keep his word. The next time I saw Denver, he'd grinned a great big I've-got-new-teeth grin, revealing a full set of pearly whites lined up neat and tight as the grille on a '54 Corvette.

"Why, you look like a movie star, Denver," I'd said, grinning back.

"Which one?"

I named the first one that popped into my head: "John Wayne!"

That seemed to sit well with him, but the teeth didn't. He wore them only to church. Said they got in his way when he ate.

He wasn't wearing them now as we sat before the fire, the burning green wood hissing and popping, soothing us down into a drowsy tranquillity. Finally, we heaved ourselves up, and I took Denver upstairs to show him the room where he could sleep. I desperately wanted him to feel welcome there. He had slept at Rocky Top a few times before, but not without coaxing. For one thing, he still preferred sleeping outside. And now that Deborah was gone, I had begun to suspect he felt like a hanger-on. I didn't feel that way about him at all. In fact, during her illness and since her death, I had come to consider him my brother.

58

I was real happy to be goin with Mr. Ron to his ranch to help fix up the place where Miss Debbie was laid. But to tell the truth, I'd never felt as comfortable around him as I had around her. Not really, even though we'd been knowin each other for a coupla years. I was purty sure that the onlyest reason Mr. Ron tried to be my friend was 'cause Miss Debbie told him to. And I figured now that Miss Debbie was gone, wouldn't be too long 'fore he'd cut me loose.

That evenin, Mr. Ron showed me the room upstairs again, even though I knowed where it was at. It's real cozy, with a little iron bed and everthing done up cowboy-style. I slept there before but always on the floor, 'cause I ain't ever been real comfortable sleepin inside in the first place. But Mr. Ron said he wadn't gon' hear 'bout that no more and made me promise I was gon' sleep in the bed.

"See you in the morning," he said and walked out the door, shuttin it behind him. I just stood there real quiet in the middle a' the room and listened to him thump down the stairs. When I heard his bedroom door close, I opened mine so I wouldn't feel so penned in. Then I wrapped a blanket around me and laid down on the bed with the blanket up over my head like a hood and just my nose stickin out, homeless-style. Didn't matter what I did, though. I just couldn't get comfortable in somebody else's bed, and I knowed I wadn't gon' be doin much sleepin.

I'd been layin there for a coupla hours, still as a dead man and wide awake, when I heard somethin—footsteps in the room.

For a minute, I froze up, real scared. But then a kinda peace came over me, and I closed my eyes underneath the blanket. Then I felt the covers slip off my head and some soft hands, light as a feather, tuckin em in around my neck. But I kept my eyes closed.

Then I heard the voice of a woman, a voice I recognized: "Denver, you are welcome in our home."

I opened my eyes and there was Miss Debbie, healed and beautiful. Then, just as quick, she was gone. As sure as I'm tellin you this, it wadn't no dream, 'cause I wadn't sleepin. It was a visitation.

I laid there for a long time, tryin to figure out why Miss Debbie had come. *You are welcome in our home.*

Our home.

I took that to mean it was her home *and* Mr. Ron's home, and that I was still welcome even though she was gone. Now, she was married to him for a mighty long time, so I figured she knowed him purty good. That's when I knowed Mr. Ron had meant it when he said he was my friend.

Right after I figured all that out, that bed didn't feel like a stranger's no more, and I fell into a deep sleep.

59

We awoke the next morning to a rose-colored sunrise that turned the frost pink, then gold, as the sun climbed into a cloudless sky. Denver seemed rested and especially cheerful. We parked ourselves on the back deck for coffee and watched as several deer crossed the pale river far below. Even from three hundred feet up, we could hear their slim hooves cracking through the ice that had formed along the riverbank in the night.

Since we'd planned to spend the day gathering rocks for Deborah's burial site, we were glad for the chill weather. Picking up rocks on a Texas ranch isn't a job you want to do before the first frost unless you feel like squaring off against an irritated rattlesnake.

Together, Denver and I gathered rocks for three days, passing over the ordinary to choose just the right ones. Then, stone by stone, we laid a wall around the square of ground where I would someday rest beside my wife. We used the best rocks to build pillars that would support a wrought-iron entry arch proclaiming the cemetery's name: Brazos del Dios. The Arms of God.

By that time, we'd been working for six days, and I thought I'd noticed a change in Denver. Something . . . *lighter* about his spirit. I couldn't pin it down. While we were stacking the heavy pillar stones, he solved the mystery for me.

"Mr. Ron, I got somethin to tell you."

"What is it?" I said, shoving a piece of rust-colored limestone into place.

"Well, you might not believe this, but I saw Miss Debbie the other night."

I had bent over to heave up the next stone, but straightened and turned to look at him. "What do you mean you saw her?"

Denver pulled off his ball cap, mopped his brow, and tucked the cloth away in his back pocket. "You know the first night we was here and you took me upstairs to show me where to sleep?"

"Yes . . ."

"Well, I never did go to sleep. And after I had been layin there for a while, Miss Debbie come into the room. 'Cept she didn't look sick no more. She looked beautiful like she did before the cancer."

Not quite sure what to say, I tilted my head a little and regarded him carefully. "Do you think you were dreaming?"

"No sir." He shook his head adamantly. "Like I said, I didn't go to sleep. It wadn't no dream. It was a *visitation*."

In my experience with Denver during Deborah's illness, everything he'd said had always turned out to be true. The prediction that something bad was about to happen. The angels. Her trying to get to heaven. Even her life expectancy. As a result, I had come to believe things I once would've called unbelievable.

I looked over at Deborah's grave then back at Denver. "Did she say anything?"

"Yessir. She said, 'You are welcome in our home.' I got to tell you, Mr. Ron, I felt a whole lot better when she said that, 'cause I was purty sure after she went home to be with the Lord you was gon' cut me loose."

"Cut you loose?" I was stunned that he would think that. I had come to take it for granted that he and I would be friends forever, just like he'd said that day at Starbucks. Then I remembered: When I first said I wanted to be Denver's friend, it was because Deborah pushed me into it. Then, for a while, I had secretly seen myself as some sort of Henry Higgins to the homeless—at least I had thought it was secret. And wasn't it true that I had promised not to catch-and-release when my wife, the fishing-boat captain, was alive? Now she was gone. Maybe I shouldn't have been surprised that Denver thought I was planning to abandon ship.

Smiling, I took a step closer to him and laid my hand on his shoulder. "Denver, of course you're welcome here. You're welcome here even when I'm not here. The kids and I consider you part of our family now, and our home is your home. When I promised not to catch-and-release, I meant it."

I thought I could see his throat working. He peered down at the ground for a long moment, and when he looked back up, his eyes were moist.

"Forever," he said. Then he smiled and turned to hoist another rock.

60

I like the big rock up there at Brazos del Dios, the flat one under the leaning oak. It's a comfortable place for me, 'cause when I goes up there, I know Miss Debbie's up there with me. We dedicated the new cemetery in May, and I was mighty glad to see that God blessed the day with a blue sky and big wide blanket a' yella flowers as far as you could see. There was about fifty people there, mostly the same ones that had come to the burial back in November. We all sang for a while and spent some time talkin 'bout God's faithfulness to carry us through this time of grievin.

Then I felt like the Lord had given me a word for the people that was gathered there. And when the Lord say "speak," ain't much you can do but get up, open your mouth, and see what comes out.

Here's what come out that day: "Miss Debbie was a close enough friend a' mine that I prayed and prayed for her, day and night—even to the point of offerin God life for life. 'Let me go in,' I said to Him. 'Let her stay here, 'cause she more worthy than me to stay here on this earth, and I would be better off to go on up to heaven 'cause I ain't had no kinda luck down here.'"

But everbody there that day knowed it didn't turn out that way. So I looked at Mr. Ron and Carson and Regan sittin over on the bench that Miss Pame put in, 'cause I knowed what I was fixin to say was gon' be hard for them to hear.

"I know when somebody you love is gone, that's the last time you feel like thanking God. But sometimes we has to be thankful for the things that hurt us," I said, "'cause sometimes God does things that hurts us but they help somebody else."

I could see folks noddin their heads. Mr. Ron and them just sat still and quiet.

"If you want to know the truth about it, nothin ever really ends but something new don't begin," I said. "When somethin ends in our sight, it begins somewhere else where we can't hear it or see it or feel it. We live in two worlds—a physical world and a spiritual world. When Miss Debbie's physical body laid down, her spirit rose up. When we come through this world, we just change form 'fore we go on to the next."

I looked over at her grave at where Mr. Ron's ranch hands had tucked some wild roses in an old bucket and set em up by Miss Debbie's head. Then I looked at Mr. Ron again, and I could see him noddin then. He smiled a little, and I thought maybe he was rememberin that I had seen Miss Debbie's spiritual body with my own eyes.

61

Summer burned through and September breezed in, its usual hot winds unseasonably cool. Denver and I spent a lot of time together. We talked about what we'd been through and tossed around the idea of writing our story down.

But to tell the story, I needed to know more about Denver's roots. Had the place he'd come from been as bad as all that? I had been to the plantation in Red River Parish many times in my mind. But the images I conjured had a back-lot quality, as though a stagehand were constructing them using props left over from *Gone with the Wind*. Denver's vocabulary, meanwhile, was short on adjectives, leaving us just one choice. I knew I had to go with him back to Red River Parish to see and touch the place that had produced this man who had changed my life. Denver had another reason for wanting to go back: to close the door on the past.

Maybe that's why he clammed up when in early September 2001, we hopped on Interstate 20 and began our pilgrimage. As we motored east in my new Suburban—the old one had logged too many miles by then—Denver was unusually quiet, and I asked him why.

"I ain't slept much lately," he said. "Been nervous 'bout this trip."

He'd been back before, to visit his sister, Hershalee, and his aunt Pearlie May. But in 2000, Hershalee had died, just a few months before Deborah, leaving Denver feeling permanently untethered from the close family bloodlines that bind us to earth and give us place.

We hadn't been driving long before Denver's head hit his chest like a rock falling off a cliff. A minute later, he started snoring. For the next three hours, the trip sounded like the scenic route through a sawmill. But once we crossed into bayou country, something in the air seemed to quicken his spirit: He didn't rouse slowly from sleep but suddenly sat straight up.

"We nearly there," he said.

The Louisiana air was warm and moist, heavy with the residue of recent rain. Soon, we were whipping by cotton fields, and Denver's eyes brightened like those of a young boy passing an amusement park. Outside the windows, acres unrolled, and vast blankets of milky-white bolls stretched away to meet rows of hardwood trees that formed a distant horizon.

"Looky-there now, ain't that purty! Just right for pickin!" Denver shook his head slowly, remembering. "Used to be hun'erds a' colored folks spread out all the way across them fields as far as your eyes would let you look. And the Man'd be standin by his wagon with his scales, writin down how much ever one of em picked. These days, all that cotton just sittin there waitin for some big ole monster-lookin machine to run through there and strip it off. Them machines cost a lotta folks their jobs. It just don't seem right."

Again, Denver's love-hate relationship with his plantation struck me. It was as though he wouldn't have minded so much being stuck in an agrarian time warp if he hadn't seen so much injustice in it.

We drove about another half-mile, Denver's nose practically pressed against the window. "Here, Mr. Ron. Pull over right here."

I eased the Suburban onto the gravel shoulder, and the tires crackled to a stop at the edge of the cotton, white rows fanning out like bicycle spokes. Denver stepped down into a muddy aisle and we walked between the rows, Denver running his hand lightly over the fluffy bolls.

"I plowed and chopped and picked the cotton in this field right here for a lotta years, Mr. Ron . . . a lotta years." He sounded wistful and tired, then brightened as he let me in on a trade secret. "This is a good day for pickin 'cause there's a little bit a' dampness in the air," he said with a wink. "Makes the cotton weigh more."

"Don't you think the Man figured that out and factored it in?" I asked.

Denver paused for a moment then laughed. "I 'spect so."

I pulled a tiny digital camera from my pocket, and Denver slipped into sepia-portraiture mode as if I'd thrown a switch. He dropped one knee into the dirt and peered seriously into the lens through designer sunglasses, looking about as much like a former cotton-picker as Sidney Poitier. I snapped off several shots, and he was still frozen in his touristy pose when the soulful call of a train whistle floated over the fields.

"Was that your ride you caught out of here?" I asked.

Denver nodded solemnly. I wondered how many times he listened to that whistle before he heard it calling his name.

62

I was mighty anxious 'bout goin back to Red River Parish. I felt better when we crossed the Louisiana line, though. There was somethin in the air . . . memories, spirits, I don't know. Ain't every spirit good, but they ain't all bad neither.

Mr. Ron took some pictures of me in one a' the fields I used to work. We didn't stay but just a minute 'fore we got back on Highway 1, which shot straight ahead, cuttin that cotton in half just like a long black knife.

We drove on for a purty good li'l piece till I told him, "Turn in right here." He yanked the wheel hard right onto a old dirt road. Set back on the left was the Man's house, and on the right was a new house I hadn't never seen before.

We bumped down the road purty slow, kickin up a little mud, cotton spreadin all about. Wadn't too long 'fore we saw a old, abandoned shack, gray and falling down, all the paint wore off it. "That was the Boss Nigger's house," I said.

Mr. Ron looked at me kind of funny. I guess he was surprised I said "nigger," but that's just what we said back then. Case you're wonderin what the Boss Nigger did, it was just what it sound like: He was the colored man that bossed all the other colored folks around.

Mr. Ron kept drivin till I said, "Stop right here."

Right there next to the road on the other side of a wire fence was a two-room shack looked like it was fixin to fall down any minute. There was weeds crawlin up over it. Wadn't no front door, just a yella jackets' nest as big as a hubcap. "That's where I stayed," I said, kinda quiet.

Wadn't no place to pull off, so Mr. Ron just stopped the Suburban in the middle of the road. We got out, climbed over the fence, and poked around a bit, pushin through the high weeds, peekin in the windows. Wadn't no glass in em. Never had been. Wadn't nothin inside but cobwebs and yellow jackets and heaps a' trash. I wondered if any of it was mine. But after so much time had gone by, I reckoned not.

Mr. Ron just kept shakin his head. "I can hardly believe you lived here all those years," he said. "It's awful. Worse than I thought."

Lookin at that shack, I could see myself as a young man, so proud to have my own place I didn't even realize it wadn't no bigger than a toolshed. I could see myself on the Man's tractor in that field yonder. I could see myself tendin a hog out back a' the shack and scrapin to make the meat last. I could see myself rollin out the bed ever mornin before sunrise, tendin the Man's cotton year after year, and for nothin.

When Mr. Ron asked could he take some pictures of me in front of that shack, I let him. But I only smiled on the outside.

63

When Denver showed me where he used to live, I could hardly process it. Made of gray plank lumber, it was half the size of the shotgun shacks I'd grown up seeing in Corsicana, nearly small enough to fit in the back of a long-bed pickup truck. I stared up the road the way we'd come and remembered passing the Man's house—a big white country house, clapboard, with a gracious porch complete with swing. The contrast disgusted me.

Denver didn't say much as we poked around the place. Then he suggested we move on down to the house where Hershalee had lived. We climbed back into the Suburban, and as we rolled over the red dirt road, he told me how the Man had let her live in the house until she died even though she didn't work the fields anymore and couldn't pay rent. Denver seemed to think that was mighty decent of him.

For a moment, my mind drifted down a road it had traveled before: What kind of man was the Man? For decades, one Man kept sharecroppers barefoot and poor, but let a little colored boy earn a brand-new red Schwinn. Another Man let an old black woman live on his place rent-free long after she'd stopped working in the fields. A third Man kept Denver ignorant and dependent, but provided for him well beyond the time he probably could have done without his labor.

It seemed a throwback to the slavery-era doctrine called "paternalism," the idea that black people were childlike and incapable of living free, and therefore better off as slaves. That it had happened to Denver in the mid-twentieth century shocked me.

About a quarter-mile down the road, we stopped at Hershalee's. It was a real house—what you could see of it. Tarpaper shingles and grayed, peeling eaves stuck up from a ten-foot tangle of johnsongrass like the last dry deck on a sinking ship. Behind the house, thirty yards off, a pea-green bayou slunk from left to right. I shut down the Suburban, and Denver and I got out to survey the place.

At one time, Hershalee's house had worn a coat of white paint trimmed in baby blue. But today it looked like a bomb had exploded nearby. All the windows were broken out. Trash and glass—mostly wine bottles—lay scattered in the few patches of bare ground that weeds had not yet overrun. The house sagged askew from sawed-off bois d'arc tree stumps, and the porch was rotten and falling away. From what we could tell, johnsongrass shrouded the house on all four sides. The parts of the windows we could see spilled forth only darkness.

Denver looked at me with a sly grin. "You scared to go in?"

"No, I'm not scared. How about you?"

"Me? I ain't scared a' nothin."

With that, we breaststroked through the towering weeds like men on safari and jumped up on the porch—having to, since the steps had fallen off. Using the few remaining boards like stepping-stones, we picked our way to the front door, which hung open, reminding me of a hungry mouth.

Denver went in first, and I heard rodents skitter for cover as I followed him into a small parlor that had been ransacked then used as a dump. A divan was piled high with trash, broken chairs, and an old record player. A table and a dresser stood against the wall at odd, unlivable angles. Clothes littered the floor. A thick layer of dust lay over it all.

I took a step, kicking paper, and looked down to find an old pile of mail. On the top, a letter from the City of Fort Worth addressed to Denver Moore in Red River Parish, Louisiana. The date: March 25, 1995. I started to hand it to him, but he waved me off.

"You open it. You know I can't read."

I slipped a thumb under the yellowed envelope flap and the glue gave way like dust. Shaking out a single sheet inside, I unfolded what turned out to be a warrant for driving without a license. Squinting in the dim light, I read aloud: "Dear Mr. Moore, we have a warrant for your arrest for the amount of $153.00."

We broke out laughing, the sound falling strangely in the dark, ram-shackle house. I tucked the letter in my pocket, a keepsake. Reaching down, I scooped up another letter, this one addressed to Hershalee from Publishers Clearing House, informing her that she may have won $10 mil-lion. Looked like she'd died on the eve of her lucky break.

Hershalee's bedroom was eerie, like walking through a life suddenly abandoned. Family photos still sat on the bureau. Her clothes still hung in the closet, and the bed was made.

Denver looked at the bed and smiled. "I remember one time Hershalee was watchin some other folks' kids, and she wanted to make em mind. So we come in here'n closed the door, and she told me to jump up and down on the bed and holler like she was beatin the tar outta me. She wanted to make them other children do what she say."

The memory turned him melancholy, but the moment passed quickly.

"Come on," he said. "I want to show you Hershalee's bathtub."

Denver had told me about the tub when he'd bought it for Hershalee, using the money I'd insisted he keep from his Colorado adventure. Hershalee bathed in it but had never had it hooked up to running water, and she kept it on her screened-in back porch. Denver and I picked our way out there, straining to see in the house's dark center. Boards groaned and creaked under our feet and the hair on my neck twitched a little. When we reached the porch, a little more light streamed in through the johnsongrass that crawled up the surrounding screens. And sure enough, there sat Hershalee's bathtub, crawling with spiders.

Only the tub-half of the porch was screened in and open to the air. On the other end, some kind of extra room, dark and boarded up, jutted out toward the bayou.

"Hershalee was mighty proud she had this new tub," Denver said. "Come on. I want to show you the potbellied stove where she heated up water to take a bath."

He started toward the kitchen, but froze and looked back at me: "Did you hear that?"

I stopped and listened in the weird silence. Then I heard footsteps, like heavy boots. Worse, I heard heavy breathing. Someone was stalking toward us from *inside* the boarded-up room fifteen feet away. But it didn't sound to me like some*one*—it sounded like some*thing*.

The hair on my neck stirred again and I looked at Denver. *Thump, thump* came the steps, then the creaking of a door handle. Denver's eyes widened until they seemed the size of pie plates. "Let's get outta here!" he whispered.

We bolted off the porch, back through the inky house, hurdling piles of trash and upended furniture. I barely beat Denver to the front door. We burst out, one-two. I leaped over the rotting porch planks and flew off the front porch, Denver airborne behind me. We hit the ground running, but a few feet from the house, pulled up and stopped.

I stared at Denver and he stared back, both of us panting with relief. Then we broke into nervous laughter.

"Do you think that was a possum or a coon?" I said lightly, as though neither of us had really been all *that* scared.

"Mr. Ron, ain't no such thing as a two-hundred-pound possum or coon that wears boots and walks like a man."

I picked up a big stick and looked back at the front porch, ready to do battle with whatever emerged. Then, instead of calling it a day, Denver and I did just what they do in the horror movies: We edged around the side of the house toward the bayou. I was fully prepared to see some kind of boot-wearing swamp monster lumbering back to his gooey lair. Less than a minute had passed when suddenly every hair on my body stood at attention. Denver and I locked eyes, transmitting shared terror.

"Let's get outta here!"

This time we both said it and raced back to the Suburban in a dead sprint. We jumped in, slammed the doors, and punched the lock buttons. I turned the ignition key and . . . nothing.

My brand-new car wouldn't start. Over and over, I cranked the key forward. Denver's head swiveled between the key and the house, the key, the house. His eyes grew wider. He punched the imaginary gas pedal on the passenger side, willing the thing to start.

The engine coughed and sputtered as though out of gas. But the tank was nearly full.

"Do you believe this?" I said, my voice up an octave.

"Sure do," he said and swallowed.

A full minute passed as I tried the ignition again and again. The hair on the back of my neck was now so rigid the follicles hurt. The engine coughed and spit and finally caught. But when I pushed on the gas . . . nothing.

Terrified, I wouldn't have been surprised if the swamp monster we *hadn't* seen out back roared out from under the truck, crashed through the windshield, and ripped our throats out. I had never before felt such fear. It was visceral, palpable. With the engine barely turning, I jerked hard on the gearshift and we rolled forward, my $40,000 SUV limping like an antique buggy. About a quarter-mile down, the road dead-ended. I bumped off into a muddy pasture to turn around, but the engine stalled. As I cranked the ignition again and again, Denver kept glancing up the road, looking for the Something.

Finally, the Suburban sputtered to life again and I pulled back onto the road, the engine popping and sputtering like an old tractor with a tank of bad gas. We crept along like that until we passed Hershalee's house. A hundred yards later, the engine roared to life then settled into a kittenish purr, gauges perfect, as if nothing had happened.

At that, Denver erupted into a belly laugh so all-consuming that if he'd been on an airplane, the oxygen mask would've dropped to help him breathe. He gasped and howled, tears squirting, until he finally blurted, "Now, Mr. Ron, you got a story to tell—a good one! You sure do!"

Then, as if an eraser had wiped the smile off his face, he turned dead serious and stared into my eyes. "Nothin keeps you honest like a witness," he said.

64

When we heard them steps thumpin toward us from inside that boarded-up room that wadn't fit for no human, I thought my eyeballs was gon' pop outta my head. We hightailed it outta there like nobody's business. But when I was runnin, I started feelin a little silly, thinkin maybe what we heard coulda been a vagrant or somebody just holed up in Hershalee's house. But when we slid around the side a' the house and my skin started crawlin, I was purty sure it was somethin, not some*body*. And when Mr. Ron's brand-new car started actin like a spooked horse, I knowed it for sure.

After we got past Hershalee's house, I told Mr. Ron that it wadn't the first time I seen strange things on the plantation. Like that time my auntie, Big Mama's sister, made it rain.

Lookin back on it, I think Auntie was what you might call a spiritual healer, like a "medicine man," 'cept she was a elderly woman. She lived out there near the bayou 'bout half a mile from Big Mama's, and I used to go over there and see her sometimes. I was scared of her. She always wore a long, dark skirt and a rag around her head, and when she laughed, sounded like a flock a' birds scared and flyin away. But Big Mama made me go to show my respect and also to help Auntie gather up the fixins for her medicines.

She used to take me with her down by the swamp where she'd be gatherin up some leaves and roots. We'd go in the evenin, just when the sunset was givin over to a cool twilight, and take us a little basket. I'd carry it for her, pickin our way through the cypress trees, while the bullfrogs and crickets were tunin up. I always kept one eye out for gators.

"Now Li'l Buddy, this here's for takin the pain out a wound," she'd say, pullin up a root and shakin off the earth. "And this here's for pneumonia."

She musta knowed twenty different kinds of roots and what have you, and what she knowed musta been a secret 'cause she made me promise I wouldn't tell nobody what she was pullin and where she was pullin it.

Auntie lived by herself. She had a room in her house with a big table in it covered with jars in all kinda sizes.

"See them jars?" she told me one time.

"Yes, ma'am."

"In each one of em, I got somethin for anything that happens to you."

Folks used to go see Auntie when they was sick. But if folks wadn't sick, they stayed away. I wadn't surprised. She had some kinda spiritual thing goin on in that house. Ever time I went in there, she made me sit on a little stool in the same spot, even facin in the same direction, like she didn't want me to mess up whatever voodoo she had goin on in there.

One day when I was sittin on that stool, she sprinkled some powder on the wood floor. Then she walked over to me and stared into my eyes and said real low, "Do you believe I can make it rain?"

I looked out the window and didn't see nothin but blue sky. "I don't know," I said, half-scared but kinda curious.

"Sit there," she said.

Then Auntie picked up her broom and started sweepin that powder around on the floor, hummin a li'l tune like no song I ever heard. She hummed and swept, hummed and swept, brushin at the floor with small strokes. She swept that powder all around the front room, then swept some onto the front porch, hummin all the way.

Then she called to me. "Li'l Buddy, walk out on the porch."

I did, and this is the truth: A cloud had formed right over the house. Just one cloud—not a whole skyful. And right when I looked up at it, that cloud flashed with lightnin and thunder cracked. I could feel it rumblin up underneath the house. Then it come a rain right there on the porch.

Auntie turned her face up into the sprinklin drops, smilin a little, like she knowed a secret. "I told you," she said.

'Cept for Mr. Ron, I never told nobody 'bout that, 'cause most people gon' say that's just superstition. They'd rather pretend things like that don't happen

65

I guided the miraculously healed Suburban back over the red dirt road that eventually spit us out onto Highway 1. We drove a mile or so looking for another dirt road, just a slit in the weeds really, so narrow we missed it a couple of times and had to double back. It was the road to Aunt Pearlie May's house. In the 1960s, she'd moved into a shotgun house out closer to the plantation and had lived there ever since.

As I eased the truck along the pitted trail, bumper-high johnsongrass parted to reveal a slice of America that most Americans never see. Six shotgun shacks squatted in a clearing in the woods, lined up like prisoners held hostage from another era. No yards divided the lots. Instead, junk huddled in heaps around every house—old tires, beer cans, car seats, rusted mattress springs. In the middle of the road, lay the bloated carcass of a dead mongrel dog.

In front of one house, a young black man and woman watched us from a molting sofa someone had dragged out into the dirt. The woman pulled on a cigarette as chickens pecked around her feet. Smoke boiled into the air from one yard, where two kids tended a pile of burning trash. Nearby, a girl pinned wet laundry to a rope that ran between the house and a dead tree. She looked about twelve and was pregnant.

I slowed down as if driving past a bad accident. The residents stared at me like I was an alien.

"Stop right here," Denver said. There, sitting on a tree stump beside the road was an elderly woman sucking on a can of beer at three in the afternoon. Dressed in men's trousers and a stained T-shirt shot through with

holes, she lit up when she saw Denver. He got out of the truck and hugged
her then handed her a $5 bill. With a wheezy giggle, she poked her hand
through one of the holes in her shirt and tucked the money in her bra.

"Y'all come on in the house," she rasped. "I got some greens on the stove
and they's fresh."

Denver politely declined and hitched himself back into the Suburban.

"She ain't no kin," he said. "Just a friend a' Pearlie May's."

We crept down to the last house, past a man working on a tractor. He
had disassembled the machine into several dozen pieces near his front door,
which wasn't really a door at all but a red-plaid blanket tacked up to keep
the flies out.

Pearlie May's house sat at the end of the row. A dozen or so plastic lawn
chairs littered the dirt out front, punctuated with huge pyramids of empty
Natural Light beer cans stacked like fire logs. Next to the porch lay a mountain of brown Garrett snuff jars, hundreds of them. From the end of a long
chain, a spotted mongrel dog yapped at a flock of unperturbed chickens,
who knew just how long the chain was.

"Li'l Buddy!" Aunt Pearlie May said when we walked up to her porch.
"Lord, if you ain't got your daddy's nose!" Denver gave her a hug—not a big
one—then she leaned on the rotten porch railing and aimed a four-letter word
at the barking hound. "Shut up, dog, 'fore I come out there and shut you up!"

She turned then and smiled at Denver, but her weathered face
telegraphed concern over my presence. To ease her mind, I nodded at the
snuff-can mountain and told her that my grandmother and great-aunts had
dipped Garrett snuff. That seemed to make her feel better.

Aunt Pearlie May invited us into her parlor, a space that measured about
six feet by eight feet and was wallpapered in a patchwork of Christmas
wrap, along with three pictures of Jesus. Somehow, someone had managed
to shoehorn two worn-out love seats into the room and arrange them facing each other. When Denver and I sat down across from Pearlie May and
her husband, our knees touched. We chatted about this and that, except for
the husband, who sat across from me expressionless, and never said a word.
Later, Denver said that was the friendliest he'd ever seen him.

"Y'all come out back and see my hogs," Pearlie May said after a short visit. "I'm thinkin' 'bout sellin em off. Want you to see em case you know anybody wants to buy em."

We unfolded ourselves and covered the distance to the back door in three long steps. Outside, two corpulent hogs snuffled and grunted, wallowing in mud up to their bellies. Pearlie May made a little porcine sales pitch, then yakked cheerfully about her new indoor toilet. She'd had it installed in 2001, and paid for it with proceeds earned over a lifetime of bootlegging Natural Light beer through her bedroom window for a buck a can. Said she still mainly used her outhouse, though, since all the kinks hadn't been worked out in her indoor plumbing yet.

We left just before dark, and as we drove away the images of poverty and squalor burned themselves into my brain like hated tattoos. I could hardly believe places like that still existed in America. I thanked Denver for taking me there, for taking my blinders off.

"Mr. Ron, they're livin better than I ever did when I was livin here. Now you know it was the truth when I told you that bein homeless in Fort Worth was a step up in life for me."

66

By the second week in September, more than half a million dollars had poured into the mission. A couple of days before the groundbreaking ceremony for Deborah's chapel, Mary Ellen called me. She wanted to share with me something that Jesus had told His disciples, a metaphor for His own death recorded in the Gospel of John: "Truly, truly, I say to you, unless a kernel of wheat falls to the earth and dies, it remains by itself, alone. But if it dies, it bears much fruit."

In prayer that morning, Mary Ellen said, she'd felt God whispering to her heart, *Deborah was like that kernel of wheat.*

The next day, Denver dropped by for a visit. Sitting across from me at my kitchen table as he had so many times, he said nearly the same thing but in the language of a country preacher. "Mr. Ron, all good things must end," he said. "And nothin ever really ends that somethin new don't begin. Like Miss Debbie. She's gone, but somethin new is beginnin."

Three days later, on September 13, we gathered to break ground on "New Beginnings," the new mission. Only two days before terrorists had crashed a pair of passenger jets into the World Trade Center, changing America forever. Carson lived in New York City. It had taken me hours to reach him by phone, as I sat before the live TV news coverage, stunned at the news, knowing it was now not only my own world that tragedy had changed forever.

The nation ground to a halt, but in honor of Deborah, the mission board decided to go ahead with the groundbreaking. I followed the familiar route she and I had driven so often to the mission, past train tracks and derelict buildings and underpasses that doubled as outhouses for the homeless. The first time Deborah and I traveled East Lancaster, she'd dreamed of bringing beauty there. And she had, but not in the way she'd first imagined. Instead of lining the sidewalks with picket fences, she'd fenced out fear, prejudice, and judgment, creating with her smile and open heart a sanctuary for hundreds. Instead of planting yellow flowers, she'd sown seeds of compassion that changed hearts, mine and Denver's only two among them.

So I stood with Regan, Denver, my mother, Tommye, and nearly a hundred friends that day, under God's blue canopy, using a ceremony program to shield myself from the sun. We listened as Mayor Kenneth Barr and State Senator Mike Moncrief spoke of the hope this new mission would bring to the homeless of Fort Worth. Behind them, a ten-foot patch of red dirt lay exposed and four shovels festooned with blue ribbons stood like soldiers, ready to turn over the soil. Ready to receive the kernel.

Now on East Lancaster Street stands a new mission that includes new services for the needy: residential rooms for women and children and the Deborah L. Hall Memorial Chapel. Both are a memorial to a woman who served the city, a woman God took home so that in His strange providence, the sick and the lost might find greater refuge and hope. Bitterly, I wondered if He could have managed to build them without taking my wife. It could have been called God's Chapel and Deborah Hall could have served Him there.

I remembered what C. S. Lewis said of the clash between grief and faith: "The tortures occur," he wrote. "If they are unnecessary, then there is no God, or a bad one. If there is a good God, then these tortures are necessary for no even moderately good Being could possibly inflict or permit them if they weren't."

The pain of losing Deborah still brings tears. And I cannot mask my profound disappointment that God did not answer yes to our prayers for healing. I think He's okay with that. One of the phrases we evangelicals like to throw around is that Christianity is "not a religion; it's a relationship." I believe that, which is why I know that when my faith was shattered and I raged against Him, He still accepted me. And even though I have penciled a black mark in His column, I can be honest about it. That's what a relationship is all about.

Still, I can't deny the fruit of Deborah's death—Denver, the new man, and the hundreds of men, women, and children who will be helped because of the new mission. And so, I release her back to God.

— — —

The Sunday after the groundbreaking, Denver and I pulled into the parking lot of the New Mount Calvary Baptist Church, a church in a depressed neighborhood in southeast Fort Worth. Pastor Tom Franklin had heard Denver speak at Deborah's memorial service and for months had kept after me to try to convince him to come and preach at his church. Finally, Denver agreed. I had prayed for a standing-room-only crowd, but by the looks of the parking lot, folks were standing somewhere else that morning.

If Abraham Lincoln had been black, Pastor Tom would have been his twin. Gray-haired and bearded, he greeted us at the church door, pulling us each into a lanky hug. Peeking into the sanctuary, I could see only a few people scattered through the pews.

Pastor Tom read my thoughts. "Don't worry, Ron. Everyone the Lord wants to be here will be here."

As the service began and the tiny congregation filled the air with old spirituals, Denver and I huddled on the back row. Pastor Tom had wanted me to introduce Denver from the pulpit but spend a few minutes telling his life story first. As I suspected, Denver wasn't having any of that. During the singing, he and I huddled on the back row to negotiate.

"It ain't nobody's business how I got here!" he whispered. "'Sides, I don't want to tell em 'bout me. I want to tell em 'bout the Lord."

"So what do you want me to say?"

He paused and stared down at the Bible laying on the bench next to me. "Just tell em I'm a nobody that's tryin to tell everbody 'bout Somebody that can save *anybody*. That's all you need to tell em."

And so, when the singing stopped, I walked down front and said just that.

Then Denver took the pulpit. At first, his voice quavered a bit, but it was loud. And the longer he preached, the louder and stronger it became. And like a magnet, his voice pulled people in off the street. By the time he wiped the sweat off his face and sat down, the pews were nearly full.

Like a cannonball, Pastor Tom shot out of his seat into the pulpit, raising his arms toward the people. "I believe God wants Denver to come back and preach a revival!" he said. The congregation, most of whom had been drawn into the sanctuary by Denver's voice, exploded into applause.

My mind flashed to Deborah's dream, her seeing Denver's face, and recalling the words of Solomon: *There was found in the city a certain poor man who was wise and by his wisdom he saved the city.*

Again, something new had begun. Something I was certain had my wife dancing for joy on streets of gold.

67

Like I said before, when Mr. Ron promised he wadn't gon' catch and release me, I was skeptical. But listen to this: Not too long after I preached at Pastor Tom's church, Mr. Ron asked me would I move in with him. And you ain't gon' believe where—at the Murchison Estate in Dallas, in a mansion where Mr. Ron said United States presidents, movie stars, and even a fella named J. Edgar Hoover used to stay.

I guess the Murchisons at one time was the richest folks in Texas and some a' the richest in the whole country. In 2001, Mrs. Lupe Murchison passed on, gone to join her husband, and their kin was wantin Mr. Ron to live on the estate and sell off all a' their art. They had hun'erds a' pictures and statues and what have you. Mr. Ron said it was all worth about a zillion dollars. So he hired me to live on the estate with him and be the night watchman. That suited me 'cause I was ready to work for a livin and earn some money of my own. The mansion was real old and grand, built in the 1920s, Mr. Ron said. A coupla nights while I was guardin it, I met some ghosts wanderin around.

Not long after I moved into the mansion with Mr. Ron, I found some paints in the garage and decided to paint me a picture. I was gettin paid to guard all them silly-lookin pictures by fellas like Picasso. Didn't look to me like they was very hard to paint. Sure 'nough, it only took me a coupla hours 'fore I had made a picture of a angel that was ever bit as good as some a' them I was guardin.

Mr. Ron liked it a lot when I showed it to him the next mornin. "How much do you want for it?" he asked me.

"A million dollars," I said.

"A million dollars!" he said, laughing. "I can't afford your paintings."

"Mr. Ron, I ain't askin you to buy it. I'm askin you to sell it like you sell them other million-dollar pictures."

After that, though, I showed my angel picture to Sister Bettie and she said it was her favorite paintin she had ever seen, so I gave it to her. She's like an angel to me anyway. Then Mr. Ron set me up my own studio in the room right next door to Lupe Murchison's five-car garage. I guess I've painted over a hun'erd pictures by now. Sold some of em, too.

Carson and Mr. Ron have done sold off most a' the Murchisons' art, and somebody bought the mansion, too. Now we're livin in another house on the estate while they sell the rest.

During the day when I ain't workin, I carry Miss Debbie's torch, the one the Lord told me to pick up so she could lay it down. I still go down to the Lot and help Sister Bettie and Miss Mary Ellen. Sister Bettie's gettin on in years, and I worry about her. Once a month, I preach at the Riteway Baptist Church. I take clothes over to the homeless people and take care of my homeboys that's still on the street, maybe give em a few dollars.

I do some travelin, too. In January 2005, me and Mr. Ron went to the presidential inauguration. Mr. Ron was invited and he asked me to go with him. That was the first time I ever went on a airplane. We landed in a snowstorm, but I didn't know I was s'posed to be scared.

So there we was, on the White House lawn, sittin on the front row, and I'm lookin around at all the astronauts and war heroes and wonderin, how in the world did a fella like me wind up in a place like this? It was somethin I never even dreamed of. I wadn't that far from the president, but I wanted to check him out a li'l better so I got up outta my seat and walked up closer to where he was sittin, gettin ready to make his speech. But this Secret Service man, a black fella like me, held up his hand.

"Sir, where are you going?"

"I'm gon' walk right up here and see the president," I said.

He looked at me kinda firm. "No. You're close enough."

Later that night, me and Mr. Ron went to the inaugural ball. The president and his wife was dancin right there in front of me. I had on a tuxedo and a bow tie. I felt purty good about that.

The next day, I got to stand on the steps at the Lincoln Memorial. I remember way back when I was li'l bitty fella, Big Mama told me 'bout how President Lincoln freed black people from slavery. That's why they shot him.

I felt mighty blessed to be able to go and see the president. Me and Mr. Ron done some other travelin, too. I been to Santa Fe and San Diego. Back home in Dallas, we still go to restaurants and cafés, the ranch and rodeos, and to church on Sundays. All in all, we's purty tight. Lotta times, we'll sit out on the back porch at the Murchison place, or out on the patio at Rocky Top, lookin at the moon shinin on the river and talkin about life. Mr. Ron's still got a lot to learn.

I'm just messin with you. Even though I'm almost seventy years old, I got a lot to learn, too. I used to spend a lotta time worryin that I was different from other people, even from other homeless folks. Then, after I met Miss Debbie and Mr. Ron, I worried that I was so different from them that we wadn't ever gon' have no kind a' future. But I found out everybody's different—the same kind of different as me. We're all just regular folks walkin down the road God done set in front of us.

The truth about it is, whether we is rich or poor or somethin in between, this earth ain't no final restin place. So in a way, we is all homeless—just workin our way toward home.

Reader's Guide

Here are some questions to provoke deeper thought and life application of the issues presented in this book. Sit down with a cup of coffee or meet with friends to think about and discuss these issues and their importance in the world today.

To see Ron's and Denver's thoughts on these topics, visit their Web site at www.samekindofdifferentasme.com.

Prejudice

1. What are some modern examples of prejudice? Other than racial prejudice, what other kinds of prejudice are common today?
2. What are three things you can do to combat your personal prejudices?
3. What does being prejudiced say about your personal self-esteem?
4. Read Micah 6:8. What does this verse say about the attitude we should have toward other people?

Homelessness

1. What is your initial reaction to encountering a homeless person or someone who is in serious financial or personal need?
2. If you were in that situation, how would you want others to respond to you?
3. Other than give money to social service agencies, what are three things you can do to provide ministry to the homeless people in your community?

4. Jesus' ministry was often focused on society's outcasts. Why did
    Jesus seek them out rather than socialize with the religious elite?
    With which crowd are you most likely to spend time—the out-
    casts in your community or the religious elite? Why?

Sickness and Suffering

1. Bad things happen to good people. What might God be trying to
    reveal about Himself through these types of situations?
2. Recognizing our mortality puts life in perspective. What are three
    things for which you want to be remembered? What are you
    doing to accomplish these goals today?
3. Refresh your memory of the Book of Job. Through all of his
    pain, Job remained faithful to God. What can you do to cultivate
    that kind of faith in your everyday life?

Forgiveness

1. Is it harder to give or to receive forgiveness? Why?
2. Why is it so hard for us to grant unconditional forgiveness? How
    can your faith help you become a more forgiving person?
3. What is the role of forgiveness in your personal life? In your
    spiritual life?
4. The ultimate expression of forgiveness is found in God's sacrifice
    of His Son. Because we have been forgiven, we should be forgiv-
    ing. How would this kind of forgiveness affect your relationships?

Faith

1. In chapter 44, Denver said, "Our limitation is God's opportunity."
    How has this statement been authenticated in your life?
2. Throughout the book, Denver's initial response to life's challenges
    often was rooted in his simple faith in God. Why is it so hard for
    society's successful people to have this kind of faith? What keeps
    you from having this kind of faith?

3. With Deborah in critical condition, the object of ministry
    (Denver) became the source of ministry. Denver had been
    through a lot and was equipped to provide for Ron's needs.
    Through what experiences has God worked to equip you for min-
    istry? How has God used you to meet the needs of others?

4. Deborah extended the reach of her ministry by investing in the
    lives of others. How are you investing in the lives of others?

5. The memorial service for Deborah was a celebration. How can
    such a somber occasion be celebrative? What does this say about
    the faith of the one who passed away?

Where Are They Now?

A Conversation with the Authors

TN: How has the telling of your story affected your everyday life?

RON: The book has become my life, as there is little time apart from speaking and handling the flood of correspondence from our readers. It is nearly impossible to go anywhere, especially in Texas where Denver and I are now recognized. Admittedly, it is flattering and the amazing stories we hear from complete strangers about how our story has affected their lives and what they are doing for others is the bonus for our loss of privacy. I tell people all the time that I became wealthy through art but my friendship with Denver has made my life rich.

DENVER: That'll be all the way around the board. The things I used to do, I can't do no more. While I ain't perfect, I don't want to do most of the bad stuff, but even the stuff that ain't bad, I have to watch it cause I can't go nowhere that somebody don't recognize me.

TN: What have been some of the ministry opportunities that have come your way since the first release of the book?

RON: I have had the privilege of encouraging many who have lost spouses, children, or other family members. Obviously, we have spent a lot of time with homeless people and relatives of the homeless. Our story gives them hope.

DENVER: I never dreamed I'd be on TV, radio, and visit many cities like New York City, Washington, D.C., and Chicago and speak to thousands of people on behalf of my brothers and sisters that are still on the streets. And

241

I never dreamed I'd be able to give money back to those who took care of me for so many years. I just couldn't think that big!

TN: Do you have any additional thoughts that weren't part of the original book?
RON: Most of our thoughts were included and the book was never meant to be a self-help or instructional book. Ours is merely a story about how a godly woman with a dream followed it to the point where a city was changed. Denver and I are not preachers or teachers, but sinners with a story to tell.
DENVER: I didn't have any thoughts for this book, I just told my story. I just want to encourage folks to be more like Miss Debbie.

TN: What is the message you hope the reader will receive from reading this book?
RON: One person can make a difference. Denver is making a difference. Debbie made a difference here on earth and continues to do so from heaven.
DENVER: You never know whose eyes God is watchin' you through. It probably ain't gonna be your preacher and it just might be someone who was livin' like I used to.

TN: Every book has a legacy. What do you hope will be the long-lasting effect of the telling of your story?
RON: Our nation, maybe even our world, (wow, now that's big!) will never look at homeless people the same way. That requires love-inspired vision to see through the rags and filth into the person's heart.
DENVER: I hope people will recycle the love they've been given to somebody that's not easy to love.

TN: What are three things we can do to bridge the societal gaps that exist in our culture today?
RON: (1) We must move beyond our comfort zone and make a friend of a

different race and socioeconomic group; (2) Be accountable to them; (3) Don't catch and release no matter how difficult it gets.

DENVER: To love 'em, serve 'em and don't judge 'em, in spite of who they are, what they look like, and what they be a doin'!

TN: Your story reveals your early perspective on life. What did you learn from reading the story of your co-author?

RON: I realized how blessed I am to have been born and reared in a family that loved me, cared for me, and was not beset by tragedies. Denver's story made me aware that my family and I shared responsibilities for the unjust way families like his were treated in the twentieth century.

DENVER: I haven't read the book but I've learned not to pass judgment on anybody 'cause I don't know the things they been through that made them who they are today. But about Mr. Ron and his friends, they changed my attitude about rich folks.

TN: In some communities, homelessness has reached epidemic status. What do you think is the ultimate solution to this problem? How has your perception of homelessness changed over the past few years?

RON: In my opinion there is no solution to the homeless problem. However, there are many ways to improve the conditions for those who fall into that state: (1) Relationships build trust and trust leads to accountability. This is the point where lives can be changed; (2) Encourage and fund the reconciliation of families. The simple cost of a phone call and bus ticket home have resulted in getting people off the streets and back at home. We have heard many stories like this from our readers; (3) My perception has changed greatly after knowing hundreds of homeless people and hearing their stories. Only by taking the time to listen can you discover that most homeless people started off in life much like everyone else but were often thrown off the track by tragedy and circumstances beyond their control. But by the grace of God, I avoided a similar fate.

Denver told me that faith-based organizations, government programs, and well-meaning individuals fed him and kept him alive for all those years on the streets, but it was the love of Miss Debbie that caused him to want to make a change in his life.

DENVER: God says the poor will always be with us. I don't believe there is a solution but if people were more like Miss Debbie, homeless folks would be treated better.

TN: What is your current definition of success? How has your story affected your understanding of what it means to be successful?

RON: A successful person is one who is living a joyful life with the hand he or she was dealt. The upscale world I lived in seemed to be filled with a disproportionate number of unhappy people. In my own case, in the last six years I've made far less money but achieved far greater success than I ever dreamed possible by allowing God to use Denver and me to encourage a hopeless part of society.

DENVER: A successful person is one who can thank God for nothin', and then He'll give him everything! Success, I have found out, comes with a great deal of responsibility. I used to stand in the middle of nowhere, where time didn't matter and there was nowhere I had to be at. And now I be standin' in the middle of everywhere and never enough time to get there so I have learned TIME MATTERS!

Don't get me wrong. God needs rich people to help the poor survive. I hope everybody tries to be successful not for selfish purposes, but to help those who can't help themselves.

TN: If you had the opportunity to go back and do it all again, would this story be different? If so, how? If not, why?

RON: Yes it would be a different story with Debbie taken to the brink of death and miraculously healed. But now, seven years after her death and more than 200 times telling her story, I can see God's hand and even His purpose for her life and painful death. But, that still doesn't keep me from wishing it had been a different ending.

DENVER: No, it would be the same. If I hadn't went through what I went through then I wouldn't be who I am now! What must befall thee, must befall thee, what must pass ye by will pass ye by!

acknowledgments

Denver and Ron would like to thank the Wednesday Watchmen, Union Gospel Mission, Sister Bettie Hedgpeth, Pastor Henry Stanford, Riteway Missionary Baptist Church, Mighty Men, Best Friends, Buckaroos, Vitas Hospice, All Saints Hospital, doctors and nurses, CTRC and a host of friends, family and business partners who prayed without ceasing, phoned, sang, cooked, wrote, cleaned house, ran errands, gave back massages, gave foot massages, walked dogs, kept dogs, cleaned up after dogs, adopted dogs, sent money to Mission and H.O.P.E. Farms, managed well wishers, prepared cemetery and loved us from near and far.

And to my agent Lee Hough, a true believer who went against protocol to read an unknown writer's manuscript and then tout it to the best people in the industry . . . and to Lynn Vincent who spent hours with Denver and me in Texas and Louisiana developing our characters and shaping our story . . . and to Caryl Avery who taught me about punctuation and verbs and encouraged me that my manuscript, with a little luck, might get published.

Thanks to Jack Temple Kirby, whose book *Rural Words Lost: The American South 1920–1960* (Louisiana State University Press, 1987) provided invaluable historical background for this book.

To David Moberg and Greg Daniel—taking a risk on an unknown first-time author telling a wild tale about people they didn't know!

And especially to my Aunt Vida who has typed this whole thing more than twenty times without complaining.

God bless you all.

To Debbie—
you fought the fight and kept the faith.

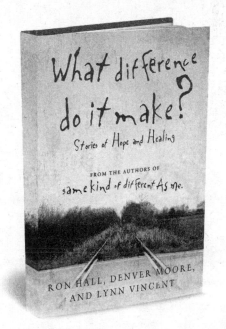

Denver's last house in Louisiana

The railroad tracks where Denver hopped the freight train out of Louisiana

"Da man's" store

Denver singing at Sister Bettie's Under the Tree Ministry

Denver at home in his gallery

Denver in Louisiana with Pearlie Mae's prize hog

Denver playing piano in
Debbie's Chapel

Denver's first birthday party at Red, Hot & Blue in Fort Worth
with Janina and Scott Walker and Ron and Deborah Hall

Ron & Denver watch the roping at Rocky Top

Deborah's last Christmas at Rocky Top

Ron and Denver joking around

Regan and Deborah dancing
in Colorado

Ron and Deborah

RockyPop and Kendall Deborah Hall, born November 27, 2007.
Her parents are Megan and Carson Hall.

Ron and Denver welcome
Ron's first grandchild, Griffin Donnell

Christmas 2007
On Ron's lap . . .
left to right:
Sadie Jane Donnell,
Kendall Deborah Hall
Standing in front:
Griffin Donnell